James Edmund Scripps

Five months abroad

The observations and experiences of an editor in Europe

James Edmund Scripps

Five months abroad
The observations and experiences of an editor in Europe

ISBN/EAN: 9783337140687

Printed in Europe, USA, Canada, Australia, Japan

Cover: Foto ©Andreas Hilbeck / pixelio.de

More available books at **www.hansebooks.com**

FIVE MONTHS ABROAD,

OR,

THE OBSERVATIONS AND EXPERIENCES OF AN EDITOR IN EUROPE.

BY

JAMES E. SCRIPPS,

EDITOR OF THE DETROIT EVENING NEWS.

ILLUSTRATED.

DETROIT, MICH.

F. B. DICKERSON & CO., PUBLISHERS.

1882.

TO

MY WIFE AND DAUGHTER,

THE

COMPANIONS OF MY JOURNEY,

THIS LITTLE WORK

IS AFFECTIONATELY DEDICATED.

PREFACE.

The following record of a European tour, made in the summer of 1881, appeared in the first instance as a series of letters in the columns of the DETROIT EVENING NEWS, and its presentation in more permanent shape was not then thought of by the author; but so numerous and apparently sincere were the solicitations that it should be reprinted in book form, that he could not, without ingratitude, allow them to pass unheeded. In preparing the work for the press much of it has been entirely rewritten, the form changed from letters to chapters, and one or two entirely new chapters added. The illustrations are mostly original, and were engraved from photographs collected by the author in the course of his journey.

The aim in the preparation of the work has been three-fold: *First,* to convey to the reader as graphic an idea as possible of what he would see and how probably be impressed were he himself to make the same journey; *Second,* to interweave with the narrative of travel such an amount of collateral historical and biographical fact as should make the book valuable as a medium of general information; and, *Third,* by frequent reference and allusion to make the work somewhat of a basis for and stimulus to culture in the realms of art and literature.

If it shall incite the reader to further reading and research, one of its principal aims, indeed, will have been accomplished.

It may be hardly necessary to add that the book is addressed in the main to western people of ordinary information—to the intelligent farmers and mechanics of Michigan and neighboring states; and that it makes no pretense to either high literary merit or infallibility in every statement. All reasonable care has nevertheless been given to render it both intelligent and trustworthy.

JAMES E. SCRIPPS.

DETROIT, January, 1882.

CONTENTS.

TABLE OF CONTENTS.

LIST OF ILLUSTRATIONS.

FIVE MONTHS ABROAD.

CHAPTER I.

HOW TO PREPARE FOR A EUROPEAN TOUR—THE SELECTION OF
A ROUTE—INTELLECTUAL PREPARATION—THE COST AND
HOW TO PROVIDE FOR IT—WHAT BAGGAGE TO TAKE—THE
VOYAGE—LIFE AT SEA.

AS a rule people who travel are of an intelligent class, though I have met persons who traveled merely for the sake of traveling, with no definite object in view, no knowledge of the history and associations of the places they visited, and little or no appreciation of the beauties and curiosities of the countries they passed through. It need hardly be said that travel in such cases furnishes but very little of either pleasure or profit.

If one contemplates a European tour the first thing to do is to decide upon the route. A list may be made of such places as the person especially desires to visit, and with a map before him a route may easily be outlined that shall take in these points and the more important intermediate ones. In my own case, as illustration, I particularly wished to see Cologne cathedral, reputed the finest Gothic church in the world, the famous Rhine scenery, Nuremberg, the best preserved mediæval city in Europe, the romantic city of Venice, art-cultured Florence, historic Rome, Pisa with its famous leaning tower, the much talked of Italian lakes, the mountain scenery of Switzerland, Paris, the world's metropolis of fashion, elegance and culture, and lastly the old cathedrals, ruined abbeys, castles and picturesque natural scenery of England and Scotland. I therefore traced out a route embracing Liverpool, London, Antwerp, Brussels, Cologne, Mayence, Frankfort - on - the - Main, Nuremberg, Munich, Innsbruck, Verona, Venice, Padua, Bologna, Florence, Rome, Pisa, Genoa, Turin, Milan, the Simplon Pass, Martigny, Chamounix, Geneva, Lausanne, Berne, Bale, Strassburg, Paris, Rouen, Dieppe, and so back to England which being a small country and easily covered less required a pre-arranged route.

The route decided upon, the next proper step is the posting up of one's self upon the geography, history, associations and attractions of the countries and cities passed through. The more fully this is done, of course, the better will the traveler be equipped for his journey. Particularly in historical matters would I recommend the jotting down in a sort of commonplace book the

THE ROUTE.

Heavy dotted lines (━━━━) national boundaries.

Light broken lines (------) the route taken by the author.

more important facts, such as dates and successions, for reference to while traveling, as such information is often very difficult to obtain away from home. In this intellectual preparation for the journey, encyclopædias, school histories, and the descriptive articles that so often appear in our leading magazines, will be found very serviceable.

The next thing is to provide money for the journey. The passage from New York to Liverpool and return may be put down roughly at from $100 to $200, according to the amount of luxury indulged in on the voyage. The railroad and steamboat fares on the continent may be put at $100 to $125, hotels about $2.50 a day, and some allowance must be made for purchases from the great stocks of pretty things that will constantly meet the eye while in Europe. I have known people to make a European tour and be home in a month or six weeks; two to three months is a very common time to devote to the trip, but I found the interest of travel to be well maintained during a period of five months. Having settled on the amount of money necessary for the trip and purchased one's passage tickets, the next step is to procure a letter of credit for such sum as will probably be required for use after landing in Europe. Such letters of credit are issued by various New York banking houses, and

may easily be obtained through local banks or
bankers.   These letters of credit may be drawn
against in any amounts, large or small as
required, at any of a hundred or more different
banks scattered through all the principal cities of
Europe.   A very small fee is charged for the
cashing of each draft, not more perhaps altogether than the interest the undrawn deposits
will earn.   The safety, economy and convenience
of this method of carrying one's funds can never
be appreciated until it has been tried.

Then comes the packing for the journey.   As
little baggage as possible should be taken, and it
is astonishing how little a person can get along
with.   One, or at most two, suits of clothes, or
dresses, will usually be sufficient, as additional
clothing can be easily and cheaply procured anywhere on the journey, should it be required.
Nor is a great amount of underwear essential, as
one can get washing done at any hotel without
much delay.   Warmer clothing should be taken
than would ordinarily be worn at home in the
summer season, as on the Atlantic, in the mountain regions, and generally through England and
Scotland the climate is much cooler than it aver-
ages in the United States.   A heavy winter over-
coat and a traveling rug will be found indispensable on the voyage, but these may be left at
Liverpool till the return, so they hardly count as

baggage. A reclining steamer chair, **purchasable** in New York for $2.50 to $3.50, will be **found of great** comfort for use **on deck** and **may also be** left at Liverpool.

Leaving **New** York we steam **down the harbor,** through the Narrows, **as** the **strait which** separates Long Island **from Staten** Island at **the** point of their nearest approach is called, past **Sandy Hook,** a long spit of land running out **from the** New Jersey shore, and, in **two hours after** casting off the lines at **the** pier in North River, **we are** fairly out at sea. Our course lies considerably to the north of east, Liverpool being about thirteen degrees, or, in round numbers, 800 miles north of the latitude of New York. The distance by the route usually taken is about 3,085 miles, and about ten days may ordinarily be reckoned upon as the time **for the** passage. Twenty-four hours, however, before reaching **Liverpool, we** touch at Queenstown, **on the** south-east coast of Ireland, to land the mails, **and** from this time the voyage seems practically at an end.

For the first few days after sailing, if the sea **be at all** rough, one is very apt to suffer from an entire loss of appetite and **more or** less sea-sickness. The sensation is **one of** great misery, especially **with the** reflection constantly haunting one that his wretchedness may **be of ten days'** continuance. However, with most people this wears off

in a few days, and the latter part of the voyage,
with the animating prospect of soon being in port,
becomes quite enjoyable.   On the leading lines
of steamers the state-rooms are clean and well ven-
tilated, and a table is set superior even to that of
the majority of first-class hotels.   If the weather
is pleasant it is wonderful how quickly the time
passes.   We get up in the morning, take a stroll
on deck, breakfast at eight, stand or lie around
in groups watching the waves or chatting, are
served with beef tea at eleven, at noon the chart
with the progress of the ship for the past 24 hours
marked upon it, and which is suspended in a
frame in the companion-way, engrosses the attention, at one comes lunch, and at six o'clock
dinner, with tea or coffee still later if one cares
for it.   The intervals are filled up with prome-
nades on deck and games of shovel-board or
quoits.   Shovel-board is played with a number
of circular pieces of wood perhaps six inches in
diameter which are slid over the smooth deck,
being propelled by a sort of cue, the object being
to place them on certain squares marked with
chalk on the deck, the squares being numbered
from one to nine and the players counting the
sum of the numbers of the squares upon which
their blocks rest after all have played.   In the
smoking-room cards help to pass the time; in the
saloon, music and reading.   Every steamer now

has its piano and library. But as we are journeying eastward the clocks have to be set on half-an-hour every day, and the fact that the days thus have but twenty-three and a half hours perhaps helps to make the time seem short.

The best months in which to cross the Atlantic are May, June, July and August, but one is liable in any of these months to encounter a rough passage, and may, in like manner, enjoy a smooth one even in December.

The intense delight of sailing into the lovely harbor of Queenstown can only be appreciated by those who have experienced it. It takes but half-an-hour to transfer a few tons of mail bags to the tender that comes out into the harbor to meet our steamship, and we proceed immediately on our way to Liverpool, keeping much of the time in sight of the Irish and Welsh coasts.

AN OCEAN STEAMER.

CHAPTER II.

ARRIVAL IN ENGLAND—LIVERPOOL AND ITS WONDERFUL COM-
MERCIAL DEVELOPMENT—CHESTER AND ITS ANTIQUITIES—
ENGLISH HOTELS—CHEAP CAB FARES.

O N the occasion of my trip the enjoyment of arriving at Liverpool was greatly marred by the fogs, which utterly obscured all sight of land even after we had dropped anchor in the Mersey, and by a drizzling rain in which we landed. The customs restrictions in this glorious country of free trade offer no annoyance to travelers, and only if there is reason to believe they have spirits or tobacco or reprints of English copyright books among their baggage, is it subject to anything like an examination. Sixpence (12 cents) for each trunk pays the dock porters' fee for all the necessary handling till it reaches our "fly," or one-horse hack, and a shilling (24 cents) carries us to any hotel in the city.

Liverpool is usually passed over by travelers, who upon landing hasten to take the first trains for London. But it merits more attention. It is one of those cities like Venice, Florence, Antwerp, and many others on the continent, which, having grown wealthy by trade, has turned its

attention to culture, art and luxurious elegance.
One wealthy merchant has founded a free public
library of 70,000 volumes, and built for its accommodation a palatial stone edifice. Another has
founded a free art gallery which already contains
many valuable treasures. St. George's hall, one
of the finest in the country, and containing one
of the largest organs, upon which weekly recitals
are given at popular prices (12 cents) to the music
loving public, is one of the chief landmarks of
Liverpool. Then within the past ten years the
city has purchased and improved, at a cost of
about $2,000,000, a fine public park, known as
Sefton park. Architecturally, too, Liverpool is
becoming a very beautiful city. It has lately
been made the see of a bishop, and an elegant
cathedral church is looked forward to. But the
docks and other commercial conveniences are
still the chief feature of the city. Extending
for eight miles up and down the Mersey there
are a great number of docks or basins in which
vessels can lie to load or unload without being
affected by the tides which here rise and fall ten
or a dozen feet. The entire area of these docks
is over four hundred and thirty acres, and twenty-
eight miles of wharf is afforded by them. They
are managed by a commission of twenty-eight
members, elected by the great body of dock
rate-payers, who serve without compensation.

The capital needed for their construction from time to time has been raised by loan. Their entire cost has reached the enormous sum of $100,000,000, and the commissioners have a debt of $70,000,000 still outstanding. Each dock is surrounded by extensive warehouses, and these again by high walls.

Two centuries ago Liverpool was an insignificant fishing village, with but about one thousand inhabitants. There were then several ports on the coast possessing equal or even superior natural advantages. In 1703 the first dock, a small one three acres in extent, was constructed, and from this beginning dates Liverpool's wonderful commercial greatness.

The landing stage is another notable work. It is an immense floating wharf, eighty feet wide and half a mile in length, anchored a few rods from the bank of the river and connected with it by eight bridges. Of course it rises and falls with the tide, and thus presents a wharf of uniform height at all times for the smaller steamers and ferries to land at. Upon it are built customs offices, waiting and refreshment rooms and all other conveniences.

The streets of Liverpool are kept beautifully clean and well paved. The American is particularly struck with the shop windows, in which goods are displayed to an extent and with an attractiveness unknown in our country. Inside, the stores are usually inferior to ours, but the street display is magnificent. Often the windows are so filled that the store behind is completely darkened and gas must be used at all times. Another striking feature, and one I think American merchants would do well to imitate more generally, is the ticketing of every article displayed in the windows with the price in bold figures, a matter of great convenience to customers.

At Liverpool, being within an hour's ride of Chester, one of the best preserved mediæval cities in England, travelers generally improve the opportunity to visit it. It is a charming little place of about forty thousand inhabitants, with nothing but its antiquity to support it. It is believed to be the perpetuation of a Roman military camp, the plan of the streets conforming to those of the usual camp of a Roman legion. It is surrounded by a wall about two miles in circuit, part of which is no doubt of Roman construction, and the summit of which forms a delightful promenade. The houses are mostly of the gabled sort with each story projecting a little farther into the street than the one below it, such as was the usual style of building three or four hundred years ago. Some have their timbers richly carved, and all present a very quaint appearance. But

the greatest oddities are the "Rows." In the
business thoroughfares both the first and second
stories of the buildings are devoted to stores,
those in the second story being recessed back
fifteen or twenty feet so as to open upon a covered gallery running over the tops of the stores
below. These are the "Rows," and all the best
stores are found in them. On rainy days ladies
can do their shopping without at all exposing
themselves to the weather, except it be at street
crossings where of course they must descend to
the street level. They are very curious and
interesting.

One of the principal antiquities of Chester is
the church of St. John the Baptist. Its erection
was begun in the year 1067, the year after the
Norman conquest. The nave is a fine specimen
of early Norman architecture, with massive pil-
lars five feet in diameter. Part of the church is
a picturesque ruin; part has in recent times been
restored for public worship. The old tower,
one hundred and fifty feet high, stands a little
detached from the church itself. It is very
massive, with walls eight feet thick and some
carvings upon them which must once have been
very rich. But the old tower looked very shaky
when we saw it, and a great part of it fell with
a crash the day after we were there, destroying
in its fall the beautiful Early English Gothic

porch of the church. It is however to be rebuilt. St. John's was at one time the cathedral church of the united dioceses of Lichfield, Coventry and Chester. It was superseded some five or six hundred years ago by the present cathedral, a fine old structure, but much dilapidated from the softness of the red sandstone of which it is built. When I last saw the cathedral, in 1864, it was in doubt whether it was worth restoring, but the question seems to have been settled in the affirmative as considerable work has already been done upon it. One of the most notable objects in it is the tomb of Bishop Pearson, author of the famous Exposition of the Creed. We attended service at the cathedral, and had the pleasure of hearing the eminent Dean Howson, the joint author with Conybeare of the well known Life of St. Paul.

The English hotels are very different from what we are accustomed to at home. Instead of the characteristic American hotel clerk, ladies are almost invariably found at the desk. There is no registering as with us, but the guest having been assigned a room is known only as the occupant of such and such a number. There are no regular meal hours, but the guest orders his meals at such times as best suit his convenience, and they are served either in his private parlor or in the coffee room, as he may prefer. There is no bill of

fare from which to select, and being thus dependent on his own knowledge of the dishes possible
to produce, it not infrequently happens that the
stranger fares rather badly from his ignorance of
how to order a meal. This having to order spe-
cially everything one eats is the chief annoyance
of English hotel life. Otherwise they are generally very comfortable places of sojourn, being
more quiet and more resembling private house-
holds than the hotels of this country. One sees
very little of his fellow guests, and may be for
days at a large hotel with a good custom and still
fancy himself almost the only visitor. The hotels
are less elegantly fitted up than those of corresponding position in America, but they are usually
not at all inferior in the matter of comfort. The
guest is charged so much per day for his room,
a certain other amount, usually one shilling or
eighteen pence, for attendance, and for his meals
according to what he orders. A plain breakfast of
bread, or toast, and butter and coffee generally
costs about eighteen pence (36 cents), with cold
meat it would perhaps be two shillings, and with
hot meat two and sixpence (60 cents). In the case
of dinner, all the different items, soup, fish, joint,
" sweets," and dessert are reckoned separately,
and the cost will range from two and sixpence to
five shillings (60 cents to $1.20). On leaving it is
customary to give the waiters who have attended

you a small fee, but this is altogether optional. English hotels would be more desirable if they were more generally equipped with elevators, or "lifts" as they are called in that country.

Cab fare is very cheap in England. For one or two persons, for any reasonable distance, the fare is but a shilling, or but about one-half what is charged in this country. So, too, with carriages hired at a livery stable, rates do not exceed one-half what we are accustomed to at home.

ARMS OF GREAT BRITAIN.

CHAPTER III.

HAVING seen Liverpool and Chester, we take our journey to London. The railways of England are, for the most part, grouped into eight or ten great systems, all centering in London, and each confining itself to a particular part of England, but so overlapping in territory that from almost any town of importance to another a choice of two lines may be had; and thus a healthy competition is maintained. Still rates are uniform and there is no cutting, the managers rather cultivating custom by seeing how attractive they can make their lines respectively. The principal railway systems are the Great Western, the London & Northwestern, the Midland, the Great Northern, the Northeastern, the Great Eastern, the London, Chatham & Dover, the London, Brighton & South Coast, and the London & Southwestern. It is very rare that either highways or other railways are crossed at grade, and consequently not only are there few accidents from collisions or obstructions on the track, but a much higher rate of speed is possible than with us. The towns and cities are usually entered at a level above that of the streets, which are crossed by viaducts, the passengers reaching the station by stairs. The stations, they are never called "depots" in Europe, are noticeably large and complete in their appointments. Even in towns of a score of thousand of inhabitants stations are often found rivaling the great Forty-second street depot in New York in magnificence. They usually consist of fine glass and iron roofs entirely covering the tracks for a distance exceeding that of the longest train, with brick or stone depot buildings on either side, the one for business bound in one direction, the other for traffic going the opposite way. The two sides are connected either by a tunnel or subway under the tracks, or by a bridge over them, and the public are never on any account allowed on the tracks. The stations are provided with cloak rooms where parcels of any sort may be stored at a charge of two or four cents a day for each article. The ladies' waiting rooms are often laid with Brussels carpet and furnished as comfortably as an ordinary private parlor. A lavatory or wash-room is provided, with an attendant whose duty it is to keep it scrupulously clean. Soap and clean towels are furnished, and to defray the expense a charge of about four cents is made to those using

them. So with the water closets. No hotel could
have cleaner or more elegantly fitted up. A person is in charge of them, generally a superannu-
ated employe of the company, and to defray the
expense of his care a charge of two cents is made
to those applying for a key. The hack stand is
generally in the depot and consequently under
cover, so there is no going out in the rain and
mud to take a carriage after leaving one's train.
In many other respects the English railway stations are models we could afford to copy from in
our own country.

The practice is growing in favor of having mammoth hotels connected with important railway
stations, the same being owned and controlled, if
not actually carried on, by the railway companies. Strangers thus land directly in their hotels,
and in two minutes after leaving the cars may be
in their bedrooms.

On many of the English railways the station
grounds at points along the line are beautifully
laid out as gardens, and are resplendent with
beds of bright flowers. The reader can imagine
how much pleasanter stops are under such circumstances than where the passengers' vision is
confined to a dusty yard strewn with old iron
and other litter, as is too often the case in this
country.

The English railways do not have their switchmen running all over their yards to operate the switches, at the cost of many lives and limbs annually, but the switches are all handled from one or two comfortable lookout stations, so situated as to command a view of all the tracks and the movements of every train. In these one man, without exposure to the weather, can manage fifty or more switches. Often, as he sits in his glass house with his long row of levers before him he is fairly embowered in the geraniums and other pot plants with which he adorns his perch and beguiles his leisure moments. Think of an American switchman indulging in flowers!

I need hardly tell the reader that English railway carriages are very different from ours. They are divided into several compartments, between which there is no communication, the seats run entirely across the car, half the passengers ride backwards, and the carriages (they don't call them cars) are entered at the side. I prefer them to ours, they are so much more roomy and so pleasantly exclusive. While very clean and comfortable the carriages are very plain—no rich gilding or veneering with costly woods. The result is, while they carry nearly as many passengers, they apparently weigh but little more than half what ours do, and I should think would cost to build scarcely a third the sum. They are hence more economical every way. The engines, too, are smaller and much less showy than ours.

The contrast between the heavy, cumbersome freight cars used in America and the light, simple and cheap ones used on the English lines is particularly noticeable. While the American freight car usually weighs about ten tons the English weighs less than five ("tare 4 tons 16 cwt.," I in one instance observed one marked), and both carry about the same load. The economy of motive power in using this light rolling stock must be apparent to everyone.

You never see the floor of an English railway carriage defiled with tobacco juice. Oh for the time when the same can be said in our own country!

They give you no checks for your luggage (it is not "baggage" on that side of the water), and you must look out for it yourself, and promptly, upon arriving at your destination. Tickets are taken up by ticket collectors at the station preceding the one they are issued for. The system in this respect is hardly so complete as ours. The railway porters are feed for handling the baggage, from four to twelve cents, according to the quantity you have.

Fares in England are about four, three and two cents a mile according as you ride, first, second or third-class. Return tickets are always sold at

a large reduction. They are made good for from
three days to a week, and the round trip costs
about fifty per cent. more than the single trip.
The railway passenger traffic of England is enormous and I have no doubt has been largely cultivated by the railway companies by their wise system of encouraging travel by the adoption of
cheap fares. All the railways are compelled by
their charters to run at least one train a day at a
penny (2 cents) a mile. At first it was regarded
as an imposition upon them, and all possible
obstructions were thrown in the way of people
availing themselves of this so-called parliamentary train. Now, however, the railway managers
find that the third-class traffic is the best part of
their business, and it is quite as much courted as
the first and second-class. Indeed, the Midland
railway, one of the most enterprising and best
managed of the great railway corporations of
England, has gone so far as to abolish the second-
class grade altogether and at the same time has
improved its third-class cars to the former standard of the second-class in comfort and elegance
and now runs them upon all its fast express trains.
Out of most of the larger cities of England, regular excursion trains are run on certain days of
the week at a fare not exceeding one cent a mile,
and this too must be found profitable or it would
not be so extensively practiced.

3

The most profitable railways in England are
not the great trunk lines, but the little suburban
branches that carry people daily from their
homes to their business and back again.   They
are very numerous in the vicinity of London.
American railroad managers might take a hint
from this and give more attention to developing
suburban traffic.

CHAPTER IV.

WE were unfortunate in arriving at London just at the Easter season, when nothing could be seen and scarcely any business transacted. On Good Friday all shops were closed and everything was as quiet as on Sunday. On Saturday business closed early, and on Monday, which is one of the great bank holidays, all London was off pleasure seeking and not even a box of matches could be purchased. This is no doubt better than our half-and-half way of keeping holidays in America, and I commend it for imitation on our Fourths of July.

All places of amusement proper were closed on Good Friday, but as appropriate to the day the oratorio of the Messiah was produced at Albert Hall, an immense structure capable of holding eight thousand people, erected as a memorial of the late Prince Consort. It is built of heavy masonry, oval in form, and so arranged that every one can see and hear, the solo singers occupying one of the foci of the ellipse. It contains one of

35

the largest organs in the world, presided at on
this occasion by Dr. Stainer, organist of St. Paul's
Cathedral. The orchestra embraced about eighty
instruments, and the chorus over eight hundred
singers. I need hardly add that it was grand.
At the Hallelujah Chorus the entire audience
rose to their feet and the effect was most intense.

By the way, Handel's Messiah was first rendered in the chapel of the Foundling Hospital,
the organ of which, still in use, was a present to
the institution from the great master. I attended
services there on Easter Sunday. The institution
was founded by one Captain Thomas Coram in
1739, and was so well endowed by him and others
that it is now a very rich corporation, owning
whole streets of elegant houses in the vicinity.
Formerly there was an aperture in the wall with a
revolving box in which any one could place an
infant she wished to get rid of, when by ringing a
bell and giving the box a turn the child became
an inmate of the establishment and all clue to it
was lost forever. Now, however, the mother must
present her child in person and give her name
and address, and she as well as the child becomes
an object of solicitude with the managers of the
institution, though of course not an inmate.
There are now about four hundred children in
the Foundling. They are kept till old enough to
go out as servants or be apprenticed to trades, and

though not pampered, are well cared for. The little girls look exceedingly pretty in their high white Normandy caps, white collars coming down to and pinned at the waist, and white aprons. The service at the chapel is choral, and the children, assisted by a quartet, supply the music. It was charming, the spirit with which they entered into it and the precision they maintained. Notwithstanding the wealth of the institution, the wardens stand at the door with plates, and every visitor is expected to make a contribution of sixpence or a shilling. After the services the children dine, and the visitors commonly remain to see them eat and afterwards to inspect the dormitories and school rooms. There is also an interesting museum containing some rare paintings, which may be seen by those who like.

On Sunday evening we attended one of the people's services under the dome of St. Paul's, at which eminent men from all parts of the kingdom preach in rotation. On this occasion the entire church was filled with hearers to the number of many thousands.

A few steps from St. Paul's is the main office of Thomas Cook & Son, the pioneer tourist ticket agents. Here at one payment we can procure tickets for thousands of miles of travel, by rail, steamer and stage coach, and traversing a dozen different countries. It is an immense conven-

ience to travelers, particularly if one is not
familiar with the languages of all the countries
visited. Our tickets, taking us from London
through Belgium, up the Rhine, through Bavaria, the Tyrol, Italy, Switzerland and France,
over the route described in a former chapter, with
the privilege of lying over at numerous places,
cost us £18 17s 6d, or $91.73 each.

Besides this we are able at Cook's to pay
hotel bills in advance for any number of days we
desire at the rate of eight and sixpence, or $2.10
per day. The tickets entitle us to a table d'hote
dinner, usually served on the continent at the close
of the day's sight-seeing, or about five or six
o'clock, a bed, with lights and attendance, and a
meat breakfast. Lunch in the middle of the
day one is supposed to procure at a restaurant
wherever he may happen to be. There are
separate coupons for each meal and the bed,
so one is not required to remain longer than
he cares to at any hotel, nor does he have
to pay for any meals he has not eaten. The
coupons are good at any of a list of three
hundred and twelve hotels at two hundred and
seventy-two different places on the continent.
Cook's is not the only tourist ticket agency,
nor, in the opinion of some, the best, but it
is an old established concern, and is every way
worthy of confidence. The senior Mr. Cook

began his enterprise by getting up temperance excursions for the poorer classes in England, in part as a philanthropic measure, and from this beginning has grown up a very extensive business, with branch offices in all the principal cities in Europe and America. It is safe to say the majority of English and American people one meets on the continent are traveling on Cook's tickets.

We spend but little time in London as it is important that we reach Rome by the middle of May, soon after which the fever season sets in and it is unsafe for strangers to sojourn there. We leave therefore the sights of London till our return, and push on for the continent.

CHAPTER V.

WE sailed from Dover with a stiff east wind blowing, confident in late trans-Atlantic experience to bring us through like old sailors, but before we reached Calais our confidence gave way, and we vowed the next time we crossed we should wait for a fine day. The steamers are small, and the heavy waves break over them to an extent that not a foot of dry space is to be found on deck. No sooner were the lines cast off at Dover than the sailors ominously passed around to every passenger a large white bowl, and devoted themselves mainly during the voyage to emptying them as occasion required.

It takes about two hours to cross from Dover to Calais, and about five more, by rail, to reach Brussels. The country we pass through in this portion of our journey is very flat, but not uninteresting. We pass through several large manu-

facturing cities and see some fine old churches, a
few castles, and near the boundary line between
France and Belgium some fortifications. Occasionally in the intervening country we see a stately
manor house, but the majority of the houses
are of the quaint, high-roofed French farm house
sort, built of stone or brick and covered with tiles
or thatch. Scarcely a fence is to be seen the entire
distance, only lines of trees, usually willows,
marking the subdivisions of the land. In the
case of the willows they are usually kept trimmed
off close about six or eight feet from the ground,
where a great unsightly knob forms itself. The
periodical cropping of the trees is for the purpose
of supplying fuel, of which the country is otherwise largely destitute. The same branch-denuded
trees—mere stumps with bushy heads of small
twigs—are commonly seen all over continental
Europe, large full grown trees being quite exceptional except in royal and public parks. The surface of the ground between Calais and Brussels is
so flat that in many cases the fields are intersected
by canals a yard or two wide—primarily for
drainage but also utilized for navigation, the
farmer using boats instead of wagons to convey
his crops from the fields to his barn. Wagon
roads are rarely seen, but what there are are
excellent, the main highways being paved with
stone like the streets of a city. So, too, draft

animals seem scarce, and manual labor appears to take their place in farming operations. Everywhere spring work was in full blast, and almost as many women as men were seen in the fields. In one case I noticed a man and a woman drawing a harrow by ropes passed over their shoulders, and in another case a like pair were drawing a roller over a newly plowed field. One of the most striking features of the route is the great number of windmills seen, and which may almost be counted by hundreds.

Arrived at Brussels, we drive to our hotel, find plenty of attaches who speak English fluently, and soon feel quite at home. The hotel is a quaint sort of a place, but withal very clean and comfortable. There is a court-yard in the center, open to the skies, across which we have to walk to the dining room, and upon which the ladies' parlor opens. It is a queer mixture of the ancient and modern, the rude and the elegant. Our chamber ceiling is low and is intersected by a great beam, the woodwork of the doors and windows, too, is old fashioned and clumsy, but the house is fitted with electric bells, a handsome French clock with accompanying ornaments occupies the mantle-piece, a good Brussels carpet the floor, and all the furniture is of solid mahogany. The beds are all single, the custom of the continent being for husbands and wives to sleep separately, and, in lieu of a sufficient supply of blankets and counterpanes, each bed is provided with a small eider-down bed, coming up about half way to the pillows, and covered with lace. This lies on top and keeps the feet and legs warm. The bed rooms are lighted only by candles, and, cheap as must be the article of soap, every guest is expected to furnish his own.

The table d'hote in our hotel is at five o'clock. The dinner bell rings and all the guests sit down together. Ten courses are served, and we sit altogether about an hour and a half. All the plates and knives and forks are removed and clean ones provided for each course. First comes soup, then ham patties, then fish, and after these in succession, roast beef and spinach, roast veal with onion dressing, asparagus with hard-boiled eggs, some kind of bird on toast, head-cheese and salad, pudding, and lastly dessert of fruit and cakes—ten clean plates to each guest, unless he chooses to omit some of the courses in which case he sits patiently till the other guests have finished and the next course is served. Almost every guest has a bottle of wine by his plate, the light German and Italian wines being much used on the continent as an ordinary beverage.

After a night's rest we take a drive over the city. A two-horse carriage and driver for two hours costs us nine francs, or $1.80. Brussels is a beautiful city. No American city, or even London, can boast such architecture for boldness and elegance. A more graceful tower and spire than that of the Hotel de Ville, a more massive creation than the new Palace of Justice, or more palatial rows of private buildings than line some of the newer boulevards it would probably be difficult to find anywhere. Even in the older portions of the city, where the streets are narrow and crooked, the houses with their gabled roofs and well-cared-for stuccoed walls, the attractive shop windows, and the stately old churches and other public buildings which stand out everywhere, contribute a charm to the place.

The boulevards of Brussels are magnificent thoroughfares, some of them two hundred feet wide. These have a macadamized roadway for pleasure driving in the center, lined with avenues of trees. On one side is a dirt road for horseback riding, and on the other a grassy walk for pedestrians. Outside of these come paved roadways for heavy traffic, and still beyond them flag sidewalks.

The cathedral church of St. Gudule is a very fine Gothic edifice, famous for the magnificent chapels that flank the choir, for its rich stained glass windows, and for a remarkable carved wooden pulpit representing the expulsion of Adam and Eve from Eden. Our first parents are

of life size, and, with the trunk of the tree of
knowledge of good and evil, support the pulpit.
Just over them is a life-sized angel brandishing
his fiery sword, while Satan, in form of a serpent
some twenty or thirty feet long and as large as a
man's leg, is coiled all about the pulpit with his
head peering over the top of the sounding board
above, where a figure of the Virgin appears
instructing the infant Jesus to crush the head
with his foot. The stair railing leading up to the
pulpit is ornamented with cocks, monkeys and
various other animals, and altogether it is a very
curious piece of work.

In the Hotel de Ville or City Hall are some
tapestries which for perfection of shading and
brilliancy of coloring rival the best art of the
painter. But the great specialty of Brussels is its
lace. There are a number of manufactories some
of very long existence. The designs are generally
very artistic, but the skill with which the oper-
atives manipulate, in its production, sometimes
hundreds and thousands of bobbins is truly wonderful. The interest in seeing lace made is only
exceeded by observing the skill and ingenuity
with which it is sold. Every hackdriver and
hotel porter seems to have a special interest in
beguiling travelers into the lace factories. Once
within the walls they are taken in charge by the
most beautiful and fascinating of young ladies,

and the stock is exhibited with so much tact and graceful naivete that I doubt if one person in twenty gets away without making some purchase.

Brussels, which has three hundred thousand inhabitants, is the capital of Belgium, one of the youngest of the family of European nations. As part of the dukedom of Burgundy, it fell in the sixteenth century to Charles V., emperor of Germany and Spain, by inheritance. The oppressions of his son, Philip II., caused the eighty years war, portrayed so graphically by Motley in his Dutch Republic. The war ended in 1648 with the independence of the protestant provinces of Holland, but the retention by Spain of the catholic provinces now forming Belgium. By the peace of Ryswick, in 1713, the latter were transferred to Austria. It was the Empress Maria Theresa of Austria who gave Brussels its park. In 1794 the province was conquered by the revolutionary army of France, and it remained under French dominion till the fall of Napoleon in 1815, when the congress of Vienna, which undertook the reconstruction of the map of Europe, united it again with the kingdom of Holland. The Belgians were not given equal rights with their new confreres, grew discontented, and in 1830 threw off the Dutch yoke and set up as a separate nation. They elected as their king Prince

Leopold of Saxe-Cobourg, the widower of the beloved Princess Charlotte of England, daughter of George IV. and cousin of Queen Victoria. He was a man of high culture and superior character, and made for thirty-five years a good and popular king. His son, Leopold II., now reigns, and it is his daughter Stephanie who was recently married to the son of the emperor of Austria.

The people of Belgium are mostly catholics, and are industrious and enterprising and fully abreast of the French and English in the development of the arts and manufactures. Besides lace, Brussels carpets, glass and iron are among the chief products of the country. The French and Flemish languages are about equally spoken in Belgium.

From Brussels we take a train for Antwerp, the principal sea-port of Belgium, and an interesting old city of one hundred and twenty-five thousand inhabitants. It is an hour's ride and the fare for the round trip is about one dollar. The country we pass through is a dead level as far as the eye can reach in every direction, neither cutting nor embankment worth speaking of being required for the railroad the entire distance. Nor is there scarcely a fence to be seen, but rows of trees mark every subdivision of land, and fine avenues line every roadway. These have a very pretty effect, and will no doubt supply future generations with much valuable timber. The land is in a high state of cultivation, and every rod is fully improved. The field labor is chiefly manual, comparatively few beasts being employed. One horse usually draws the plow, and in one field I saw a single ox harnessed to this implement.

Antwerp, once the commercial metropolis of the world, a position to which London has now succeeded, is a well built but rather quiet and sleepy old city. It lacks the brilliancy and gaiety of Brussels, but is clean, in good repair, and presents an air of stately respectability. The houses are of great architectural variety, but the steep gabled fronts predominate. All are built up closely in solid blocks. We first visit the cathedral, one of the finest in northern Europe, and dating from 1352–1411. It is remarkable for having three aisles on either side of the nave, giving great breadth to the church. Its lofty, light, graceful spire very much resembles that of the Hotel de Ville at Brussels. The two master-pieces of Rubens, "the Elevation of the Cross" and "the Descent from the Cross," for which the cathedral is noted, hang in the two transepts of the church, and are only uncovered for public inspection at certain hours. Antwerp was the home of Peter Paul Rubens, the greatest of Flemish painters (born 1577, died 1640), and his

best works **are** to be seen here. Some are collected **in a small** gallery at the house he resided
in and which is still **preserved in good** condition,
but the principal collection is **found at the**
Museum, a public gallery **open free** on **certain**
days of the **week.**

The Belgians of past ages seem **to** have especially excelled in the art of wood carving. **I**
have already mentioned the wonderful pulpit **in**
St. Gudule's. In Antwerp cathedral is **one very**
similar to it, and in **the church** of **St. Paul** the
wood carvings are perhaps nowhere surpassed for
abundance and richness. Every confessional
consists **of a** group of figures of life size, and the
walls **of the** large church all around **for some**
height **above** the pavement are **a mass of rich**
carvings in oak.

A scarcely less **notable feature** of St. Paul's
church **in Antwerp** is its "Calvary." **This is**
outside **the church but** adjoining **it, and consists**
of some sixty life-size marble statues, representing all the great bible worthies, leading **up to an**
artificial mountain, upon which **appears in full**
the scene of **the** crucifixion in white **marble.**
Below the mountain is a cave **in which a dead**
Christ is seen, and back of the **mountain** a representation of purgatory, **with** men tortured by
devils and writhing in marble flames. It is altogether **a very** curious conception, and **is a favor-**

4

ite place of resort for meditation and prayer with the pious catholics of Antwerp.

One of the inconveniences in Belgium is the lack of a uniform language. All notices to the public have to be in polyglot form, involving an immense amount of printing and sign painting. Thus, as illustration, the refreshment room at the railway station usually bears a sign reading:

BUVETTA.
TAP-ROOM.
DRINKPLAATS.
TRINKSTUBE.

And the outlet from the station is indicated by the words:

WAY OUT..
WITGANG
SORTIE.
AUSGANG.

So all official papers appear printed in two or more different languages, side by side.

A POLLARD WILLOW.

CHAPTER VI.

LEAVING Brussels for Cologne we pass
through Louvain with its great catholic
university from which so many priests are
sent to America, and the important manufacturing city of Liege. In this direction the country
is much more rolling, and after passing Liege
becomes decidedly rocky, if not mountainous.
Soon after, we cross the boundary line into Germany and stop at the old city of Aix-la-Chapelle.
The place is famous in history as one of Charlemagne's capitals and as the scene of several
important treaties of peace, including that effected by the congress of 1818 held for the settling
of the affairs of Europe after Napoleon's defeat
at Waterloo in 1815. It it is a quiet, modern-
built town with only one or two objects of any
considerable interest to the ordinary traveler.
These are the cathedral, part of which was built
by Charlemagne more than a thousand years ago,
and in which he was buried, and the Rathhaus, or

city hall, which occupies the site of the great
emperor's palace, some remains of which are
embraced in it. The cathedral is octagonal in
form, with square piers and semi-circular arches,
and is of exceedingly massive construction. At
a later period an elegant Gothic choir or chancel
was added to the plain Carlovingian portion.
The tomb of Charlemagne was in the center of
the octagon, and he was buried originally in a
sitting position in an arm-chair of marble. This
chair or throne is now exhibited in the gallery of
the church. For many generations it was used as
the coronation chair of the emperors of Germany.
After reposing in it for three hundred and fifty
years Charlemagne's body was removed from
the chair to a richly-carved marble sarcophagus
brought from Rome, and said to have been the
coffin of the Emperor Augustus. This coffin is
also exhibited, the remains having at last found
a place as sacred relics in the treasury of the
church.

The Rathhaus is remarkable chiefly for an
exceedingly fine vaulted hall one hundred and
sixty-five feet long and sixty wide, called the
. kaisersaal, and which contains some very fine
modern frescoes.

A two hour's ride brings us to Cologne, where
our baggage undergoes the formality of a customs inspection. The celebrated cathedral so

overshadows everything else at Cologne that one
hardly cares to visit the objects of lesser interest,
though the city contains several fine mediæval
churches, the tomb of the famous thirteenth century British scholar and theologian Duns Scotus,
who died in Cologne where he occupied a chair
in the university, and numerous interesting antiquities, for Cologne was founded in the year 51 by
Agrippina, mother of the Roman emperor Nero,
and doubtless derived its name from being the
chief Roman colony in north Germany. But it
is not a pleasant city to stay long in. The streets
are narrow and crooked, the slops of the city
flow down the open gutters of the streets, and the
seventy-two distinct smells of which Coleridge
wrote seem now blended into one not unlike that
of some of our American sulphur springs. So
we confine our attention to the cathedral, the
grandest Gothic structure in the world, to see
which is well worth a journey to Europe to any
lover of architecture.

Cologne Cathedral was begun in 1248 by an
archbishop who was ambitious of a church
comporting with the wealth and commercial
greatness of the city at that period. The east
end, or choir, was first erected, and this was completed in 1322, when the nave, transepts and
towers were begun. In 1447 one tower was high
enough to receive its bells. The enthusiasm then

subsided, a temporary roof was thrown over the
nave, and for more than three hundred years all
hope of the church ever being completed was
abandoned.   It had fallen greatly to decay, when
in 1796 the French stripped the lead from the
roof, used the interior as a hay magazine, and
left the church little better than a ruin.   In 1816
the king of Prussia caused the building to be
examined with reference to its restoration, but it
was not till 1823 that work upon it was begun.
The work was then carried on under the supervision of one Zwirner, an architect of rare talent
who died in 1861, and he was the person who first
suggested the entire completion of the edifice.
Between 1842 and 1876 the immense sum of
$3,500,000 was expended upon it, the greater part
being contributed by the Prussian government.

The cathedral is four hundred and forty-four
feet long, two hundred and one feet wide at the
nave and two hundred and eighty-two at the
transepts.   The walls rise one hundred and fifty
feet and the ridge of the roof is two hundred and
one feet from the ground.   The two towers at the
west end rise grandly to the height of five hundred and eleven feet, and their walls one hundred
and fifty feet from the ground, as I measured
them, were twelve feet in thickness.   Inside the
church the vaulted ceiling is one hundred and
forty-five feet above the pavement.   But these

figures will utterly fail to give the reader anything like an idea of the immensity of the structure or the deep impression it makes on one's mind. But even this impression fades before the admiration inspired by the intrinsic beauty of the structure. Its magnificent proportions, its graceful outlines, its apparent lightness and its chaste yet elaborate ornamentation all combine to render it the most beautiful Gothic church in the world. What Handel's Messiah is in music Cologne cathedral is in architecture. It is above comparison and can only be worshiped.

After drinking in the grandeur of the nave, with its double aisles lighted with thirteenth and fourteenth century stained glass, we ascend to the galleries, which perforate the walls a hundred feet from the ground, and look down on the pigmies worshiping below. Then we climb fifty feet higher to the vaulting of the nave, at which level we entered the belfry where in one of the towers hangs a thirty-ton bell cast from French cannon captured in the war of 1870 and presented by the Emperor William. This bell requires twenty-eight men to ring it. Then we ascend into the lantern, over the intersection of the nave and transepts, two hundred and fifty feet from the ground, and gaze up at the beautiful openwork spires towering still two hundred and sixty feet above us.

That portion of the river Rhine visited for its
scenery is comprised between Cologne and Mayence, a distance of one hundred and seventeen
miles, though it is in fact only the seventy-five
miles between Bonn and Bingen that possesses
interest to the American traveler. The rest of
the distance the banks are low and contain few
objects of attraction. Between Bonn and Bingen,
however, the scenery is very fine, far surpassing in my opinion our much boasted Hudson.
Mountains rise on either side hundreds of feet in
height, and the river so winds among the hills
that it seems perpetually land-locked. The sides
of the hills are wonderfully improved in the cultivation of the grape, and terrace after terrace
rises along their steep sides, sometimes to their
extreme summits. Wherever on their rocky
slopes a dozen square yards of soil can be secured
by the erection of a sustaining wall there we find
a dozen grape vines. Tens of thousands of acres
must be thus employed, and hundreds of miles of
stone wall. One ceases to wonder where all the
wine comes from, or that it can be retailed at so
low a price as from thirty to fifty cents a bottle.
On our way up the river we pass, near Bingen,
the famous Johannisberg vineyard of forty acres,
the average product of which reaches a value of
$40,000 a year. It belongs to the family of the
late Prince Metternich.

The vine-clad hills are not the only attraction.
At intervals of a few miles the tops of the hills
are crowned with old castles, sometimes mere
ruins, sometimes restored for habitation. They
are often very picturesque. They are the product of a barbarous age, when might made right,
and when positions of inaccessibility, with strong
walls and towers, were the only safeguards for
life and property. They were particularly
numerous along the Rhine and its tributaries, as
the commerce of the river afforded a tempting
revenue in the way of tolls to any one who was
powerful enough to collect them. The traveler
remains on deck every minute of the time during
the trip up the river and enjoys the panorama
exceedingly.

The Rhine is a very swift stream, and is navi-
gated by sharp and powerful steamers, which
nevertheless require in ascending the river about
eight hours to accomplish what they would in
five in going down. To enjoy the scenery one
should always ascend the river. We made the
trip in April, too early in the season for comfort,
the weather on the river being quite chilly. The
large express steamers also had not begun their
season's trips and the smaller boats made two
days of it, leaving their passengers over night at
Coblenz, a point at the confluence of the Moselle

with the Rhine, about midway between Cologne
and Mayence.

Coblenz is a strongly fortified town of thirty
thousand inhabitants. The extent of its fortifications may be judged from the fact that after
they had been dismantled by Napoleon I. the
Prussian government expended $6,000,000 in
their restoration. One can hardly find a square
yard of space anywhere in the vicinity that is
not covered by some loop-hole or embrasure in
some piece of fortification. Eight thousand soldiers are stationed there—a useless provision, one
would think, in time of peace, but every able-
bodied man in Germany must render three years'
military service, and the large army thus enlisted
must be disposed somewhere, so the little town
of Coblenz sleeps secure with a guard of about
two soldiers to each house.

The Empress of Germany has a summer palace
at Coblenz, and during the season it is a place of
considerable fashionable resort. In the way of
antiquities it possesses one church, at least, that
of St. Castor, over eight hundred years old.

Near the close of our second day's voyage we
call at Bingen, the "Fair Bingen on the Rhine"
of Mrs. Caroline Norton's beautiful poem.

Mayence, or Mentz, is an interesting little city
of fifty thousand inhabitants, opposite the mouth
of the river Main, and also strongly fortified. It

is particularly interesting as being the birthplace
of Gutenberg and the art of printing. Johann
Gensfleisch von Gutenberg seems to have per-
fected his invention about 1438. He was then
residing in Strassburg. He returned to Mayence
in 1443 and soon after formed a partnership with
a capitalist named Faust for the establishment of
a printing office. His first production was a
Latin bible, the precise year of the appearance
of which is not known. The building, however,
in which the business was carried on is still in
existence, and a tablet on it fixes 1447 as a period
of its occupancy by Gutenberg. The poor
inventor was subsequently cheated out of the
property by his rich partner, and having procured other assistance he was compelled to begin
again, his original office being now carried on by
Faust & Schoeffer as a rival concern. Gutenberg died in 1468, and his fame is perpetuated by
a fine bronze statue by Thorwaldsen in one of the
public squares of Mayence.

Mayence has also a very interesting old cathedral dating from 1180, combining the Roman-
esque with the Gothic styles of architecture, and
very rich in sepulchral monuments.

Leaving the Rhine at Mayence we turn eastward (the Rhine flows nearly due north) and an
hour's ride by rail brings us to Frankfort-on-the
Main, until 1866 one of the four free cities of

Germany and the seat of the Germanic Diet. In the Austro-Prussian war Frankfort took sides with Austria, and for a time stood in great danger of being sacked by the victorious Prussians. As it was she was mulcted in a war indemnity of $1,250,000, about half a million of which was, however, assumed by the emperor individually and a like amount by the imperial government, so that on the whole the city got off quite easily. The policy of the empire has been very conciliatory toward Frankfort; and while the loss of her ancient sovereignty is still bemoaned by the older inhabitants, she never was more prosperous than since her incorporation into the empire, and altogether she is as loyal to-day as any other part of Germany. Frankfort is a splendid old city. A good portion of it is as quaint and old-fashioned as can be, with narrow, crooked streets and tall overhanging buildings of frame work filled in with brick and plaster, many of them richly carved and ornamented. Part of the city, however, is modern and quite elegant, and altogether it possesses an air of business, and presents attractions in the display of its wares that we have seen nowhere else since we left Brussels. Frankfort also contains some of the finest hotels in Germany. It is the seat of great wealth and has a splendid Bourse or stock exchange.

Frankfort has some old churches of consider-

able interest, and the Rœmer, or town hall, dating from the year 1406, in which the elections
for emperor of Germany were accustomed to be
held.   The kaisersaal, or large hall in which the
banquet was held after the election was complete,
and from a window of which the new emperor
was presented to the people, has been restored in
recent times, and now contains fine oil portraits
of all the emperors from Charlemagne down to
the dissolution of the empire in 1806.

In one of the quiet back streets of Frankfort is
a large and old-fashioned house bearing a slab of
marble in its front wall with this inscription:

In diesem hause
wurde
JOHANN WOLFGANG GOETHE,
am 28 August, 1749,
Geboren,

signifying that in that house the immortal Goethe
was born August 28, 1749.   A fine bronze statue
of the great poet adorns one of the public
squares.

Another birthplace I took the pains to ferret
out was that of the famous Rothschild family.
It is in the Jews' quarter, in a miserable, dirty,
ruinous row of tall houses. Here, three generations ago, Mayer Rothschild kept a small bank,
and having the good fortune to preserve through
a period of invasion the treasures of one of the
German princes at the sacrifice of his own prop-

erty, obtained favors from the government which
laid the foundation for the immense fortunes his
descendants still enjoy.   A branch of the Roths-
childs' banking business is still carried on in
Frankfort, a plain four-storied modern building
being occupied, only a stone's throw from old
Mayer Rothschild's narrow quarters in the Juden-
gasse.

CHAPTER VII.

BAVARIA—THE ANCIENT CITY OF NUREMBERG—MUNICH AND ITS
  PICTURE GALLERIES—ITS BRONZE FOUNDRY—GERMAN TREE
  CULTURE—GERMAN COINAGE—FREEDOM FROM PAUPERISM—
  CONTINENTAL SUNDAYS.

"In the valley of the Pegnitz, where across broad meadow lands
  Rise the blue Franconian mountains, Nuremberg, the ancient, stands;
  Quaint old town of toil and traffic, quaint old town of art and song,
  Memories haunt thy pointed gables, like the rooks that round them throng."
  —*Longfellow.*

HALF a day's ride from Frankfort brings us
to the interesting old city of Nuremberg.
This we had long looked forward with
pleasure to seeing, as the best preserved mediæval
city on the continent. Nor were we disappointed. It is surrounded with a splendid stone
wall and a moat at least fifty feet wide. It also
has dozens of towers for defense, some of them of
great height and strength. The streets are usually of good width, and the houses broad and
large, indicating a prevalence of wealth and comparative luxury at the time they were erected.
They are usually three or four full stories high,
with high roofs above containing from two to six
additional attic stories lighted by dormer windows. The houses are commonly of stone with
walls of great thickness, though the projecting
fronts of filled-in frame work are also common.

63

The predominating feature of the town is the immense quantity of elaborate stone carving which ornaments walls, towers, churches and private buildings, rendering the city extremely picturesque and interesting. This feature results, first, from Nuremberg being in early days a famous center of art, and second, from the city being built mainly of a species of soft sandstone, in which sculptures can almost be whittled out with a jack-knife. This combination of circumstances has given almost every other house some quaint device in stone, while no churches I have elsewhere seen have been, for their size and importance, so rich in sculptures. The two principal churches are those of St. Lawrence and St. Sebald, both quite cathedral-like in their proportions and artistic beauty, and each claiming a good two hours for its inspection.

Albert Durer, Germany's greatest painter and engraver, was a native and resident of Nuremberg, and both the house in which he was born, in 1471, and that in which he lived in mature life are still to be seen. Nuremberg reverences Durer as Antwerp does Rubens, and memorials of him stand out in every feature of the place. Besides Durer, Nuremberg was the home of Peter Vischer and Adam Krafft, both eminent sculptors, some of the best works of whom adorn the churches of the place. We stayed at Nuremberg

a day and a half, and could with difficulty tear
ourselves away. Nuremberg is situated on the
river Pegnitz, a tributary of the Main, and now
contains about one hundred thousand inhabitants. It is peculiarly a protestant city, possessing but one catholic church, and that a small one.
It is within the jurisdiction of Bavaria, but from
remarks dropped by people there I fancy the
emperor of Germany is far more popular than
king Louis II.

Munich, the capital of Bavaria, is five hours'
ride south of Nuremberg, and is described in all
the guide books and foreign letters as one of the
finest little cities on the continent. Perhaps I
had been led to expect too much, for I certainly
was grievously disappointed in it. Its streets, it
is true, are broad and straight and reasonably
well paved and clean, but architecturally Munich
stands nowhere. It has scarcely a single really
fine church that I can discover, although the
Basilica, a recent structure, is immense in its size
and gorgeous with rich marbles and frescoes. The
public buildings, as a rule, are pretentious, but
lacking in beauty. One very imposing structure
when seen from a little distance, known as the
Hall of Fame, we find on approach to be a mere
portico with nothing back of it. It contains
busts of about a hundred of the eminent men of
Bavaria, including Durer, Krafft, Jean Paul

Richter. etc. Another costly building, the New Pinakothek, instead of being of stone with bold cornices and pilasters, is of brick finished with plaster almost perfectly flat, and depending for its exterior ornamentation on a series of enormous frescoes by Kaulbach, which have already faded to an extent that renders them an eye-sore rather than a thing of beauty. Stucco takes the place of stone almost universally, and not only is but little constructional ornamentation possible, but everything is left of a dirty yellow color that gives it a cheap look.

Munich has two very pretentious picture galleries, the New Pinakothek, containing the works of modern artists, and the Old Pinakothek, containing works of the old masters alone. The latter was founded by Maximilian I., first King of Bavaria, in 1822, and the building was completed and opened in 1836. The collection of pictures was formed by the consolidation of several previously distinct collections, including that of Dusseldorf. The pictures are so arranged as to illustrate the progress of the art in the last four centuries.

The royal bronze foundry is one of the lions of Munich. The charge for admission is forty pfennigs (10 cents). The first thing that caught my eye on entering the inclosure was the model from which the statue of Michigan, which surmounts the Detroit Soldiers' Monument, **was cast.** The museum of the foundry contains a large number of the original models from which the more famous statues have been made including that of **Wash-ington (colossal equestrian)** at Richmond, Va., **Clay, Webster,** Jefferson, **Chief** Justice Marshall, Lincoln, **Everett,** Benton, **and other prominent** Americans; **Goethe, Schiller,** Marshal Bernadotte, king of Sweden, Prince **Milan** of **Servia,** Gen. Bolivar (the last three magnificent equestrian statues) **and** many **others,** also the **models of** the bronze **doors of the** Capitol at Washington. America seems to have been by **far** the best cus-tomer of **this** royal foundry, though statues have been cast in it for almost every civilized nation on the globe. The works are **now** employed **on a** colossal statue of Germany to be erected at **Bin-gen.** It **will be** represented **as** a buxom female forty **feet** high, **and** will require three **years to** complete. **A still** larger **statue** representing **Bavaria** was **turned** out **at this** foundry some years since, and **is** now one **of the** sights **of** Munich. It is **fifty-four feet high and** stands **on a** pedestal **forty** feet high. **Steps in** the inte-**rior** lead up to the lady's head, which will **hold** eight grown people at one time.

The bricks used in Munich **are twelve and a** half inches long, **six wide, and three thick.** Very coarse mortar is used **with them.** Partition walls are built six inches thick and plastered directly on the brick work. For ceilings, after lathing with wood, a cross lathing of wire is used in some buildings, the wires being half an inch apart. For sidewalk paving hard burned tiles eight inches square and one and a half thick are used. They make a nice walk and are probably cheaper and more durable than stone.

The only kind of heating apparatus we saw on the continent was a tall rectangular stove made of tiles, usually white and glazed, but sometimes ornamented. It stands six or seven feet high, looks very neat, and is probably economical of fuel.

One of the noticeable features of the country in traveling through Germany is the extent to which tree culture is practiced. We often pass on the railway large tracts of land covered with pine trees, all planted in rows like corn, and so thickly that they grow up tall and straight with no lateral branches. The question suggests itself, might it not pay to plant similar tracts to timber in the United States? One might have to wait some time for returns, but they would be certain and lucrative when they did come.

Another feature is the great number of crosses, crucifixes and images of the Blessed Virgin that are seen along the highways and in the fields. Some are quite large, others small and protected by little shrines.   In the villages and cities, notably Nuremberg, almost every corner house has a little niche in the angle from which a little gaudy image looks down upon the passer-by.

We began to notice in Brussels that the horses were of superior quality.   Down in Bavaria the heavy draft horses are simply magnificent.   A team of four attached to a heavy brewer's truck, as seen in the streets of Munich, would be a notable sight in America.   Oxen are very much in use and are often driven singly.   Instead of the heavy cumbersome yoke used in this country, they are made to draw by their heads, a padded stick being placed across their foreheads, suspended from the horns, and traces being attached to the ends.

Under the present imperial government there has been a reconstruction and unification of the coinage of Germany.   The unit in their system is the mark, as the franc is in France, the pound in England, and the dollar in our own country. The value of the mark is twenty-four cents in our currency, and it is subdivided into one hundred parts called pfennigs, the value of a single pfennig being about a quarter of a cent.   The coins struck are one and two pfennig pieces in copper; five and ten pfennigs in nickel, twenty and fifty pfennigs, and one, two, three and five marks in silver; and five, ten and twenty marks in gold.

The necessity for the smaller coins may be questioned, but everything is cheap in Germany and they are frequently required, as for illustration in paying the tolls over the Rhine at Coblenz, which are two pfennigs per head, or a scant half cent.

Germany, at the time of our visit, was suffering from "hard times"—the reaction from the era of prosperity which followed the unification of the German states, the conquest of France, and the re-establishment of the Empire. It is a noteworthy fact that even in such times of depression there is in Germany no poverty apparent on the surface, and no poor laws or boards of associated charities. There is no need for them; the prudent, independent German shapes his expenses to his income, and if he has but ten cents a day he will manage to live on it. I submit that this is a condition of things infinitely superior to our American system, where a large percentage of the population has to be constantly supported by the remainder. In this branch of social science I am strongly inclined to believe our Teutonic cousins are far in advance of us, and that sooner or later we shall have to adopt their theories. Our American system is a mere cultivation of pauperism.

In Munich we had our first experience of a so-called "continental Sunday." The first thing we saw from our windows on the Sunday we were there was the shopkeepers taking down their shutters and arranging their goods in their windows. Then a large load of beer barrels came along; then a load of sand and all the ordinary traffic of a week day. As we passed through the streets on our way to church, people could be seen at work in all the various shops, trucks were delivering goods, and altogether it was hard to believe it was really Sunday. We went into three or four churches, Catholic and Protestant, and found only mere handfuls of worshipers.

CHAPTER VIII.

IT was cloudy when we arrived at Munich, and we did not notice the beautiful mountains which lay to the southward of the city; but on our departure, as soon as we were clear of the houses, the panorama which met our view in the snow-clad Bavarian Alps glistening in the mid-day sun was truly magnificent. It took us three hours to reach their base. Meanwhile the scenery greatly changed. North of Munich we were very much reminded of the Illinois prairies, both by the lay of the land and the methods of cultivation, but as we approached the mountains a decidedly Swiss aspect began to be assumed. The farm houses began to exhibit a peculiar style —oblong in shape, with the residence portion at one end and the barns and stables at the other. The roofs became rather flat and projecting, and one or two verandas usually ornamented the fronts. Stone was the material of the walls and shingles of the roofs, the latter being held down by heavy stones laid upon them.

The railroad penetrates the mountains, following the valley of the Inn, a tributary of the Danube. At Kufstein, a little place shut in by lofty mountain peaks, we enter the Tyrol. We are now in Austrian territory, and here have to undergo that always annoying process, the examination of our baggage. This causes a tedious delay, and it is late in the evening before we reach Innsbruck, one hundred miles south of Munich. We find prices higher, and the people more grasping, in Austria than in Germany.

Innsbruck is a delightful little city of twenty-three thousand inhabitants, dropped right down in a deep valley among the mountains. The latter seem to rise on every hand but a few blocks away from the beholder, and they tower up thousands of feet and are capped with snow for the greater part of the year. Innsbruck is the chief city of the Tyrol, and is a place of some historic note. The German emperor Maximilian I. (1459–1519), made it one of his capitals, and himself lies buried in one of the churches of the place. Seventy-two years ago it was the scene of the famous exploit of Andrew Hofer, who, a poor peasant inn-keeper, raised the Tyrol against Napoleonic dominion, defeated the emperor's ablest general in a pitched battle, and compelled Bonaparte to vary his usual tactics and conclude an armistice with other foes in order to concentrate against the Tyrolese an overwhelming force. Hofer was then defeated by sheer force of numbers and compelled to take refuge in flight. He was subsequently betrayed to the French, taken to Mantua, and shot like a dog. He now lies buried in the Hof church at Innsbruck, in company with the great Maximilian. The scene of his great battle in which he defeated the French in the spring of 1809, is a low hill just south of and overlooking the city.

The newer portions of Innsbruck are finely built, with broad streets and palatial looking structures. The older part has narrower streets, with low arcades on either side through which the sidewalks extend, and upon which the curious but well-stocked little stores open. These arcades are very quaint and pleasant to walk through.

Maximilian's tomb, referred to above, is reckoned the very finest in Europe, and certainly we saw none more beautiful or interesting. It stands in the center of the Hof church, and with its accessories pretty much monopolizes all the space in it. Extending down the nave of the church, facing and flanking the tomb, are a series of twenty-eight fine bronze statues something more than life size, and all of sixteenth century work. They represent the famous ancestors of Maximilian, male and female, in the armor or costume of their day, and include the renowned crusader Godfrey de Bouillon, King of Jerusalem. The tomb itself contains twenty-four panels of marble, each exquisitely carved in high relief, for which the Tyrol is so famous, and each representing some scene in Maximilian's life. We had seen plenty of fine bas-reliefs, but none before that so filled us with wonder and delight. In the space of a yard in length there would be hundreds of figures, with arms, armor and costume, even the embroidered dresses, faithful to life. Maximilian was the immediate predecessor of the emperor Charles V., and reigned from 1493 to 1519.

The Tyrol embraces eleven thousand square miles of mountainous country lying to the east of Switzerland. About one-third of this territory is perpetually covered with snow, another third is covered with dense forests, and the remainder is mostly pasture land. The population numbers nearly nine hundred thousand souls, two-thirds being of German stock and speaking the German language, and one-third Italian. The former inhabit the northern slopes and valleys of the Rhætian Alps, the latter the southern. The Tyrolese are notably fond of music and athletic exercises. Education is widely diffused. Innsbruck boasts an extensive university. The province has belonged to Austria since 1363.

The Tyrol is famous for its wood carvings, and

particularly for its pictures carved in relief, which are exquisitely beautiful and artistic, and if one only has a well-lined pocket book Innsbruck is a very seductive place for its depletion. The place has also good hotels, and is altogether a desirable point for a few days' sojourn.

An afternoon's ride over the Alps, by the famous Brenner Pass railway, brings us into Italy. This railway was opened in 1867, and is regarded as one of the most difficult pieces of railway engineering in Europe. Leaving Innsbruck we rapidly ascend to a height of four thousand six hundred feet above the sea, with mountains all around us rivaling our own Mount Washington in altitude. In a distance of seventy-eight miles the road passes through twenty-two tunnels and over sixty bridges. Its grades are in places one foot in forty, and very powerful engines are employed to draw the trains, notwithstanding which we travel very slowly — probably not over six miles per hour while making the ascent. We follow in the ascent the course of a little mountain stream, so have a deep valley on one side of us. The scenery is very interesting. Twice in the distance, in order to effect an abrupt elevation to a higher level, the road branches off up a lateral gorge, and after proceeding some distance, in one case a few miles, enters a tunnel in which it describes a complete semi-circle, when it returns to the point of divergence at a few hundred feet higher level, the tracks to and from the **turning tunnel being** parallel to and in sight of each **other the** whole distance. This **is** probably **the only** railway in the world where **a** passenger **can leave** his train, walk leisurely **a few** hundred **yards and sit** down at a **cafe** to a **glass** of beer and **wait** for **his** train **to overtake him.** This **can** literally be **done at one of** the points of **diverg-ence** just **mentioned.**

Botzen, **at the foot of the** mountains **on the** Italian **side, is a** place of considerable **import-ance, and** lies **in** a rich valley thickly **surrounded by** vineyards. A hundred miles more through **the** fertile valley of the Eisack, which lower down **becomes** the Adige, with **mountains in** the **back-**ground on either **side, brings us to** Verona in Italy.

CHAPTER IX.

ITALY—VERONA, ITS ARENA AND CHURCHES—PADUA—ARCADED STREETS—THE SHRINE OF ST. ANTHONY—ITALIAN AGRICULTURE.

OUR first experience of Italy was in Verona, and we were not favorably impressed. It is a dirty place, abounding in beggars, and with very little of interest to see except its Arena or ancient colosseum, resembling the famous one at Rome but smaller and in much better state of preservation. The Arena is oval in form and built wholly of stone. There is a level space in the center, eighty-three yards long and forty-three wide, for the games and other exhibitions, and from this, tiers of stone seats rise all around like the seats in a circus. There are forty-five rows of these seats, and it is estimated that they would seat twenty-five thousand spectators. Above the uppermost row was originally an arcade or gallery in which still more people could stand and watch the performances. Only a small portion of the exterior wall remains standing, but enough to show the design of the whole in its completed state. The outer wall is one hundred and six feet high, and presents three stories of arched openings. **The entire** building **is** five hundred and four feet long and **four** hundred and two wide. **It** is constructed with **massive piers** of stone, connected by vaultings, so as to form **inter**-secting passages, one set radiating from **the center,** the other encircling it. In the lower **story** there are three of these encircling arcades or passages, in the second two, and in the third the one mentioned above as surmounting the seats. The vaulting is partly of brick, and partly of concrete and cobblestone boulders. The seats are all **of** native marble, dressed but not polished. The Arena is believed to have been built in the **time** of the Emperor Diocletian, **A. D. 284,** which would make it about sixteen hundred years old.

The tombs of the Scaligers are perhaps the next object in order of interest. As the famous Medici family by their wealth and abilities made themselves **rulers** of Florence, **so** did the Scaligers supplant **the** republic of Verona, and establish in their family an hereditary rulership. This lasted from 1260 to 1389, and it was the golden age for Verona. The proud Scaligers scorned **to** have their tombs hidden **away in** churches and **fixed up a** little cemetery for themselves **in** the heart **of** the city, where every passer-by **would be** reminded of their greatness. The tombs are very rich **and** costly, but after **all** do not create very much **of** an impression on the **average tourist.**

The churches of Verona are rather magnificent
as to size, but like most of the churches of Italy
were commenced on so grand a scale that they
never could be completed. They are for the
most part immense ugly piles of rough brick-
work, the unfulfilled intention having been to
encase them with marble. Interiorly they are
finished with plaster and faded frescoes, and.
come far short, in elegance and impressiveness,
of the Gothic cathedrals and churches of England
and northern Germany.

As our omnibus drives through one of the gates
of Verona on the way from the station to the
hotel it suddenly stops. An official thrusts his
head in and rattles off a few words in Italian. We
have not the slightest idea what he says, so we
make no reply. He seems satisfied, and we drive
on again. We then remember that French and
Italian cities raise part of their municipal revenue by levying a tax on all articles of food
brought into the city. This is called an octroi,
and officers are posted at all the gates to inspect
every vehicle entering the same, and collect the
tax should provisions constitute any part of the
load. The man was simply inquiring if we had
anything in our baggage liable to octroi duty.

We lay over for three or four hours at the
sleepy old city of Padua, the seat of the once
famous university, founded in 1238, and which

throughout the middle ages made Padua a place
of renown. Although possessing sixty-six thousand inhabitants Padua presents scarcely any
signs of life. The streets are narrow and lined
with arcades such as exist in the older portions
of Innsbruck. Indeed, there is hardly any sidewalk exposed overhead. On hot days these
Italian arcaded streets are very delightful. I
wonder we have never adopted the idea in America. There is very little to see in Padua beyond
a few interesting old churches. The principal of
these is the church of St. Anthony, founded
about 1250. It is of immense size and contains a
great number of very fine monuments, but its
great central attraction is the chapel and shrine
of the patron saint. The chapel is entirely of
marble, elegant in design and rich and beautiful
in its elaborately carved ornamentation. It was
designed by the great Venetian architect Sanso-
vino, who was born in 1477 and died 1570.
Around the chapel are a series of fine bas-reliefs
illustrating incidents in the life of the saint, and
each one is the work of a master in the art of
sculpture. St Anthony's tomb forms the altar of
the chapel, and at the time we visited it a crowd
of devotees thronged its rear, laying their hands
upon it while reciting their prayers.

Two other churches contain in dilapidated condition much prized frescoes, those in the one

6

painted by Giotto, one of the earliest Florentine artists; those in the other by Andrea Mantegna, the great Paduan master.

Such draft animals and vehicles as they use at Padua would fairly make a western man laugh. Of the latter there seem to have been no new ones built for a century at least, or if there have been they were built after last century's pattern. · We saw horses at work that could not have weighed over three hundred pounds; but little donkeys were most numerous, and they drew loads that would shame an American horse.

The country in northern Italy in May looks very beautiful—vegetation quite a month in advance of what it is in our northern states. Rows of trees at intervals of a few rods intersect every field and line every road, giving the country an attractive appearance. The practice is universal of pruning down the shade trees till they grow with great ugly knobs a few feet from the ground. The prunings supply the people with fuel, and the trees do not by their shade affect the crops cultivated beneath them. In this part of Italy they are also used instead of trellises to support the grape vines. On the Rhine the vines are cut off close to the ground, only one or two shoots being left for bearing. These are tied to a single upright stake four or five feet long. At Botzen and above Verona the vines grow up straight for two or three feet, then are trained over a sloping trellis five or six feet wide —a much more complex system, but one exposing the leaves and fruit to the sun and keeping the ground below well shaded. South of Verona trellises are dispensed with altogether, and the vines are trained from tree to tree like clotheslines. All the horned cattle we see in Italy are uniformly of a grayish white color, with extraordinarily long horns. The rivers are all above the level of the adjacent country, and require to be diked.

CHAPTER X.

IN crossing the Alps one is struck with the perishable quality of the rock, and the great quantities of alluvium that are carried down by the rapid streams. The rivers of north-eastern Italy rival the Missouri for muddiness, and their mouths are a repetition of the large areas of alluvial deposit found at the mouth of the Mississippi. Places once on the coast are now in some cases fifteen miles inland. The lands are low, and waters shallow. A mile or two off the main shore a series of low islands has been formed by the combined action of the rivers and the sea. On a group of these islands the city of Venice has grown up.

Under the Romans north-eastern Italy had become very rich and populous. When the country was over-run by the barbaric Lombards in the seventh century, many of the people took refuge on the islands off the coast, and some of these being found easily defended they became the seat of a populous colony. Having no lands

to cultivate, the inhabitants turned their attention
to commerce, and like all commercial peoples,
soon became very rich and powerful. The trade
of the world was carried on by Venice. At the
height of her prosperity the little islands numbered a population of two hundred thousand
souls, possessing three hundred ships and a fleet
of forty-five armed galleys. For the convenience
of her trade Venice had conquered possessions
on all the coasts of the Mediterranean, and at one
time was even master of Constantinople. Coeval
with the discovery of America its decay began,
and continued steadily for three hundred years.
In 1797 Napoleon occupied Venice—the first
foreign foe who had ever held possession of it—
and at his downfall in 1815 the territory was
given to Austria, by whom it was held till 1866,
when, as a result of the weakening of the
latter's power by the war with Prussia, Venice
was united to the kingdom of Italy.

As we approach Venice the country becomes
flat and low. Bits of marsh land appear. Then
we find ourselves on the bridge, two and a half
miles long, which connects Venice with the main
land. The water crossed is shallow, and still as a
mill pond, and is called the lagoon. A few fishing boats are scattered over it. In a few minutes
we are in a large covered railway station, from
which we emerge on a fine stone quay fronting

on the grand canal. The sight that meets the
eye is a curious one. Dozens of funereal gon-
dolas are crowding their way to the landing,
and one by one they receive their passengers and
quickly row away. We get into one, with all our
baggage. It is about thirty feet long, and armed
at its prow with a tall iron meat-cleaver sort of
ornament. It is painted black and a black pall
is hung over the little covered cabin in the center.
Arriving in the evening, as we did, this being met
by hearses at the depot is quite impressive. It
seems that an old law required this mourning,
and the law has never been repealed. Two men
row the boat—one at the bow, the other at the
stern. Each uses a single oar and rows standing and facing in the direction we are going. The
delicacy and precision with which the boat is
managed is quite remarkable. We turn off into a
minor canal perhaps twenty feet wide. Houses
rise on both sides of us directly from the water's
edge. Scarce a light is seen in them and all is
still as the grave, save for the plash of the gondo-
liers' oars. Presently we meet another boat; a
sharp, clear word in Italian indicates on which
side we are to pass. Another word, shouted just
as we are about to turn a corner, prepares any
boat that may be coming through the intersecting
canal, to meet us, and prevents a collision. But
for these occasional cries and the plash of the

oars we should scarcely know that a living soul
was within miles of us. The boat at last pulls
up at a flight of stone stairs. A posse of clerks
and waiters assist us to land and escort us into
the hotel. We cross courts, ascend stairs, look
down into other courts, traverse corridors and at
last find ourselves in a pleasant suite of rooms in
the excellent Hotel Victoria. Inside, all is bright
and gay, and in striking contrast with the gloom
and loneliness of the watery streets.

There are said to be one hundred and fifty
canals in Venice, crossed by three hundred and
seventy-eight bridges. The grand canal winds
through the city like a reversed letter S, and is,
perhaps, one hundred and fifty feet wide. The
rest I should think were from twelve to thirty
feet. Some have narrow streets running along
their banks, others are bordered directly by the
houses. The tide, which rises and falls about two
feet, keeps the canals tolerably pure. All the
heavy traffic is done by boating through these
canals, for, excepting the four bronze horses stolen
from Constantinople and contributed to the decoration of St. Mark's (they stand over the front
portal), there is not a beast of burden in all Venice. The streets are mere foot paths, rarely over
six feet wide and often less than four. They are
all well paved with flagstone or concrete, and
upon them the houses and shops open. The city

is a perfect labyrinth of these little streets, and the stranger has great difficulty in finding his way about, as the houses close in on him so closely that he can have no sort of landmarks. But some of these little four-foot streets are as bright and cheerful, and trade is as lively upon them as on the best retail streets in any of our western cities. The shops get but little light, but they are shallow and need but little. The principal part of their stock occupies the windows. The better houses are constructed on the oriental plan, with a court-yard in the center, and generally with an imposing arched entrance into the court-yard, and an arcade or colonnade around the latter. From this court-yard the main staircase ascends, and upon it most of the windows open. The exterior is dark and gloomy, but a peep through the open gateway often reveals a paradisiacal home.

Fronting the Cathedral of St. Mark is a large open square about six hundred feet long and two hundred wide, known as the Piazza. It is paved with marble and surrounded on three sides by a handsome colonnade upon which all the principal stores and cafes of Venice front. No street in London makes such a brilliant display of pretty things as is seen in this Piazza. Books, photographs, pictures, jewelry, toys and confectionery predominate, and the shop windows are in themselves quite one of the sights of Venice. In the evening the Piazza is brilliantly lighted up and is thronged by thousands. In front of the cafes hundreds of chairs are scattered about, with small tables occupied by merry groups drinking coffee or eating ice creams. It is altogether a novel and fascinating scene. Prices are quite reasonable in St. Mark's Piazza.

St. Mark the Evangelist, is the patron saint of Venice. A thousand years ago, when her religion outweighed her commercial acquisitiveness, it was a penal offense for any Venetian navigator to enter an infidel port. By stress of weather however, a certain ship was once forced to put into Alexandria, where the remains of the saint then rested in the care of a small Christian church. The mariners found the Christians greatly alarmed for the safety of the precious relics, as the reigning pasha had a mania for building palaces, and to secure material for them found the demolition of Christian churches a ready and convenient method. The Alexandrian Christians did not care to have poor St. Mark left out in the cold, so arranged with the Venetians to transfer the body to the more Christian city of the Adriatic. The sailors were glad enough of the commission, for by the sacred treasure they brought home they hoped to gain immunity for their breach of law. The Venetians were of course delighted with their acquisition, and at once prepared a fine church for the reception of the precious relic.

Some time later there was a riot in Venice over some little political matter, and the mob set fire to the Doge's palace, which adjoined the church of St. Mark. The latter was consequently burned to the ground, with all its contents. Then a new church was determined on, and one which should correspond in grandeur with the wealth and greatness of the city at that time. It was begun in 976, and took nearly a century to complete. Meanwhile the Venetians sailed to all countries, and the shipmasters vied with each other in bringing home the richest contributions for the new St. Mark's. The rarest marble and alabaster, and antique sculpture despoiled from many a heathen temple, found its way into the stock heap, and skillfully did the architects make all contribute to the beauty of the edifice. The church is hence a medley of rich materials more or less artistically disposed. When completed, a tomb was provided under the high altar for the patron saint, great faith being felt that his remains would yet be restored. But the tomb was never occupied. We looked into it. By a miracle however, the saint's relics were still preserved to the church. On the occasion of some great festival—perhaps the consecration of the building—as a procession was passing up the broad nave, suddenly an explosion occurred in one of the main piers, and there exposed to view lay the body of St. Mark. It was then thought best, to prevent the possibility of its ever being stolen or again lost, that it should be deposited in some secret receptacle, and accordingly the officers of the church proceeded to hide it, and to this day no man knows the part of the building where the sacred deposit was made. Such is the story of St. Mark's final burial.

The church is built of brick in the form of a Greek cross, with domes over the intersection and each arm of the cross—five in all. Both exterior and interior are completely encased with various colored marbles and bright mosaics. The latter alone cover a space of forty-five thousand eight hundred square feet, and are composed of small pieces of colored stone, so set in cement as to form pictures which from a short distance cannot be distinguished from rich frescoes. The ground work is in all cases gilt, and the pictures are usually representations of bible subjects with Latin inscriptions explaining them, the inscriptions likewise being of mosaic work. The ceiling of the main porch in front of the cathedral we found some amusement in studying out. We found it to illustrate in a long series of large and brilliant pictures, the creation of the world, the fall of man, the death of Abel, the flood, the confusion of tongues, and other events in old testament history—all most expressive, and as bright and perfect as when first produced eight or nine centuries ago. The floor throughout is of great varieties of marble arranged in hundreds of different patterns, and is of itself quite a study. There is scarcely a particle of wood work to be seen in the entire church, nor a square yard of fresco—all marble and mosaic. When new, it must have looked very beautiful indeed, but dirt and decay have given it a subdued, not to say dingy, look. The different parts of the building have settled unequally, and, while too massive to be in any sense ruinous, it is sadly out of shape, the floor in particular resembling the surface of a river just after a large steamer has passed. They are now at work restoring the edifice, and have already made considerable progress with the work.

St. Mark's is less wonderful for its size (two hundred and ten by two hundred and fifty-eight feet, inside measurement), and its architectural beauty, than for the costly material of which it is constructed. It suggests a plain woman overloaded with rich dress. It is of course well worth seeing, and one could even spend days in the study of it, but its merit from an artistic standpoint is open to discussion.

The Campanile, or bell-tower, as is the custom
in Italy, stands detached from the church.   It is
three hundred and twenty-two feet high, and was
begun in the year 911, but not completed till 1591.
To this day it has never been veneered with marble, as was undoubtedly the intention originally.
It is a fine piece of masonry, constructed of bricks
each twelve or fourteen inches long and six wide.
It is ascended, not by steps, but by a series of
inclined planes extending around its inner surface.   The summit commands a fine bird's-eye
view of Venice, with the Adriatic sea stretching
away to the east and south, the snow-covered
Alps in the north-west, the Apennines in the south-
west, and the lagoon, which separates Venice from
the main land, in the immediate fore-ground.

The churches of Venice are mostly large and
pretentious, and well stocked with paintings by
the Venetian masters.   It is unnecessary to enu-
merate them.   One thing particularly worth mentioning is the beautiful wood carving with which
the stalls of the choir of St. Giorgio Maggiore are
ornamented.   In a series of forty-eight panels the
history of St. Benedict is illustrated in rich alto-
relievo carvings, very beautiful and interesting.

To see the churches we took a gondola.   A
franc an hour (20 cents of our money), with a
small gratuity to the boatman, is the tariff for
gondola service.   Cheap enough, is it not?

The Academy of Fine Arts of Venice contains a great number of pictures, but almost exclusively the works of Venetian masters—Titian, Paul Veronese, Tintoretto, Bonifacio, and others. To the uncultured eye, none of the masters of the Venetian school, even Titian, accounted one of the five greatest of the Italian painters, possesses very great attractions.

In the palmy days of Venice it was governed by an aristocracy of nobles, and these elected from among themselves a chief executive who was styled Duke or Doge. His official residence, with the halls in which the oligarchy held its elections and other meetings, adjoins St. Mark's church, and is known as the Palace of the Doges, or the Ducal Palace. It forms three sides of a quadrangle, the church filling the fourth. The building is now used chiefly as a library and gallery of art. Some of the rooms have been restored in recent times, and are very handsome. A great number of the works of the great Venetian artists, Titian, Paul Veronese, and Tintoretto, are found in them. In the rear of the church and ducal palace is a small canal, and crossing this canal, connecting the second story of the palace with the corresponding floor of a building on the other side, is a covered stone bridge, popularly known as the Bridge of Sighs. It was across this bridge that in the tyrannical days of the oligarchy those who had given offense to the all-powerful nobles were led from trial in the palace to execution in the prison across the canal; whence the name of the structure. Another notable bridge is the Rialto, a stone structure spanning the grand canal about ,midway its length. It is a single arch with a span of seventy-four feet. It was built in 1588, and is said to rest on twelve thousand piles.

We bid good bye to Venice with regret, for it is a cheerful place, notwithstanding its gloomy first reception, and the Venetians know how to attract and entertain us foreigners. Venice is particularly a favorite with the English, and at the table d'hote each day English was almost the sole language of conversation.

A VENETIAN GONDOLA.

CHAPTER XI.

A PLEASANT five hours' ride from Venice through a somewhat flat but highly culti- vated and fruitful country brings us to the ancient city of Bologna, pronounced Bolognya by the natives. It is situated at the commence- ment of the foot-hills of the Apennine range, has about the same population as Detroit, Rochester or Milwaukee, and is rich, and substantially built. Its principal church of which the nave only was ever finished, was begun on a stupendous scale in 1390, in rivalry with the immense cathedral at Florence. But the buildings by which Bologna is best known are its two leaning towers. They stand side by side in a small open space at the junction of several streets and lean in contrary directions. The one is three hundred and twenty feet high and leans four feet from the perpendic- ular, the other is one hundred and sixty-three feet and leans ten feet. Both were erected seven hundred and seventy years ago. By the way, almost all towers and even tall chimneys seem in Italy to have a penchant for leaning. Whether

THE LEANING TOWERS OF BOLOGNA, ITALY.

it is from a peculiarity of the soil or carelessness in the workmen in not plumbing them properly I cannot say, but I have noted a number of instances of more or less deflection. I cannot believe that they were in any case built intentionally leaning, as even the bad architectural taste of Italy could never have perpetrated so monstrous an eyesore. The streets of Bologna are universally arcaded, and usually in a very stately and substantial manner.

Bologna was once the center of a school of painting peculiar to itself. It included among its great masters Domenichino, Guido Reni and the brothers Carracci. An academy of fine arts is still maintained. Its gallery is of course particularly strong in the works of the Bologna masters but it has one famous picture of Raphael's— St. Cecilia, attended by St. Paul, St. John, Mary Magdalene and one other saint, with broken musical instruments at her feet and a choir of angels in the clouds above. But to the average sight-seer the salon containing the modern pictures which have won the first prizes of the academy from year to year is much more interesting and attractive than any of the old masters, even than the Raphael.

We happened to spend Sunday in Bologna, and before breakfast I took a stroll around the principal square. Half the population seemed to be in the streets. All the shops were open and pedlars thronged the sidewalks. Wagons loaded with furniture and boxes of merchandise passed and repassed. From the great number of people abroad in holiday attire I was forcibly reminded of a Fourth of July morning in our own country. Comparatively few people went to church, and still fewer visited the public picture galleries which government had opened free on this day for their benefit. The noise and bustle on the streets was far greater than on other days. Such is an Italian Sunday.

The railroad from Bologna to Pistoja (the place where pistols were first made and whence they derived their name) lies across the Apennine range of mountains. The latter are not equal to the Alps in height or rugged grandeur, but are still high enough to retain considerable snow on their summits in the middle of May when in this warm climate haymaking is in progress in the valleys below. We gradually ascend to a height of two thousand feet, following the valley of the Reno, which flows westerly into the Adriatic, and, having passed the summit, descend through the valley of the Ombrone, a tributary of the Arno, which latter flows through Florence. It is a most interesting ride. In a distance of forty-four miles we pass through no fewer than forty-four tunnels—one for each mile—and as they must certainly average half a mile each, it is pretty safe to assert that on this portion of the road we are underground fully half the time. The remainder we are winding around mountain ledges and crossing tall viaducts, hundreds of feet above the picturesque valleys and gurgling streams beneath us. The ever-changing panorama between the tunnels is most enchanting. The tunnels are monotonous, but not disagreeable like our American tunnels, where we are stifled with smoke. At one point we catch a glimpse of a broad plain, with a walled city with its domes and campaniles set in the midst, and with smaller villages scattered over it. Such a bird's-eye view of a wide extent of country is rarely enjoyed. We are looking down upon Pistoja and the fertile plains of Tuscany from an elevation of between fifteen hundred and two thousand feet. Half an hour later we reach the station at Pistoja, and from thence on to Florence our journey is through the hot but fertile plain.

CHAPTER XII.

FLORENCE, the city of flowers, is beautifully situated in the lovely valley of the Arno, with the snow-capped Apennines skirting the landscape to the northwest. It is most interesting for its historic associations; as the home of the famous Medici family, which made it the great center of literature, art and civilization, and which gave the church her most brilliant pope in Leo X., and to France two of its best known queens; but is above all famous as having no superior in the world either in its collection of art treasures or in the quantity and beauty of the art productions which it still furnishes to us outside barbarians. Florence is a charming place; and halting here within a few minutes walk of its noble cathedral, of the home of Michel Angelo, of the original Madonna della Sedia (Madonna of the chair), Raphael's most popular painting, of the famous Venus de Medici, of Savonarola's cell and the place where he was burned at the stake, and of the old monastery where the monk Fra Angelico lived and painted his exquisite delineations of holy men and women, one has no care to see either Rome, Naples or Paris. Florence in itself is all-satisfying. Weeks could be spent there without satiety.

Upon arriving our first step was to take a drive about the city and learn its geography, and so it happened that one of the first things we visited was the noted Protestant Cemetery, where so many well known foreigners, including the esteemed poet, Elizabeth Barrett Browning and our own Rev. Theodore Parker, lie buried. Indeed it is filled almost exclusively with English and American graves; and the inscriptions, mentioning New York, Philadelphia and a score of other places in our own country, make one feel quite as if he were on American soil. The cemetery evidently at one time was situated just outside the walls of the city, but within the past few years all the fortifications have been leveled, and on the ground occupied by them, broad and beautifully ornamented boulevards have been constructed. And so it happens that the cemetery has become a little oval park in the center of one of the finest boulevards. It cannot be more than an acre in extent. It rises in the center to a height of fifteen or twenty feet above the roadway and rounds off to the fence on every side except the north, where it terminates with an abrupt wall. It is surrounded by an iron fence, and is nicely kept. We had no trouble in finding the tomb of Mrs. Browning, although it bears no inscription except the simple initials "E. B. B.—ob. 1861." It consists of a marble sarcophagus supported by six short columns. Theodore Parker's we were unable to find without inquiry. It is a plain grave with an old-fashioned dark-colored headstone bearing the inscription, "Theodore Parker. Born at Lexington, Massachusetts, United States of America, Aug. 24, 1810. Died at Florence, May 10, 1860."

Our first walk is directed to the Duomo, or cathedral, a structure of great historic and architectural interest. It was projected at a period of great ambition in the building line, when the various cities of Italy vied with each other to produce the church of greatest immensity. It was begun from the plans of Arnolfo di Cambio in 1294, and was nearly one hundred and sixty years building. Arnolfo dying in 1310, was succeeded by Giotto, the famous pupil of Cimabue the father of Italian painting. (Painters and sculptors were also the architects of those days.) Three or four generations of architects and builders passed away, each more or less changing the plans, and more or less destroying what its predecessors had built up, until at last the structure was ready for the dome. This was in 1418. No such large dome had up to that time ever been attempted, and now the question arose how was it to be built? Architects from all over the known world were invited to send in plans, and serious controversies arose as to its being at all practicable. One difficulty that suggested itself was the construction of a centering to support the stone work while in progress, it being argued that there was not timber enough in all Italy for the purpose. Then some wise head proposed filling up the interior of the church with earth and using a mound of this material as a center. In order to facilitate the removal of the earth afterwards, he proposed scattering money through it, when he thought the poor of the city would be glad enough to cart away the dirt for the chance of finding the coin. At last a really scientific architect turned up in the person of Filippo Brunelleschi, who insisted that it was possible to construct the dome without any centering. He was at first hooted as a lunatic, but finally got the ear of the building committee and secured the adoption of his plans with the appointment of supervising architect. He did not live to see the work completed, but his plans were fully carried out, and his fame as one of the greatest architects of the middle ages fairly established. Even when the church was considered complete and was dedicated, the west front or facade, was left a mere rough brick wall, the intention being to

encase it with marble at some future time when it
might be convenient to do so. But thus it
remained for four hundred years, or down
to 1860, when the work of completing it was
undertaken. It is still in progress. The entire
building is of brick, faced with black and white
marble in panels. While very rich and beautiful,
it lacks the dignity of churches built of plain
stone. One is reminded of inlaid work of ivory
and ebony, and its application to so immense a
structure has a belittling effect, and destroys very
largely the sense of imposing grandeur. The
interior is very disappointing. Even its immensity fails to impress, so well, or so badly, is everything proportioned. One cannot realize that the
dome is three hundred feet high, or that the
rotunda and dome of the capitol at Washington
could stand under it. The walls are plain, and
in great part of a gloomy brown color ; the building is insufficiently lighted, and is remarkably
bare of monuments. It has nothing, therefore,
but its size, to interest the visitor.

Much more interesting every way is the old
church of St. Croce, begun at the same time and
by the same architect, and nearly as large as the
cathedral, but much less pretentious. It is very
rich in the tombs of Italy's great men, including
those of Michel Angelo, Galileo, Macchiavelli the
statesman, Raphael Morghen the eminent engra-

ver, Cherubini the musical composer, and many others scarcely less well known. There is also a fine monument to Dante, though his remains are buried at Ravenna. In its magnificent sepulchres of departed greatness it is the Westminster Abbey of Italy. Among the other principal churches of Florence are the church of St. Lorenzo, built at the expense of a few wealthy Florentines by Brunelleschi, and finished by Michel Angelo, and which contains the tombs of the Medicis; that of St. Maria Novello, and the Baptistery. The latter stands opposite the cathedral, and is an octagonal structure surmounted by a dome ninety feet in diameter. It is chiefly remarkable for its three bronze doors, constructed between four and five hundred years ago, and covered with reliefs representing bible scenes. They were the work of Lorenzo Ghiberti, whose name is immortalized mainly through them, and they served in some degree as models for the bronze doors of our own capitol at Washington.

The Campanile, or bell tower of the cathedral, stands, as is the custom in Italy, a little apart from the church itself. It is a handsome square tower two hundred and ninety-two feet high, of black and white marbles, designed by Giotto and completed in 1336. It has recently been restored, and has quite a new and fresh look.

On the principal public square of Florence is

the fortress-looking Palazzo Vecchio with its tall tower. It was originally the seat of government of the republic, and was later the residence of Cosimo I. It is now the city hall of Florence. We walked through the principal rooms, including the great hall where Savonarola's council was accustomed to meet. Just at the corner of the building Savonarola himself was burned in 1498.

THE PALAZZO VECCHIO.

Also facing this square is a large open hall or piazza filled with sculpture, the work of famous artists. It is exposed to the street, and forms a sort of loafing place for the idle. It is called the Loggia dei Lanzi, loggia being the Italian for hall or gallery.

Close by is the entrance to the famous Uffizi (pronounced "Uffeetzy") picture gallery, one of the most extensive in the world. It comprises all the rich collections of the Medicis, with additions made by the later dukes of Tuscany. It occupies the upper story of three sides of a long court. There are two parallel corridors, each about six hundred feet long, and a shorter

one connecting them at the end, with some
twenty-five or thirty rooms opening from them.
The corridors and rooms are hung with pictures and filled with antique statuary. The
most precious pictures and statues are collected
in an octagonal room called the Tribune. Here
is the famous Venus de Medici, believed to be
the work of a Greek artist about one hundred
years before Christ, and discovered, some three
hundred years ago, in the ruins of Hadrian's
palace at Tivoli. Among the pictures in this
room are Raphael's Madonna of the Goldfinch,
in which the infant John is represented presenting a bird to the babe Jesus; also his well
known picture of the young St. John. In other
rooms the different schools of painting, as the
Tuscan, the French, the Dutch, the German, etc.,
are kept distinct. One room is devoted to gems
of wonderful size and most exquisite workmanship. Another contains only cameos and intag-
lios of rare artistic value. Still another is filled
with ancient bronzes, and another with ancient
inscriptions carved in stone, the records of an age
long anterior to the Christian era. One room
contains hundreds of portraits of eminent painters, ancient and modern, mostly painted by themselves. It is a very interesting collection. But
few rooms possess more intense interest than the
salon of Niobe.

In Grecian mythology Niobe was the mother of six sons and as many daughters, and, proud of her offspring, she snubbed Latona, one of the wives of Jupiter, who had only two, Apollo and Diana, and officiously interfered with their worship as divinities. Thereupon Apollo and Diana revenged themselves upon the silly mother by shooting all her children with their arrows. Diana, as the goddess of hunting, was of course a good markswoman, and so the whole dozen were slaughtered. Niobe's grief was so excessive that the gods, out of pity, turned her into stone, but even that failed to mitigate her terrible sorrow. The scene of the slaughter was portrayed in stone by some ancient Greek sculptor, probably Praxiteles, and the group was discovered in Rome in 1583, buried in the earth, and more or less broken. They were restored, and now occupy the room I am speaking of. Never have I seen anything more striking. Niobe's face is a picture of the deepest grief, while the attitudes of her children endeavoring to shield themselves from the arrows of their assailants are, perhaps, the most wonderful achievements of the sculptor's art the world has ever seen.

Across the river, a quarter of a mile or more from the Uffizi gallery, is the Pitti palace, so named from the family who built it in 1440. It is now one of the royal palaces of Italy. It

also contains a very extensive gallery of rare pictures, and this portion of the palace is connected
with the Uffizi gallery by long passages, crossing
the Arno by one of the bridges. We pass from
the Uffizi gallery down a flight of stairs, through

THE PONTE VECCHIO.

a long zigzag passage hung with old and rare
engravings ("prints" is the proper word), then
through a long corridor filled with drawings,
many of them by the old masters. Looking out
through a window we find we are now over the
river. A narrow, dark, crooked passage follows,
in which some less-cared-for pictures are hung,
and then begin the tapestries. These hang from

the ceiling to the floor on both sides of us, and, though some centuries old, are quite brilliant in their colors, and as admirably shaded as if done with the artist's brush. They are exclusively needle work, and depict, often in life size, bible incidents, battle scenes, and other like subjects. Then we ascend more stairs, and find ourselves at last in the six salons of the Pitti gallery.

Among the more important pictures here are Raphael's well-known Madonna of the Chair, his portrait of Pope Julius II., and his vision of Eze- kiel, besides which there are some five hundred other pictures embracing some of the best works of almost all the great masters. In fact this gal- lery is reputed the best in Italy in the fewness of its works of subordinate merit. Unfortunately however the rooms were not originally designed for picture galleries, and are not properly lighted, so the pictures do not show to the best advantage possible.

We pay a franc or lira each to enter either gal- lery, and can go from one to the other at pleas- ure, but on Sundays and Thursdays both galler- ies are open free.

Back of the Pitti palace are the extensive Boboli gardens, open to the public on certain days, and commanding a magnificent view of the city, of the plains beyond, and of the Apennine range in the background.

Besides the Uffizi and Pitti galleries, there is a valuable collection of pictures in the Academy of Fine Arts. In all the galleries there are constantly a great number of painters engaged in copying. Many are ladies. Their works, when finished, are sold to dealers, or left for sale on commission, and thus pictures can be bought in large numbers in Florence, and at reasonable rates. Copies of old masters range in price from twenty to two hundred dollars, according to the size and quality of work. Carved frames are also a specialty of Florence, and are made in great variety.

But Florence's great specialty is her mosaics. Different colored marbles are cut up and so skillfully joined as to form in some cases very life-like pictures. They are made of all sizes, from a sleeve button up to a large table top, and range in prices from a dollar or two up to several hundred. Jewelry, paper weights, pictures for easels, and table tops, are the forms Florentine mosaics are most frequently found in. They are generally inlaid on a black marble ground, but sometimes the whole surface is occupied by the picture. The art has been practiced at Florence for over three hundred years.

CHAPTER XIII.

SOMETHING over five hundred years ago there lived in Florence a worthy old gentleman named Salvestro Medici (pronounced Medeche—three syllables, with the accent on the first, and the "ch" soft), who had grown very rich in trade, and who, enjoying the esteem of his fellow-citizens, had been elected gonfalonier or chief-executive of the then republic of Florence. He had a son John (Giovanni is the Italian for John), a chip of the old block, being distinguished for his commercial enterprise and patriotism. John, who was born in 1360, died in 1428, leaving a son, Cosimo, who, being immensely wealthy and very liberal, likewise enjoyed great popularity. Having no need to devote himself to business he went into politics, and so managed matters that for thirty-four years he was practically the sole ruler of Florence. He looked out well for the public interests, stole nothing from the public treasury, and maintained his popularity to the last. When he died in 1464 and at his own desire was unostentatiously buried in a plain grave in front of the altar in the church of St. Lorenzo, the senate passed a resolution styling him *Pater Patriæ* (the father of his country). The family was thus established by three generations of energetic, honest and public-spirited men.

Cosimo was succeeded in his estates and political influence by his son Peter, who, however, was killed in a popular revolt five years later, 1469. He in turn was succeeded by his son, Lorenzo the Magnificent, who was born in 1448 and died in 1492, the precise year of the discovery of America by Columbus. Lorenzo inherited, besides a princely fortune, all the ability of his ancestors, if not all their virtues. He was a man of culture and refinement, and spent liberally of his fortune in the beautifying of Florence and in the cultivation of literature and the arts. He ransacked Europe for books for his libraries and pictures and sculpture for his galleries. The best that was to be found anywhere was purchased and carried off to Florence. Learned men and skillful artists were encouraged to make Florence their home, and in all matters of civilization and culture it became the metropolis of the world. Lorenzo lived in the grandest style and indulged in the most munificent hospitality. No prince in christendom was surrounded by such learning

8

and elegance. While nominally still a republic, Lorenzo was practically autocrat of Florence for twenty-three years, and this was emphatically its golden age.

LORENZO THE MAGNIFICENT.

Lorenzo left three sons—Peter, John and William. As they could not all succeed to the political power of the father, John was trained for the church, and, animated by the Medici ambition and backed by the family influence, he in due time reached the highest position in the ecclesiastical hierarchy, and in 1513 was elected pope under the title of Leo X. As pope, Leo fully maintained the reputation of the family in the brilliancy of his career. He controlled the politics of half of Europe, elevated his relatives to the highest positions, gave a new prosperity to Rome, gathered there men of fame and objects of art from all parts of the world, and made the city as gay and brilliant as it had ever been in the palmiest days of the emperors. Of course true vital religion did not thrive amid so much temporal prosperity, and it was the profligacy of Rome and its priesthood at this time that attracted the attention of Martin Luther and caused that great split in the christian church which, notwithstanding the reforms that came in due time in the Roman branch, exists to this day between the Roman Catholic and Protestant bodies. Leo's chief energies were directed to the building of St. Peter's church, which he determined should be the largest and most splendid church in the world. The famous painter Raphael was one of Leo's proteges, and lent his talents to the adornment of his patron's churches and palaces. Christian Rome was then at the zenith of its power and splendor. Leo was born in 1475 and died in 1521.

Meanwhile his father had died, and his brother Peter had succeeded to the government of Florence, but had immediately been deposed by the people, an outburst of republican spirit having followed upon Lorenzo's death. It was about twenty years before the family were restored to power, and it was during this interval that Savonarola founded in Florence his theistic republic, of which I shall speak presently. Then Peter's son, Lorenzo II., resumed the government with the title of Duke. It was his daughter, Catharine de Medici, who married Henry II. of France, and upon her husband's death in 1559 governed France as regent. She is notorious in history as the promoter of the horrible massacre of St. Bartholomew in 1572, whereby she hoped to wipe out protestantism from her realm. She was a woman of great ability, a lover and patron of the arts, and she it was who built the palace of the Tuilleries in Paris, which was destroyed by the commune in 1871. She died in 1589.

Florence continued to be governed by the Medici family until 1737—a period in all of nearly three hundred and fifty years. After Lorenzo the Magnificent the greatest of the line was

Cosimo I., 1513–1574, who much resembled him in his patronage of art and learning. Pope Clement VII., elected in 1523, was also a Medici, being a cousin of Leo X. Besides thus contributing to the church two popes, the Medicis furnished two queens to France. Catharine has already been mentioned. The other was Marie de Medici, who was born in Florence in 1573, and married Henry of Navarre, the famous champion of the French protestants. He assumed the throne of France as Henry IV. in 1600, and became the founder of the famous Bourbon family as kings of France. Marie led an unhappy life with her husband and was probably accessory to his murder by Ravaillac in 1610. She succeeded as regent. The nation grew restive under Italian rule. Cardinal Richelieu was constantly a thorn in her side, and in 1631 she was deposed, and eleven years later died in great poverty at Cologne. She, too, was a famous patron of art, and was the builder of the palace of the Luxembourg in Paris.

Thus, altogether, few families have made a more notable record in history than these Florentine Medicis. We visited the Palazzo Riccardi, an immense, massive and imposing palace, the home of Lorenzo the Magnificent and birthplace of Leo X., and which contains highly esteemed frescoes painted over four centuries ago. In one room

one of these ceiling paintings represents a man
plowing with a yoke of oxen. Standing opposite
to it the oxen appeared to be going directly from
you. Stand at one end of the room and the oxen
are going at right angles to their former course,
and seen from the other end are going in the
opposite direction. The illusion is very curious.

On the same street with the Palazzo Riccardi is
the once famous, but now suppressed, monastery
of St. Mark, the home of the eminent painters
Fra Angelico and Fra Bartolommeo, of St.
Anthony and of Jerome Savonarola, who was
also prior of the institution. Savonarola was
born in 1452, became a monk at twenty-two, and
at thirty-seven had become renowned for his
piety and the earnestness of his preaching. People flocked from all quarters to hear him. From
attacking the sins of the laity he proceeded to
assail the low state of religion in the priesthood,
and, led on by the attention given to his dis-
courses, ultimately turned his batteries of elo-
quence upon the oppressions of the political powers of the day. The revolution which drove the
Medicis from power in 1492 was perhaps the
immediate result of his sermons. Being without
a ruler the people naturally turned to Savonarola
for leadership, and he jn his piety pointed them
to the Jewish theocracy as a model of civil government. He was called upon to organize a sys-

tem, and did so, naming Jesus Christ as the supreme head of the Florentine republic, and establishing a large legislative and executive council to act under him. His own functions were to be akin to those of Moses and Samuel in the Jewish republic, viz.: those of prophet and expounder of the Divine will. I don't know how the plan worked, but probably not well, for it was of short duration. In four or five years a popular reaction had set in. Savonarola's enemies gained the ascendancy, and he was deposed from his prophetic office and thrown into prison on a charge of heresy. They made short work of heretics in those days, and a charge of heresy was a capital way to get a political rival out of the field. The unfortunate man was brought to trial, easily convicted, and in accordance with the practice of the day was first tortured and then burned at the stake in the principal public square in Florence. A fountain now occupies the precise spot upon which the execution took place. But the most remarkable part of the story is yet to come. Savonarola, who in 1498 was burned as a heretic by the authority of the holy church, was some years later canonized by the same authority, and now ranks among the saints in the ecclesiastical calendar. Such is in brief the history of this remarkable man. We visited his cell in St. Mark's convent, saw his very noticeable portrait painted by his colleague, Fra Bartolommeo, his desk at which he wrote, and the books he studied, with their copious marginal annotations in his own handwriting.

The cells in St. Mark's are about twelve feet square, well lighted, and altogether quite pleasant retreats for studiously or artistically disposed monks. The frescoes on the walls of the cloisters, refectory and other rooms, painted four hundred years ago, are to-day as fresh, bright and beautiful as ever. The institution is now a public museum. In the fine old library we saw in glass cases a large number of the immense folio ritual books of mediæval times, collected from various monasteries. They are beautifully engrossed on parchment, with the music, and each page bears more or less elaborate illumination in colors, the work of the monks in their leisure hours. The music is written on a staff of but four lines instead of five as now in use, and the notes are square instead of round or oval.

SAVONAROLA, FROM AN OLD PAINTING.

CHAPTER XIV.

THE journey from Florence to Rome requires about seven hours. The first half is through an intensely beautiful country. We follow the valley of the Arno, having the Apennines on our left. The surface of the country is much broken, but very picturesque, though thickly populated and under high state of cultivation. Metaphorically speaking there is not a square rod of land that has not a tree growing upon it.

Between Arezzo and Chiusi we pass through a particularly beautiful district, the trees here having been allowed to grow to full size, instead of being pruned down to a bare trunk. Then we begin to follow the valley of a branch of the Tiber.

The scene changes, and we are in a poor, rough, thinly-populated country, with no vineyards. Immense rocks frequently shoot up perpendicularly from the prevailing level, and form the sites for castles and cities. The latter are compactly built, but show scarcely any signs of habitation.

They look like the ghosts of towns of a departed
age.   The sides of the rocky hills are honey-
combed with catacomb-like excavations.   Droves
of pack animals with huge saddles take the place
of vehicles.   The view is an exceedingly dreary
one.   Suddenly we come upon a heap of ruined
masonry, and directly after a long line of ruined
arches extending across the plain.   We know
now that we must be nearing Rome, and while
we are reflecting on it we pass under an old gateway.   More extensive ruins, and then blocks of
five and six-story modern houses, appear.   The
train stops.   We are in Rome.

Rome, since 1870 the capital of united Italy,
has about twice the population of Rochester or
Detroit.   I was agreeably disappointed in it.   It
was much cleaner and more attractive every way
than I expected to find it.   The eastern portion
is being extensively rebuilt in Parisian style, with
broad, well-paved streets, and elegant five and
six-story blocks.   The leading business streets
compare favorably with other principal cities of
Europe in the brilliancy and attractiveness of
their stores.   The streets are alive with fashion
and gaiety, and the old city seems fairly to have
entered upon a new era of prosperity.   While
thus as a modern city a pleasant one to sojourn
in, Rome presents the double attraction of being
able to exhibit the remains of twenty-six centu-

ries of antiquity, and some of the finest ruins
perhaps to be found anywhere. The reader must
not suppose that the antiquities are remote from
the modern city. On the other hand they are
closely intermingled. Within a stone's throw of
one of the most elegant quarters are the ruined
fora of Augustus and Trajan; and one of the
most interesting old heathen temples, fully nineteen centuries old, is doing regular duty as a
catholic church in a crowded business quarter.
I refer to the Pantheon. Fifteen minutes walk
from our hotel takes us to the Colosseum, the
Roman Forum, and a dozen other interesting old
ruins.

Rome is situated about ten or twelve miles
from the sea, and about the same distance from
the foot of the Apennines, a level plain known as
the Campagna lying between. The Tiber runs
through the city from north to south in a serpen-
tine course, dividing it into two unequal portions.
The larger and older lies on the left bank, or east
of the river; St. Peter's and the Vatican, or palace of the popes, on the west side. The whole
city is surrounded by a wall about fourteen miles
in circuit. It was originally built by the Emperor Aurelian, about the year 271, but has been
much repaired by later rulers. It is built of
stone and brick—chiefly the latter—and is fifty-
five feet high, but hardly massive in proportion.

It would be no defense against even small cannon of the present day. Twelve gates enter the city.

The streets, though generally narrow, and in some portions very crooked and irregular, are on the whole rather symmetrically laid out, so that the geography of the city is soon mastered. Except on the newer streets, there is either no side-walk at all, or so narrow a one that if a body meet a body one must step into the roadway; but this one does not mind, for the streets are beautifully clean. There are a great number of open squares or "piazzas," as they call them, and these are usually decorated with Egyptian obelisks of larger or smaller size. The city being originally built on seven hills, is still quite undulating, some localities being from a hundred to a hundred and fifty feet higher than others. The Corso is a comparatively narrow street running north and south through the heart of the city. It is the fashionable retail street of Rome, is filled with brilliant stores, thronged with people at all hours, and in the afternoon is alive with gay equipages.

The larger mansions are built in the oriental style, with a quadrangle or open court in the center reached from the street by a broad arched entrance, into which carriages often drive. The court is usually filled with trees and plants, often has a fountain in the center, and affords a very refreshing peep as one passes the entrance arch. The walls of all buildings are very much thicker than we usually construct them. Ceilings are frequently vaulted, stairs are almost invariably of stone or marble, and the roofs are covered with heavy tiles laid in cement. Houses built in this way very rarely burn down, and last for centuries.

I liked the Romans, and, indeed, the Italians generally. They are a cheerful, good-natured, courteous people. Black eyes prevail, but otherwise the Italians are very much like other people, though individuals giving a strong impression of a tinge of negro blood are quite common. The dress, too, is one quite like our own, but one frequently meets the picturesque peasant costume—a folded towel worn flat on top of the head and hanging to the neck behind, forming the female head-dress, and full white sleeves with bodice, neck-kerchief, apron, etc., of bright colors, as red, blue and yellow, completing the attire. The men wear felt hats with pointed crowns, knee breeches, red stockings, etc. The costume of both sexes is very picturesque. Beggars abound, but not to the extent I had been led to expect. Most of them have deformities of some sort—some very disgusting cases, the sins, no doubt, of the fathers visited upon the children to the third and fourth generations.

Every one is familiar, through pictures, with the massive round tower on the west bank of the Tiber known as the castle of St. Angelo. It was built in the first quarter of the second century by the emperor Hadrian as a tomb for himself. The base is three hundred and forty-two feet square, and upon this base rises the circular tower two hundred and forty feet in diameter and altogether one hundred and sixty-five feet high. With the exception of passages through it, and the burial vault in the center of the structure, which is about twenty feet square and arched over at the top, this building is a solid mass of masonry. It was originally encrusted with marble and surmounted by marble statues, but these have long since disappeared. For four hundred years it was the mausoleum of all the Roman emperors. Then in the troublous times of the invasion of the Goths it began to be used as a fortress. A chapel erected on its summit and dedicated to the Angel Michael, and a large bronze statue of an angel which surmounts its highest point, gave it its present name. We procured a "permesso" and visited it. The summit is reached by an inclined plane and steps passing in their course through the tomb chamber. The summit is quite a miniature city, with its numerous small buildings and streets paved with flagstones. A large hall is shown us in which the trial of the beautiful

Beatrice Cenci for the murder of her brutal father who sought to corrupt her virtue, took place in 1599, and adjoining it the room in which she was put to torture. The view from the summit is very fine. St. Angelo, down to the time of Pius IX., was the stronghold of the popes, and is connected with the Vatican by a private passage. It is now garrisoned by the royal troops.

We spent altogether six or seven hours in St. Peter's, and could have spent as many days without fatigue. It is the largest and most imposing church in the world, the great masterpiece of Michel Angelo's genius. The longer one walks its aisles and gazes up into its beautiful dome the more deeply is he impressed. In the broad lofty nave alone five or six of our largest churches at home could stand, barring of course the steeples, with plenty of room to drive around them with a carriage; and this is saying nothing of the broad double aisles on either side, or of the transepts. Under the dome a respectable American church steeple could stand twice over and still have something to spare in the matter of height, it being four hundred and three feet from the pavement to the mosaic-covered vaulting above. In superficial area the church occupies a space equal to about two-and-a-half ordinary blocks of one of our western cities—say blocks three hundred feet square. Probably the largest church in the west could stand under the dome without touching walls at any point.

The cost of the building has far exceeded fifty millions of dollars, and it.costs thirty-five thousand to forty thousand dollars a year simply to keep it in repair. Notwithstanding this immense cost it is still far from complete. The walls and piers of the aisles are beautifully overlaid with variously colored marbles and finely sculptured reliefs, but the pilasters of the nave and transepts are simply covered with plaster, slightly colored in veins to imitate marble. Of course it was the intention some day to enrich these portions correspondingly with the aisles. So, too, while the inscription in mammoth letters around the inside of the dome is in imperishable mosaic, that extending around the nave and transepts is simply painted on cloth like the political campaign streamers we indulge in at home.

But these imperfections are lost sight of in presence of the exquisite beauty of the mosaic altar pieces (copies of famous pictures by the old masters in the Vatican gallery), of the magnificent sculptured tombs of deceased popes, and of the general effect of the grand proportions of the edifice.

Under the dome is the high altar, with St. Peter's tomb beneath it and a massive bronze canopy ninety-five feet high, but which scarcely

looks twenty, above it. In front is an enclosed
space with steps leading down to the tomb
and eighty-nine ever-burning lamps around it.
Near by is a bronze statue of St. Peter in a
sitting position, with his right foot projecting a
little beyond the pedestal. It is an insignificant
looking figure, but is very ancient. It is the
habit with good catholics to kiss the projecting
foot, and this has been done to such an extent
that the foot is worn to about half its original
thickness. As we were looking at it several persons of various classes came up and went through
the ceremony. They would whip out their
pocket handkerchiefs, give the toe one smart
rub, kiss it, press their foreheads against it and
pass on.

Among the more noticeable objects in the aisles
are the tomb of the daughter of the protestant
king of Sweden, Gustavus Adolphus, who became
a convert to catholicism; the monument of Pope
Gregory XIII., who reformed the calendar two
hundred years ago; that of Gregory I. (the Great),
who died nearly thirteen hundred years ago; that
of the late Pius IX., a plain sarcophagus resting
on the cornice over a doorway, and the tombs of
" James III." of England and his sons, Charles
Edward and Henry, " the last of the Stuarts."
These were the sons and two grandsons of James
II., deposed at the revolution of 1688 for his

attempt to restore the Church of England to Catholicism. In English history the line of the Stuarts ends with James II., and these gentlemen are styled "Pretenders;" but catholic Europe recognizes their legitimacy and honors them with royal tombs.

On every Thursday the ascent of the dome is permitted to the public. We first ascend to the roof of the church by a spiral inclined plane in a circular tower adjoining the north aisle. In the wall are marble tablets recording the ascent of notable personages, and among them we notice the names of the late Emperor Alexander II. of Russia, Queen Isabella and the present King Alfonso of Spain, and the unfortunate Empress Carlotta of Mexico. We are now on the roof, one hundred and sixty-five feet from the ground. It is unlike the roof of any other building we ever saw. Part is paved with large flagstones, part with brick, and here and there a section is covered with lead or tiles. There are a great number of cupolas and other buildings—quite a little village in fact—a number of people making their regular homes upon this immense roof. The dome still rises over three hundred feet above us, but so easy are the stairways that it is ascended without much fatigue. Unlike the dome of St. Paul's, London, the outer shell of which is of timber covered with lead, this one is of stone throughout. It is constructed in two shells, an outer and inner, and the stairway to the top is between them. The summit commands a splen- did view—mountains to the north and east, with broad plains intervening; more plains to the west, with the blue waters of the Mediterranean in the distance, and all the hills and vales, domes and palaces, gardens and groves, of Rome at our feet. We spend an hour in the hot sun, and still can hardly tear ourselves away.

Pictures of St. Peter's always show the dome disproportionately flat. In fact its proportions are admirable, but from no point of view can they be seen to advantage, owing to the bad taste of later architects, who changed Michel Angelo's plans by lengthening the nave so as to give the building the form of a Latin instead of a Greek cross as was originally designed. The effect has been to throw the dome so far back from the main front that the lower part, or drum, is wholly obscured from view.

The building is also disfigured by the vanity of the popes, who for three centuries have seemed to vie with each other as to who shall record his name on the building in the greatest number of places. The principal facade bears, in letters probably ten feet long, instead of an ascription of praise to the Almighty, the vain record that the building was erected by Paul V., Borghese, in

1612. But even this is less disgusting than the inscriptions on the various objects in the Vatican and other museums, where, instead of finding the title or explanation of the object we only find the name of the pope by whose "munificence" it was placed there. This papal self-glorification is peculiarly the eye-sore of Rome.

CHAPTER XV.

BESIDES St. Peter's, Rome has several other
nearly as famous churches. Among them
is the basilica of St. John's, Lateran, a very
large and handsome church, bearing little evi-
dence in its rich marble front and perfect state of
repair, of its fifteen centuries of antiquity. But
then it has been destroyed by fire and earthquake
several times, and as often rebuilt. It takes its
name from a Roman family who formerly occupied the palace it adjoins. Notwithstanding that
it is the cathedral church of Rome it is situated
in the extreme outskirts of the city, with open
commons all around it. As a compliment to the
pope, the precincts of this church, as well as the
Vatican, have been ex-territorialized by the Italian
government, so as to be entirely outside King
Humbert's jurisdiction. In the cloisters of St.
John's the visitor is shown two small columns
which once formed part of the temple at Jerusalem. It can readily be believed, for they certainly belong to no existing order of architecture.

Another curious instance of large churches being built remote from any population worth speaking of is the case of St. Paul's beyond the walls. This is situated a mile or more from the city, and with no settlement around it. While smaller than St. Peter's, and with a very plain exterior, it is interiorly perhaps the most beautiful church in the world. The floor of polished marble shines like a mirror. Eighty large columns, each a single block of polished granite, support the roof of the nave and aisles. Above them in circular panels are portraits in mosaic of all the popes, from St. Peter down to Leo XIII., over two hundred and fifty in all. The ceiling of the nave and transepts is of wood, richly ornamented and gilded. The church is very large, being three hundred and ninety feet long, one hundred and ninety-five wide and seventy-five high. It was founded in the year 388, and was claimed to contain the remains of St. Paul himself. It burned down, however, in 1823, and has since been rebuilt, the work being hardly yet complete. Its cost must have been enormous, and it puzzles one to conjecture where all the money could have come from. The great variety of rare marbles and malachites, the beauty of the mosaics and richness of the stained glass, render it certainly, for its size, one of the most beautiful and costly structures in the world.

Space will not permit mention of all even of the notable churches of the city. St. Maria Maggiore, another ancient basilica, we were unable to get away from in less than an hour. It contains two particularly beautiful chapels, the burial places of four sixteenth-century popes. St. Croce, a very old church in the outskirts of the city, is interesting as having been erected by St. Helena, mother of the Emperor Constantine the Great, in the fourth century. The inscription that Pilate wrote and set up over the cross is said to be preserved in this church, though of course we did not see it.

Talking of churches, the American chapel in Rome is one of the prettiest little modern churches I have found. Prior to the fall of the papal civil power in 1870, it was the only protestant church permitted within the walls.

The palace of the Vatican, the residence of the pope, adjoins St. Peter's, and is said to be the largest palace in the world. It is an irregular pile of old-fashioned, and, in many portions, unsightly buildings. It is guarded by a corps of oddly uniformed soldiers known as the Swiss Guard. Only a small portion of the building is actually occupied by the private apartments of the pope, the remainder being taken up with offices for the transaction of the immense business of the church, and extensive museums and galleries of art. The picture gallery contains but comparatively few works, and these all of religious character. It was begun with the pictures plundered by Napoleon I. from the churches of Italy and restored at the close of his career in 1815; to which collection some later additions have been made. But the galleries of antique sculpture are very extensive and interesting. The salon of animals, which is filled with sculptured animals of all sorts, is simply wonderful. The Vatican also contains the famous antique group known as the Laocoon, also of the Apollo Belvedere.

The Sistine chapel, the private chapel of the Vatican, noted for its elaborate frescoes by Michel Angelo, is rather disappointing. It has the appearance of a dingy lumber room, and there are no indications of its having been used for religious purposes for years. The walls are plain, and the ceiling is a simple arched vault. It is so dark that the frescoes are hardly distinguishable, and famous as they are it is difficult to see any beauty in them with everything so much of one color. So, too, with Raphael's celebrated frescoes in the former private apartments of the pope; it is difficult for the uninitiated fully to appreciate them, although these Sistine chapel and Vatican frescoes are considered the most famous in the world.

There is another very interesting collection of antique statuary in a museum on Capitoline hill. Here are the famous "Dying Gladiator" and the "Capitoline Venus," with many other beautiful pieces of ancient work.

The principal collection of pictures, besides that in the Vatican, is at the Borghese palace. It is very tame, however, after seeing the Uffizi gallery at Florence. At the Barberini palace is a small collection, including Guido Reni's pleasing portrait of Beatrice Cenci, of which copies are so numerous. While Rome stands pre-eminent for its sculpture, Florence must have the palm for pictures.

There is a very pretty protestant cemetery in Rome, near St. Paul's gate. It is filled chiefly with graves of English and American people who have died in or near Rome. We stumbled upon a plain flat stone bearing this inscription:

PERCY BYSSHE SHELLEY,

Cor. Cordium.

Natus IV Aug. MDCCXCII.

Obiit VIII Jul. MDCCCXXII.

"Nothing of him that doth fade
But doth suffer a sea-change
Into something rich and strange."

The poet Keats, too, is buried in this cemetery.

The most elegant post office I have seen anywhere is the one at Rome. It has a court-yard in

the center filled with fountains, shrubbery and
flowers.   Around this is an arcade upon which
the general delivery, stamp windows, and all the
different offices open.   It is a charming place.

Rome is no exception to the rule in Italy in the
matter of the ignoring of the sabbath. Sunday
is a good day to haul building material apparently, from the number of wagons that throng
the streets loaded with stone and bricks. Stone
cutters chip away all day, carpenters shove their
planes as we pass their shops on our way to
church, and blacksmiths file away at their vises
just as on week days.

Rome overflows with priests, friars and students. They all look jolly, and appear to go in
for enjoyment much more than our priests at
home. The picture galleries and other places of
popular resort are full of them, and it is not
uncommon even to see black gowns, students,
perhaps, escorting ladies about. The nuns, too,
take an interest in the bonnets of the ladies they
meet to an extent that would shock our good
American sisters.   The brown-gowned monk
reads the secular papers and chats on the street
corners just as any one else might do.

Rome is famous for its Roman mosaics and
cameos.   The latter are cut from shell, the
antique statues in the public galleries serving for
models.   These sell at four to five dollars apiece,

unset, and are very beautiful. But for fifteen to twenty dollars anyone can have his own portrait cut in cameo, a photograph in profile being taken for a pattern for the artist to work from.

Mosaics, or pictures formed of small pieces of stone skillfully cemented together, are of three distinct classes, Venetian, Florentine and Roman. The Venetian mosaics are made of minute pieces of colored glass, put together so as to form pictures of flowers, buildings, etc., and are generally, if not always, in small sizes, adapted only for jewelry or small trinkets. The more beautiful and artistic Florentine mosaics have already been described. Roman mosaics are somewhat similar to Venetian, the whole surface being filled up with pieces of uniform size and shape, but stone or colored tile taking the place of glass, and being used in larger pieces; in the case of large pictures for wall decorations half an inch square or more. Roman mosaics are found mostly in the shape of pictures for framing, wall or ceiling decorations, and ornamented pavements. The cost of a picture in Roman mosaic is probably about four or five times what the same would cost painted in oil. Really artistic ones are hence quite costly, but they are very beautiful and enduring.

CHAPTER XVI.

AS remarked before, the remains of ancient Rome are scattered through the city in close conjunction with comparatively modern structures. Thus we may often see a rude building only a few centuries old, in the wall of which is imbedded the upper part of a massive antique column. The column has, perhaps, stood there for two thousand years. The level of the earth around it has been gradually raised by deposits of rubbish and the leveling of the hills, until only its upper portion is visible above ground, and this, standing in the way of the more modern wall, has been incorporated as part of it. All over Rome we find such antique fragments, sometimes a piece of wall, sometimes an isolated column, and occasionally a frieze and pediment, still in their place. The stone is generally badly broken, split and decayed, and such fragments are frequently strapped up with iron to prevent accident.

The remains are most numerous, however, in

140

the southern part of the city, and during the
present century considerable work has been done
in clearing away the modern houses in certain
sections and then excavating the earth down to
the old level, carefully preserving all fragments
of antique stone work found. In this way the
sites of many ancient temples have been determined, ancient streets identified, and fora, or
places of public gathering, with their rostra or
pulpits from whence the people were addressed
by their great orators, laid bare. At three localities in particular have these excavations been
extensively prosecuted, viz.: the Forum of Trajan, the Roman Forum, and the Palaces of the
Cæsars. In the case of the Forum of Trajan,
now embraced in one of the public squares of the
city, the pavement was found at a depth of ten
or twelve feet below the present roadway that
surrounds it. The earth was cleared away down
to the old level, and a brick wall constructed
around the excavation to prevent the sides from
caving in. At one end of the excavation rises
the richly-carved column of Trajan, erected as a
monument to his victories, and which, before the
excavation was effected, had ten feet of its base
under ground. In the center are the stumps of
some thirty or forty huge granite columns, which
once entered into the construction of a basilica or
large covered hall. Scattered all around are frag-

ments of these columns, with sculptured stone
work, broken statues and carved inscriptions, all
found in the work of excavating. The pit or
excavation can be looked into from the parapet
wall that surrounds it, or can be entered by steps
at one end. It is open free to the public.

The Roman Forum in some respects is more
interesting even than Trajan's. It lies at the foot
of the Capitoline hill, and contains the ruins of a
number of temples. The most conspicuous objects
are the arch of Severus and eight tall Corinthian
columns, once forming the front of the temple
of Saturn. The ancient Romans clearly were
not a church-going people, and small temples
sufficed them, for in an area of two hundred feet
square we have the remains of three distinct
temples. A little beyond are the remains of an
immense basilica over three hundred feet long by
a hundred and fifty feet wide, believed to have
been built by Julius Cæsar forty-six years before
Christ. It evidently consisted of rows of brick
piers, connected above by arched vaulting, but
with an elegant stone exterior. On one side of
this is the paved open space where the people
gathered for public meetings and other purposes,
and at each end of this space are rostra for the
speakers. Through the entire length of the
Forum extends a path, three or four yards wide
and paved with large flat stones, which path is

believed to have been the Via Sacra, leading up
to the Capitol. Besides those mentioned, there are
the colonnades of two or more other temples in
this excavation, which is altogether over eight
hundred feet long, by three hundred or four hundred feet wide. The space is inclosed by a retain-
ing wall and parapet, and is full of sculptured
remains.

But the most extensive and interesting of all
the archæological excavations is that on the site
of the Palaces of the Cæsars, on Palatine hill
overlooking the Roman Forum. The summit of
the hill for some acres in extent is one mass of
stupendous ruins. These prove to be the remains
of a series of magnificent palaces erected by the
emperors Augustus, Domitian, Caligula and others, with some foundation walls extending back
even to the times of Romulus and the Tarquins,
—six hundred to seven hundred and fifty years
before Christ. A first glance at the ruins shows
only a wilderness of brick walls, arches and vaultings, the walls being from three to six feet thick
and sometimes fifty to sixty feet high. A closer
inspection, however, convinces one that these
walls have once been encased with rare marbles
and have exhibited facades of the finest workmanship. Exquisitely sculptured stone cornices,
capitals, bases, etc., and beautifully inlaid marble
and mosaic pavements show that the structures

were not the rough barbaric edifices we had at
first been led to suppose.   In one case we have
well defined remains of a spacious hall surrounded
with a row of elegant marble columns.   Farther
on is the ruin of a magnificent fountain; elsewhere a suite of rooms with mosaic floors that
would put to blush the work of the present day,
and frescoed walls really beautiful even now.
Fragments of marble found amid the ruins and
collected in the museum at the entrance show
that the builders were familiar with a great many
varieties and used them freely in ornamenting.
With the extent and magnificence of these palaces
the spectator is strongly impressed.   A charge of
a franc apiece is made by the government for the
viewing of the remains.

In inspecting the ruins of ancient Rome one is
struck with the closeness with which the temples
and other buildings were crowded together; with
the smallness of the temples; with the great
extent to which brick and concrete were used by
the early Romans, and particularly with the mas-
siveness of their walls and vaultings.   A piece of
the vaulted ceiling of the Basilica of Constantine,
originally one hundred feet above the pavement
but now lying on the ground, measures nearly a
yard in thickness.   The vaultings of Cologne
Cathedral, by contrast, are only nine inches thick.
The Roman bricks were very thin compared with

ours, one and one-fourth inches being the usual thickness, while I have found them as thin as one inch. The Romans used mortar very liberally, the joints being sometimes as thick as the bricks themselves. But they possessed the art of making a mortar nearly as hard and durable as stone. The Basilica of Constantine mentioned above must have been a magnificent piece of masonry, its brick ceiling of eighty feet span being admirably constructed in series of octagonal panels.

Proceeding southwestward from Capitol hill we have a constant succession of interesting ruins. At the foot of the abrupt hill lies the Roman forum, described above. Then to the left the Temple of Romulus and the Basilica of Constantine; to the right, Palatine hill with the Palaces of the Cæsars. The road now passes under the Arch of Titus and down a long slope with temples of Venus and Roma on one side and piles of brick ruins, said to have been private dwellings, on the other. Beyond these we come upon the Arch of Constantine and the Colosseum. The general character of this latter stupendous work I have described in connection with the Arena at Verona. It was an immense out-door theater, capable of seating over eighty thousand spectators. It is oval in form, six hundred and fifteen feet long, and five hundred and ten feet wide. The outside wall rises to a height of one hundred and fifty-six feet, and

10

from near the summit of this, stone seats formerly sloped down in tiers to the edge of the arena
in the center. It was built by the emperors Ves-
pasian and Titus about the year 80. An idea of
the immense quantity of masonry involved in its
construction cannot be conveyed in writing. I
suppose there is more brick and stone in it than
in all the buildings in an ordinary city of one
hundred and fifty thousand inhabitants put
together. When it ceased to be used for the purpose for which it was originally designed, it
became for generations the great quarry from
which all the building material required for Rome
was derived. Its general appearance everyone is
familiar with. It is a story higher than the
Arena in Verona, or four in all, and the exterior
was originally handsomely finished with Tuscan
columns in the first story, Ionic in the second,
Corinthian in the third and Corinthian pilasters
in the fourth. It is in a sad state of ruin, and
much of what we see in anything like complete
form is mere modern restoration. It should be
understood that this is not the only ancient
amphitheatre in Rome. There are at least three
others, viz., the Theatre of Marcellus, the Circus
of Maxentius, and the Amphitheatre Castrense,
but these are comparatively small, and in an even
less perfect condition than the Colosseum.

But the finest remnant of the architecture of

the early imperial age of Rome is the Pantheon.
This was originally built B. C. 27, by Marcus
Agrippa, son-in-law of the emperor Augustus,
and was originally designed as a temple for all the
gods who were not fortunate enough to have
special temples of their own. It is an immense
circular building, one hundred and forty feet in
diameter, with walls twenty feet thick, and covered with a large flat dome of solid masonry, the
height of which above the pavement is also one
hundred and forty feet. It has a massive portico,
supported by sixteen monolithic columns, each
about four feet in diameter and thirty-nine feet
high. The building has no windows, but is
lighted by a large round hole in the center of the
dome, open to the weather. Any rain that comes
in is carried off by drains in the pavement below.
There are seven large niches in the interior wall,
each of which originally contained a statue of
some divinity, but the places of which are now
occupied by christian altars, the structure having
for centuries been in use as a catholic church.
The Pantheon contains among others the tombs
of Raphael and the late King Victor Emmanuel.

One afternoon we drove out for a few miles on
the Appian Way, a military road constructed
three hundred and twelve years before Christ by
Appius Claudius Cæcus, and still a useful turn-
pike road. The old road had become, like every-

thing else, buried up with debris, but Pope Pius IX. caused it to be excavated for several miles, and we are thus enabled to see it to-day in nearly its original state. The roadway itself is about eighteen feet wide, with a curb of rough stone on either side. The gutters are laid with flat, irregularly shaped stones, and occasionally these extend entirely across the street. Back a few yards from the curb, on both sides, are constant successions of ruined remains, said to be tombs. It is just as if all the monuments in one of our western cemeteries had been for some miles strung along both sides of one of the principal thoroughfares leading out of the city. These Appian Way monuments are now for the most part large piles of rough brick or concrete masonry, the facings of marble which once encased them having been stripped off by the vandals of the dark ages. Now and then, however, sculptured stonework and inscriptions are seen, and occasionally some resemblance to a perfect tomb. The most noticeable tomb is that of Cæcilia Metella, which takes the form of a circular tower, sixty-five feet in diameter and perhaps an equal height, erected upon a square pedestal of even larger size. At a later period it was used as the keep or stronghold of a castle which grew up around it, but which is now even more ruinous than the tomb itself. The latter is covered with dressed stone with

wreaths and skulls of oxen carved on it. Slave
labor must have been very abundant at the time
of their erection to have made such large and
massive buildings possible.

TOMB OF CÆCILIA METELLA.

There are in the vicinity of Rome a number of
different catacombs, or ancient subterranean bury-
ing places. We visited those of St. Callistus, a
mile from the city, on the Appian Way. We
descend some thirty or forty feet into the ground,
and then by the light of candles traverse a
quarter of a mile or more of narrow passages cut

through the stiff earth, with tiers of horizontal
niches on each side of us. In these niches the
dead were laid and afterwards walled in with tiles
and plaster. Economy of burial space, I imagine,
was the prime object of these catacombs, as
thus no surface land was wasted.

Another subterranean locality we visited was
the Mamertine prison, a sub-cellar under some
ancient Roman structure, now replaced by a
christian church. There can be no doubt of its
antiquity. Here Peter and Paul are said to
have been confined, and here Jugurtha, king of
Numidia, was starved to death one hundred and
six years before Christ.

A week is all too short a time in which to see
Rome. One should stay at the very least a fortnight. Our short stay of eight days, necessarily
short by reason of the lateness of the season and
rumors of increasing prevalence of Roman fever,
prevented our giving more than a hurried visit to
many objects that would well have merited more
careful examination. Among these slighted
objects were the Tomb of Augustus, the Baths of
Titus and Caracalla, Hadrian's Villa at Tivoli,
the Farnese Palace and the Ghetto, or Jew's quarter, in which, up to within a very few years, all the
Jews in Rome were securely locked every night,
it being a penal offence for a Jew to be found at
large in the city after nightfall.

CHAPTER XVII.

PISA AND ITS LEANING TOWER—GENOA, THE BIRTHPLACE OF
COLUMBUS—THE BATTLE-FIELDS OF ITALY—TURIN—ARCADED
STREETS.

A JOURNEY of nine hours northward along
the shore of the Mediterranean, through
a flat, level, malarial country, brings us to
Pisa, once an important commercial and political
center, but now a dead old place with only
twenty-five thousand inhabitants, but house room
enough, apparently, for twice the number. It is
situated near the mouth of the Arno, but seems
to have no trade left. It is well built, and boasts
many old palaces, but its only attractions to
tourists are its cathedral and leaning tower. The
former is interesting for its age (built 1063), for
its being constructed of marble throughout, and
for its columns being mostly trophies of war
plundered from temples and other buildings, and
therefore very diverse in size, style and material.
It is also notable for being the church in which
Galileo, who was a native of Pisa, discovered by
the swinging of a chandelier, the principle of the
pendulum. The same chandelier is still pointed
out to visitors.

The leaning tower is one hundred and seventy-
nine feet high, and deflects thirteen feet from the
perpendicular.   It was built for, and still serves,
as the bell tower of the cathedral.   A small fee
is charged for ascending it.   Like the cathedral,
it is of marble, circular in form, with eight
stories, each ornamented with arcades of semi-
circular arches.   It is held by some that the
tower was intentionally built with an incline to
the south, and since observing some of the eccen-
tricities of eleventh-century architecture in England, I can half believe it possible, though at the
time of seeing it the impression made on my mind
was that it had settled into its present position.
The leaning tower stands just east of the cathedral.   About the same distance west is the Baptistery, a circular dome-covered marble building, not
unlike, in its general features, the Baptistery at
Florence.   A few rods north of this trio of stately
eight-century-old buildings, is the Campo Santo,
or burying-ground of Pisa.   It is rectangular in
form, and surrounded by a high wall and broad
and lofty arcade or cloister, under the shelter of
which most of the monuments are placed.   The
walls of this cloister also contain some curious
and interesting old mediæval frescoes—interesting as illustrating the theology of the period with
respect to death, hell, and the final judgment.
That the soil in which the good Pisans of the

middle ages reposed might be the more sacred, many ship loads of earth were brought from Palestine and deposited in this Campo Santo. It was here, by the way, that we saw our first Italian funeral. The coffin was carried on men's shoulders, and was followed only by a bevy of priests and acolytes mumbling a sort of liturgy as they walked at a brisk pace through the streets. Some of these followers were dressed in gowns of black cambric, and wore black dominoes or veils over their faces, with holes cut for their eyes. When the procession breaks up, these masked individuals circulate through the city begging for money for masses for the repose of the soul of the deceased. To have one come upon you suddenly is apt to unsettle your nerves for the rest of the day, so unearthly an appearance do they present.

In the eleventh century Pisa was an independent republic and an important military power, and took a leading part in the crusades against the Turk. Later, her fleets ruled the seas, but in the twelfth century she suffered a fatal defeat at the hands of her commercial rival, Genoa, and two centuries later was conquered by and annexed to the then independent · republic of Florence.

From Pisa to Genoa the railroad continues to hug the shore of the Mediterranean, but as the

Apennine range does the same, and as the mountains often rise directly from the water's edge, the work of constructing the line, as may be fancied, was a difficult one. Between Pisa and Genoa there are over eighty tunnels, and many of them quite long. For a considerable part of the way we are under ground by far the greater part of the time. Where we do catch a glimpse of the country it is very beautiful, olives, figs, oranges and lemons growing in great abundance, and the blue Mediterranean as smooth as glass, stretching away to our left.

Genoa, the leading commercial port of Italy, is built in the form of a crescent, encircling its fine harbor. Hills and mountains lie behind it, and the houses extend far up their slopes. So limited is the space available for building, that the streets, except a few of the newer ones, are very narrow—mere lanes eight or ten feet wide, and the houses are run up to extraordinary heights, seven, eight and nine stories being quite common. The only garden space is on the roofs, and we frequently see a mass of green enshrouding the cornice and roof of a lofty structure. Genoa has many fine old palaces, but no antique remains or any edifices of especial note. The bay is filled with shipping, but owing to the shallowness of the water, cargoes have to be landed by the aid of lighters. Along the water's edge is a row of

VIEW OF GENOA, ITALY.

massive stone warehouses, and on their summit is a beautiful esplanade or grand terrace paved with stones. It is over fifty feet wide and several hundred long, and commands a fine view of the harbor. Genoa, once an independent republic, was long a bitter contestant with Pisa and Venice for the naval and commercial supremacy of the Mediterranean. It was at Genoa that Christopher Columbus was born in 1435 or 1436, and a fine marble monument to his memory, is seen near the railway station.

Leaving Genoa, we again have to cross the Apennines, a comparatively inconsiderable range at this point, our greatest altitude being about twelve hundred feet. We then descend to the fertile plains of Sardinia, or Piedmont, drained by the river Po which flows eastwardly into the Adriatic. The valley of the Po is formed by the Alps on the north and the Apennines on the south, and constitutes a broad and fertile plain extending entirely across the northern part of Italy.

On the route between Genoa and Milan via Turin, we pass several important battle fields, including that of Marengo, where Napoleon I. won his decisive victory over the Austrians after his famous passage of the Alps in June, 1800; Novi, where the year previous the French had been terribly defeated by the Austrians and Rus-

sians; Novara, where the Sardinians were badly
defeated by the Austrians in 1849; and Magenta,
where Napoleon III. and Victor Emmanuel so
totally defeated the Austrians in 1859 that they
were compelled to abandon their possession of
northern Italy. A grand monument marks the
scene of the latter achievement.

Turin, the late capital of the little kingdom of
Sardinia, which within the past twenty years has
expanded into the kingdom of Italy, is a fine
modern city of over two hundred thousand inhabitants. It is laid out with Philadelphia regular-
ity, with streets of good width, and several handsome squares, or piazzas, as they call them, ornamented with equestrian statues. Street railways
are fully introduced, and they even use steam
as a motive power with success. In Turin we
again come upon the practice of building the
houses with arcades covering the sidewalks, but
here they are much more imposing than in the
other cities we have seen, being broad, and
extending up two full stories in height, and uniform in construction for whole blocks together.
The shops are well stocked and make a fine
appearance. Turin is undoubtedly the finest
modern city in Italy.

Talking of arcades, I wonder the system of
covered sidewalks has never been introduced into
America, where the shade would be so agreeable

in our hot summers and the freedom from ice and
snow so advantageous in winter.   Fancy a leading street with long rows of columns or brick
piers extending along the line of the curbstone,
with arches spanning the intervals at the level of
the second story ceilings, and between this colonnade and the line of the houses a vaulted ceiling,
covering the sidewalk.   Above this there might
be an open terrace, or, what is more usual in Italy
and Paris, is for the upper stories of the houses to
be built out to the line of the curbstone.   Where
built uniformly, such arcades have a very pleasing
effect, and naturally attract custom to the stores
fronting upon them.   Such an experiment was
once tried on Regent street in London, but it
did not answer there owing to the fog and darkness of that city, which, for the abutting stores,
the arcade intensified.   It would be different,
however, with our bright American atmosphere.
But it is nevertheless best adapted for streets
where the stores are not of great depth, and, by
the way, I am convinced that the public good
would be promoted if there were more small
stores, and if business were less concentrated into
the hands of a few large concerns.   In Europe, if
a lady wants a parasol, she does not go to a mammoth dry goods house to select one, but to a little
store, perhaps twenty feet square, where nothing
but umbrellas and parasols are sold, and where,

of course, a superior assortment is kept. So
every other branch is subdivided. The number
of independent businesses is increased; men of
small capital can do business successfully because
they do not have to carry such multifarious
stocks; landlords are benefited by the wider
distribution of trade, and the public, not only by
the better assortments that are possible, but by
not having to go long distances to the center of
the city to do their trading.

Just out of Turin a few miles is a magnificent
hill sixteen hundred feet high, known as the
Superga, from the summit of which a rare view
of the plains of Savoy, studded with cities and
villages, is obtained. It was from the top of this
hill that one of the dukes of Savoy viewed a
battle on the plains below, between his own troops
and an invading army, and, as the legend goes,
made a vow that if his forces were victorious he
would, on that summit erect a worthy temple to
the Virgin. The church was duly built, with
accompanying monastery, and has since formed a
sort of ducal mausoleum. It is one of the sights
of Turin, and the walk to it affords a rare bit of
exercise. Ladies make the ascent on donkeys.

CHAPTER XVIII.

MILAN—ITS CATHEDRAL—THE GALLERIE—DA VINCI'S LAST SUP-
PER—THE ITALIAN EXPOSITION—SAN CARLO AND THE BOR-
ROMEAN ISLES.

ETWEEN Turin and Milan the country is
very level, the predominating feature
being the extensive rice fields flooded
with water by artificial means.

Milan, like Turin, is essentially a modern city.
Upon its emancipation from Austrian rule something over twenty years ago, a spirit of enterprise
was awakened, which to this day has kept it in
the front rank, among Italian cities, for commercial thrift and progressiveness. It has about two
hundred and fifty thousand inhabitants, extensive canal and railroad connections, and no insignificant manufacturing interests. It is best
known to the world through its cathedral, the
third largest church in Europe and probably the
most elaborately ornate of any. The latter is
built of marble and granite from foundation to
summit, the closest scrutiny discovering in the
structure itself neither brick nor timber. In this
respect it is the most complete piece of mason
work I have yet seen. The roofs of other great

churches are more or less covered with lead;
this is entirely roofed with slabs of marble.   In
another respect it is unique: so complete is
the ornamentation that no difference is made in
the richness of the sculptured work between
those portions prominently exposed to view and
portions entirely hidden, where the question of
symmetry at all enters in.   Every pinnacle is
surmounted by a statue in marble, and these,
with the statues occupying niches, bring the
whole number displayed on the exterior up
to two thousand.   But with all its magnitude,
richness of ornamentation and conscientious
workmanship, it has faults which every one
familiar with it through photographs or engravings will appreciate.   Its ground plan is so large
that, notwithstanding the nave is one hundred
and fifty-five feet high, the whole building has,
in contrast with Cologne and the best English
cathedrals, a decided appearance of flatness, and
the tower, though three hundred and sixty feet
high, looks insignificantly small on so large a
church.   It should have been at least five hundred feet high, and have tapered much more
gradually.   Then, too, the external ornament in
the shape of delicately sculptured marble pin-
nacles, flying buttresses, screens, parapets, etc.,
is decidedly overdone, and considerably detracts
from the dignity and grandeur of the building.

The interior is less open to criticism, and if the vaulted ceiling were really perforated stone work, instead of painted imitation, it would perhaps be unsurpassed for beauty among the great Gothic churches of Europe. Altogether it is certainly a beautiful thing, but, artistically, far inferior to the cathedral of Cologne.

Next to its cathedral the pride of Milan is its Gallerie Vittorio Emanuele, the finest arcade in the world. Fancy two intersecting streets, each forty-eight feet wide and five hundred or six hundred feet long, lined with elegant five-story stores, and entirely roofed in with glass at a height of ninety-four feet from the marble pavement. The two streets form a cross, and at their intersection is an immense glass dome, octagonal in shape and one hundred and eighty feet high. The buildings are ornamented with statues and brilliantly lighted in the evening, when half Milan assembles there for a promenade. Most of the best stores in the lines of jewelry, fancy goods, statuary, pictures, books, music, confectioneries, etc., with a number of cafes, are assembled here, and it has become the great center of the best retail trade of the place. The Gallerie was completed about three years ago. Of course it is not a thoroughfare for vehicles.

Another special pride of this ambitious little city is its cemetery. Milan is famous for its

11

marble sculpture, and naturally the cemetery is
exceedingly rich in beautiful monuments and
elegant private vaults.   There are also very
extensive public vaults and spacious arcades for
cenotaphs and tablets.   This cemetery is also
provided with a crematory furnace, which is in
regular use, Milan leading all other cities in its
practical adoption of the plan of thus disposing
of the dead.

There is one other thing for which Milan is
famous, viz., its possession of Leonardo da Vinci's famous picture of The Last Supper. Every
one is familiar with it through prints—with its
long table formed of boards supported on carpenters' horses, and the Saviour in the center with
six disciples on either side of him, all facing the
spectator.   It is reckoned Leonardo's greatest
work.   We went to see it.   It is in the refectory
or dining-room of an old monastery connected
with the ancient abbey church of St. Maria delle
Grazie.   We pay a franc for admission.   The
picture occupies the entire width of one end of
the room, and is painted on the plastered wall in
oil colors.   As Da Vinci died in 1519—three hundred and sixty-two years ago—it may be readily
fancied the picture is in an advanced state of
decay.   In fact, very little can be seen but the
positions of the figures—the expressions must be
in great part conjectured.   When new, however,

it must have been a very grand picture. With this conviction we have to be content, so faded are the colors and chipped and broken the plaster. I fancy with another generation or two it will have become altogether a thing of the past.

We happened to be in Milan during the progress of the great Italian Exposition held there through the summer of 1881. It was gotten up by the enterprise of Milanese capitalists, aided by a liberal appropriation made by the national government. Very extensive buildings were erected for its accommodation, and every way the Exposition was a great success, and gave tourists a better idea of the resources and industrial condition of Italy than could have been gained in any other way. In paintings and sculpture the exposition hardly came up to what I should have expected of a country the nursery of art, but the evidences of mechanical progress were very creditable. Italy turns out as handsome steam engines and other machinery as we can build in America, though it costs more to produce them. In optical and mathematical instruments and scientific apparatus she always excelled. In everything pertaining to building, except woodwork and builders' hardware, they are in advance of us; in agricultural machinery far behind. One of the most interesting departments, and one fully represented, was the culture and manufacture of silk, all the processes, from the incubating of the silk worms' eggs to the weaving of the richest satin damask, being seen in full operation. The wine and honey industries also occupied considerable space. Cremation was exemplified in models of furnaces, glass jars showing the remains of numerous subjects, and an assortment of modern cinerary urns.

Just as Leipsic is the most famous place in the world for education in instrumental music, so is Milan for vocal culture. It is the Mecca of all great singers.

Milan has a very precious treasure, in a chapel under the choir of her cathedral, in the bones of St. Carlo. San Carlo Borromeo was born in 1538. He was a nephew of pope Pius IV., who was somewhat given to nepotism, and who made Carlo Archbishop of Milan and a cardinal, when but twenty-two years of age. Unlike most men thus favored, the young prelate laid himself out to merit his promotion, and by austerity of life and severe labors he brought himself to an untimely grave when but forty-six. Soon it was found that miracles were worked at his tomb, and ultimately, in 1616, he was canonized and became Saint Carlo. He is the patron saint of all the region around Milan. In the city itself, besides his splendid shrine, there is a large church dedicated to him, and at Arona, on a hill overlooking

Lake Maggiore, is a colossal bronze statue of the reverend gentleman seventy feet high, on a pedestal of forty feet.

A few miles up Lake Maggiore from Arona are the Borromean isles, the property of the same family to which St. Carlo belonged, which still maintains its name and identity. The principal islands are Isola Bella and Isola Madre, both originally mere rocks rising above the surface of the lake, but two centuries ago transformed by artificial terraces and imported soil, into the loveliest of gardens. Upon each island a palace was erected, and trees and shrubs for the grounds were brought from all parts of the world. The present appearance of the islands, rising out of the water in a succession of arcades and terraces, reminds one very much of the fanciful pictures sometimes seen on the drop curtains of theatres.

Arona is a small village at the foot of Lake Maggiore, two hours' ride north of Milan. It is the Italian terminus of the carriage road across the Simplon pass, and here we bid adieu to Italy.

Many of the hotels in Italy were formerly old palaces, and the rooms are spacious and elegant. All Italian buildings are very substantially constructed. The stairs and landings are almost universally of stone, and houses are commonly built without joists or other woodwork in the floors, the walls being made very heavy, with a flat arch of brick springing from each side of the room and meeting in a point at the center. The haunches are filled up with Portland cement concrete, and a concrete or tile floor is finally finished for the room above. A style of floor very much in use in Italy is made of a concrete of Portland cement and various colored marbles in irregular pieces, from the size of a dime to that of a quarter-dollar, polished to a smooth surface. Sometimes the different colors are kept separate and laid in patterns.

The Italians are also splendid railroad builders. Rarely is finer constructive engineering to be seen than some of the Italian roads display. Railroad travel is cheap in Italy. First class fares are about three and a half cents a mile; second class, two and a half cents; third class, one and three-fourths cents. Their second class is superior in comfort to our first.

The money of account in Italy is the lira, which is identical in value with the franc of France and Belgium. Like the franc, it is divided into one hundred centesimi. Five centesimi make a soldo, or sou, equivalent to our cent. An irredeemable paper currency forms the sole circulating medium of Italy, and it ranges from one and a half to three per cent discount as compared with silver.

CHAPTER XIX.

ITH every traveler in Italy, the art collections of that country rank among the foremost of its attractions, and yet, I fancy, but comparatively few fully appreciate and enjoy them. Most tourists visit the galleries because they are set down in the guide books as principal attractions, and because everybody else visits them, but I am vastly mistaken if they do not inwardly vote them a bore. It is certainly a very laborious occupation; for standing about looking at pictures for hours together is far more tiring than even brisk walking. Then the character of the pictures, too, is not usually such as would be fascinating to a person of ordinary tastes. Mythological and religious subjects predominate, and in a great majority of cases they are handled in a fanciful and extravagant manner that has few charms for the hard-headed realist of the present day. I am referring now to the paintings of the mediæval period. Madonnas greatly abound, but comparatively few of them would be set down by the average observer as models of female beauty. Other favorite subjects are the martyrdoms of the saints, and sensational, revolting subjects they most usually are. St. Sebastian is perhaps the most frequently depicted, bound nude to a tree, with his body stuck full of arrows, like pins in a pin-cushion. St. Lawrence comes next, in condition of being broiled on a gridiron and prodded with tridents, as a cook fumbles over the broiling steak with her fork. When we come to bible scenes, which of course are very numerous, we see little or no attempt to reproduce the ancient and oriental, either in landscape, architecture, dress, or any other accessories. Patriarchs and prophets will be pictured in middle-age Italian costume, and Corinthian architecture be introduced in connection with the rudest and most barbarous periods of scripture history. So, too, not infrequently the painter utterly fails properly to interpret his subject, as when a feast is almost invariably represented as a debauch. Still, there must be some real merit in these old paintings, or students and connoisseurs could not so dote on them; but I am strongly inclined to the opinion that very much of the reverence with which the so-called old masters are regarded, is factitious and unmerited. Well authenticated works of the early Italian painters of note are of course limited in number, and in the strife of collectors for possession of them their value has become enormously inflated, and, being valued at extravagant figures it is only natural that people should come to believe them possessed of extraordinary merit. I go farther and assert as a plain, common sense, unprejudiced observer, that I believe that as good pictures are painted in the nineteenth century as any the fifteenth or sixteenth centuries produced. And why should there not be? The world has made wonderful progress in all other branches of intellectual and æsthetic culture; and with all the attention that the present age has given to art, with the unprecedented opportunities for study and the wealth that is lavished on works of high merit, is it reasonable to suppose that in painting alone, we have so sadly retrograded?

It is, nevertheless, interesting and profitable to see and study the works that, whether justly or not, are so much prized, and to know something of their authors. The number of old Italian masters is very large and a list of them would be tedious and unprofitable; but there are some twenty-five or more, whose names and works soon become familiar to the traveler in Europe, and these may be noticed here as a very slight introduction to an acquaintance with Italian art.

Not quite the oldest painter known but still

one regarded as the father of Italian painting, was
Cimabue, who was born in Florence in 1240.   In
his day oil colors had not come into use, but the
pigments were mixed with glue or size and laid
on wood instead of canvas.   All the earlier paintings were executed on gold grounds.   They were
almost exclusively confined to religious subjects
and, compared with the works of later artists,
have a stiff and doll-like appearance.   Artistic
grouping was unknown and the pictures represent but little more than a collection of figures
very little dependent on each other.

Cimabue walking in the fields one day found a
shepherd boy drawing pictures in the sand with a
stick.   He thought he detected genius in the lad,
took him into his studio and trained him.   In
time the pupil, whose name was Giotto and who
was born in 1276, far surpassed his master, and
his remaining works are perhaps as highly prized
as those of any other painter.   Most of his paintings are frescoes, that is, are painted on plaster
walls in water colors, and hence are generally in
a dilapidated condition.   Even the unlearned in
art will quickly discover that Giotto was far in
advance of the painters of his age in the life-like
naturalness of his figures and groups.   Besides
being a great painter he was the architect of the
cathedral at Florence, as related in a former
chapter.

The next great painter was Fra Angelico, a monk of the convent of St. Mark at Florence, the cells of which he decorated with frescoes still in an excellent state of preservation. Fra Angelico was born in 1387. He was a most prolific painter, most of his works being religious scenes embracing a great number of figures of small size, but all most exquisitely drawn and a character depicted in every countenance. We greatly admired the little gems of art that the good monk was so facile in turning out.

Bellini, born in 1422, was the founder of what is known as the Venetian school, and the master of Titian, the greatest of the Venetian painters.

Then came Mantegna of Padua, who was born in 1431. He was noted for the laborious fidelity with which his pictures were worked up, but they are nevertheless strongly marked with the crudeness of the early painters.

Next may be mentioned Perugino, who enjoys the honor of being regarded as the master of Raphael, the greatest of all painters. Perugino was born in 1446.

We now come to the five pre-eminently great Italian painters: Leonardo da Vinci, 1452–1519; Michel Angelo, 1474–1563; Titian, 1477–1576; Raphael, 1483–1520, and Correggio, 1494–1534.

Leonardo da Vinci was born in Vinci on the Arno, near Florence. He was a universal genius, being equally talented as a painter, an architect, a sculptor, and an engineer and scientist. At the age of thirty he accepted a position in the service of the Duke of Milan, and in that city he accomplished his greatest works. His famous painting of The Last Supper, one of the greatest pictures of all ages, has already been described. His other pictures are not numerous, and being greatly darkened with age are not particularly attractive to the non-professional.

Michel Angelo, like Da Vinci, was a man of rare and diversified talents. He also was a Tuscan by birth. From the age of fourteen to twenty-six he devoted himself to sculpture, producing during that period his colossal statue of David, now in the Academy of Art at Florence, and others of his most famous works in marble. For the next thirteen years he was engaged chiefly in fresco painting, his principal production being the ceiling of the Sistine chapel in the Vatican, heretofore mentioned. Then he took up architecture, ending his career as the principal builder of the church of St. Peter at Rome, and the designer of its splendid dome. He left few or no paintings in oil.

Titian was a Venetian and a painter only. The greatest collection of his works is at Venice, though a great many are found in Spain, where he probably resided for a time under the patronage of the emperor Charles V. His paintings are quite numerous, but are not attractive, commonly presenting great masses of dark color with only a small portion distinguishable as a picture.

Strictly as a painter, Raphael is accounted the greatest of the five. He was born at Urbino, a place one hundred and thirty miles north of Rome, and seventy east of Florence. After residing eight years at Perugia and four at Florence, he settled at Rome where he spent the remainder of his short life, dying at the early age of thirty-seven. Among his most famous works are the "Stanzas," or pontifical dwelling rooms in the Vatican, the frescoed walls of which vie with the ceiling of the Sistine Chapel for the pre-eminence as the grandest mural paintings extant. One of his most notable oil paintings is his Transfiguration, in which the upper portion of the picture represents the scene on the mount, while the lower portion depicts the disciples at the foot of the eminence, endeavoring to cast out the devil from the lunatic lad. This picture hangs in the Vatican. Another of his masterpieces is St. Cecilia, in the Academy at Bologna. In this the tuneful saint is represented in a rapture of bliss, with her broken musical instruments at her feet and a choir of angels overhead taking up the strain she has just been playing. On either side of her stand St. Paul, St. John, St. Augustine, and Mary Magdalene, wrapped in contemplation. Still others are his famous series of seven cartoons, copies of which are so familiar to every reader. The originals, belonging to the British government, are exhibited at the South Kensington Museum in London. Then the visitor of the great galleries of Europe will be struck with a magnificent portrait of Pope Julius II., which Raphael painted in triplicate, two copies being at Florence and the other at the National Gallery in London. His Madonnas are very numerous, and some of them are among his most esteemed works, but with few exceptions his Virgins wear a sleepy look which detracts very much from our modern idea of beauty.

Correggio, the fifth of the famous quintette, was a native of the province of Modena. His greatest works are the frescoes in the cathedral at Parma, but oil paintings of his are moderately numerous, and are found in all the principal galleries. The story of Correggio's death has often been told. He had painted an altar piece for a monastery at Parma, and the monks, for a trick, or for spite, or to humiliate him, paid him off in copper coin. The labor involved in carrying home his heavy burden brought on a fever, which carried him to his grave at the early age of forty.

The fifteenth century produced in Florence two admirable painters, Fra Bartolommeo, a monk of

St. Mark's convent, born 1469, and Andrea del Sarto, born 1488. Carlo Dolci, born 1616, was also a Florentine.

In the sixteenth century two important schools of art arose—the Venetian school, numbering among its adherents Bassano, born 1510, Tintoretto, 1512, and Paul Veronese, 1528; and the Bolognese, of which Lodovico, Agostino and Annibale Carracci, two brothers and a cousin, born respectively in 1555, 1557, and 1560, Guido Reni, 1575, and Dominichino, 1581, are the shining lights. Guido has a world-wide fame from the frequency of copies of his portrait of Beatrice Cenci, the original of which is in the Barberini Palace at Rome, and for his Aurora. The latter is a fresco in one of the palaces at Rome, and is regarded as his finest work.

Classed as of the Roman school are Gulio Romano, 1492, and Sassoferrata, 1605. Salvator Rosa, 1615, was a Neapolitan painter, and Canaletto, 1697, a Venetian. The latter was very prolific with his brush, and in subject and tone all his pictures are very much alike, being almost exclusively Venetian canal scenes, and all utterly innocent of bright colors.

Two celebrated Spanish painters may appropriately be mentioned here, Velasquez and Murillo. The former, born 1599, especially excelled in portraits, and is reputed the greatest of all Spanish painters, though to the uninitiated in art his works are not by any means particularly attractive. This however cannot be said of Murillo, born 1618, whose pictures, whether of homely beggar boys or glorified saints, possess a grace and beauty that no one can be insensible to.

ECCE HOMO, AFTER GUIDO RENI.

CHAPTER XX.

AMONG THE ALPS — THE SIMPLON PASS — BRIEG — MARTIGNY — CHAMOUNIX — MONT BLANC — A GLACIER.

AT Arona we take the diligence at eleven o'clock at night, so as to get over the mountains before dark next day. The diligence is a heavy, cumbersome vehicle drawn by five horses, two at the pole and three abreast as leaders, each wearing a string of sleigh bells. Fancy an old-fashioned stage coach with half the body of another attached in front, and a seat with a buggy top perched up behind. The baggage is piled on the roof of the center compartment which, inside, holds four persons. The driver and guard sit over the front section, which is called the coupe and which holds two persons. Under the rear seat, known as the banquette, is a large locker for the mails and small parcels. Seats in the coupe and banquette are preferred, as affording a better view, and are charged for extra. The driver devotes himself chiefly to cracking his whip, and applying the brakes at the down grades. Horses are changed every ten miles, and well they need to be, for they are kept on a brisk trot, and the vehicle and loading must weigh several tons.

12

The road from Arona to Brieg, over the Simp
lon, is seventy-five miles in length, forty of which
lie directly through the mountains. The whole
road was built by Napoleon I. between 1800 and
1806, as a military road, for the purpose of affording the French armies ready access into Italy.
It cost three million six hundred thousand dollars, half of which was paid by the French Government and half by the Italian. It was the
second carriage road across the Alps, the Brenner road having been completed some time before.
It is a beautiful macadamized highway, about
twenty-five feet wide and lined at intervals of
from ten to twenty feet with substantial stone
posts. It winds along the sides of deep gorges,
traverses rocky ledges, passes over numerous
bridges spanning mountain torrents, and through
several tunnels. In places where exposed to danger from avalanches, it is roofed over with a stone
vaulting, through which water percolates like rain.
At nine or ten points on the route refuges are
maintained—substantial stone houses in which
persons are constantly in attendance to relieve
snow-bound travelers or any needing help.

After leaving Arona the road skirts the shore
of Lake Maggiore for a dozen miles, then follows
the valley of the river Tosa, a tributary of the
lake. Forty miles from Arona we turn up a
lateral valley, that of the Dovera river, a braw-

ling mountain stream capable of furnishing power enough for all the machinery in half a state. Soon a granite column by the side of the road indicates the boundary line between Italy and Switzerland. At the next stopping place a Swiss custom house officer inquires of each passenger if he has anything to "declare." If he replies in the negative, that is the end of it. It is only in the case of tobacco and cigars that they are at all strict.

We now ascend mountain gorges, with almost perpendicular cliffs rising thousands of feet on each side of us. At last we are ourselves six thousand six hundred feet above the sea and the summit of the pass is reached ; but mountains still tower far above us, their tops enveloped with snow and half hidden by clouds. At the summit a large hospice, kept by the monks of St. Bernard, is located, and here all travelers are entertained gratuitously, but those who are able are expected to put something in the poor-box of the institution for the support of the house.

All along the road thus far the telegraph poles have been square strips of stone sixteen or eighteen feet high. Stone poles are also used for grape trellises in the valleys, and flat slabs of stone, a sort of mica slate, are employed universally for the roofs of the houses, and are set up on edge for fences.

The descent on the Swiss side of the mountains
is more rapid and dangerous.   So late as in June
we pass great banks of snow reaching as high as
the top of the diligence.   In an hour and a half
we are in the beautiful valley of the Rhone—a
lovely green plain, bordered with high snow-
capped mountains.   In the center stands the
pretty little Swiss village of Brieg, with its old
chateau, its quaint houses, its rustic street scenes
and its clean tidy hotel.

We rest a night at Brieg, and then take the
train down the valley of the Rhone forty-eight
miles to Martigny.   It is a beautiful ride.   The
valley is of nearly uniform width, with ranges of
mountains on either side, which usually rise
abruptly from the level valley, though in some
places their bases are lost in beautiful green
slopes.   Villages are numerous in the valley.
The Rhone here is a small but rapid stream, perhaps twenty yards wide, but is liable to freshets
which inundate the country and do much dam-
age.

Martigny is a small village at a point where the
Rhone makes a sudden bend to the northwest,
twenty-four miles before it flows into Lake
Geneva.   It is an old-fashioned place, chiefly
important as a starting point for mountain excursions.   Here we hire a small pony carriage,
drawn by two strong horses, to convey us to

Chamounix, twenty-two miles south. The route
has until recently been only a bridle-path, and it
still would be impassable to anything but a very
small vehicle. For those who are not hampered
with baggage the road from Martigny to Chamounix affords a good opportunity for a little pedes-
trianism, the scenery being very wild and interesting, and the mountain air exhilarating. By
the carriage it takes nine hours to make the trip.
We begin by ascending the mountain ridge at the
back of the village by tiresome zig-zag slopes.
We are fully four hours in getting out of sight of
Martigny, by which time we have reached an
elevation of thirty-five hundred feet above the
level of that place, or five thousand above the
sea. With a rough and stony road, as may be
fancied, the ascent is a tiresome one, but upon
looking back, the view up the Rhone valley for
twenty or thirty miles is most beautiful, and goes
far toward repaying the labors of the journey.

The road from the summit to Chamounix, by
what is known as the Tete Noir route, is a succession of ups and downs, but with an aggregate
descent of about fifteen hundred feet. The region
traversed is wild and much of the way desolate.
We descend the deep valley of a roaring mountain torrent, with rocks rising almost perpendicularly thousands of feet all about us. Sometimes
the road lies among masses of rock that have

rolled down the mountain sides—masses often as
large as small cottages, yet piled up one upon
another as if shoveled there by Titans.   Once the
road gets through an otherwise impassable point
by a tunnel through an immense projecting rock.
The noise of the water dashing its way through
the great boulders that often fill the bottom of
the chasm is almost deafening.   A wild, awe-
inspiring solitude prevails.   Now we ascend the
valley of another stream, and are soon again out
of Switzerland and in the province of Savoy,
formerly part of Italy, but ceded to France in
1859.   We pass several small but comfortable
looking hotels, and numerous way-side shrines—
little stone buildings open to the weather in front,
with more or less artistically sculptured madonnas, or crucifixions, or dead Christs, or sometimes
only pictures—cheap engravings of sacred subjects exposed in them.   Occasionally we encounter
a little saw-mill driven by water power and apparently cutting a thousand feet a week, though
with power available sufficient to run all the saw-
mills in Michigan.   Two or three little villages
we pass, with their churches and little graveyards
filled with little black iron crosses, the churches
sometimes protected from destruction by avalanches by immense stone barricades in their rear.
The houses in these villages come quite out to the
six-foot roadway, are built of stone and wood in

combination, and are so intimately associated with goat stables that it is impossible to tell what is stable and what is house. Every one greets you with a "*Bon jour*," and buxom maidens emerge from the houses of refreshment and rattle away French at you in the most welcoming and hospitable manner. They are clearly a simple, polite, good-hearted people. For several miles there is no house in sight, nothing but a boulder-strewn valley with high mountains all around. Large flocks of goats, with an occasional cow, all with loud-tinkling bells, alone give life to the scene. A bend in the road and we are in full sight of the famous Mont Blanc range and of our first glacier.

The valley of Chamounix (also spelled Chamonix and Chamouny), extends nearly north and south, and is fifteen miles long. The river Arve runs through it. On the east lies the Mont Blanc range, with a dozen or twenty peaks ranging in hight from eight to fifteen thousand feet. The highest is Mont Blanc itself—fifteen thousand seven hundred and eighty-one feet above the level of the sea, or about twice the hight of our own Mount Washington. On the west side of the valley is another range of high, but by comparison inferior, mountains. The Mont Blanc range forms the dividing line between France and Italy. These mountains are peculiar

for their sharp, jagged peaks, which rise almost
like church steeples from the great mass of snow
with which the whole range is perpetually covered. At least four great glaciers pour down
from them into the valley.

In the case of mountains so high that the snow
never melts on their summits, it piles up from
year to year until the weight becomes so immense
that it is forced out at the bottom, and under the
tremendous pressure it emerges in the valleys in
slowly-flowing streams of the hardest ice. These
are glaciers. We visited one in immediate proximity to Mont Blanc. Seen from a distance, the
upper part has the appearance of a mountain
gorge filled with snow, rough and dirty as if it
had been shoveled there from all the aggregated
sidewalks in the world. The mass narrows as it
descends toward the valley at an angle of about
forty-five degrees from the horizontal. It also
grows rougher and dirtier on the surface. What
look like slight furrows from a distance, we find
on approach are great ridges, requiring ladders to
surmount. On either side of the mouth of the
glacier are great embankments of earth and small
stones deposited by it, and these extend out a
long distance from the original line of the mountain, like deposits of alluvium at the mouth of a
swift river. These are called moraines. Between
them the ice becomes blacker and more intermin-

VIEW OF A GLACIER IN THE VALLEY OF CHAMOUNIX.

gled with boulders, and is at last lost in a rollick-
ing stream which hastens away to join the Arve.

We hire mules and guides, and by a tortuous
route at last reach the summit of one of the
moraines at the point where it joins the mountain
proper. We are now several hundred feet above
the valley, and look down forty or fifty feet into
a chasm between the bank and the mass of mov-
ing ice, which, instead of spreading over its entire
channel like water, apparently heaps itself up in
the center. We descend into this chasm, and by
ladders mount upon the glacier. It is strewn
with boulders that it has brought down from the
mountains above. Here and there it is intersected by deep fissures, into which, if a person
were to slip, he would go down twenty to fifty
feet, or perhaps more. We climb down into one
of the furrows which run longitudinally along the
glacier, and enter a tunnel which has been cut
right into its bowels. This we penetrate for
eighty-five yards. It is lighted by candles. The
ice all about us is as pure as crystal and as solid
and hard as stone. And this solid mass of ice, the
guides assure us, moves at the rate of about two
hundred and fifty feet a year. The remains of a
guide, lost in 1820, were found in the glacier in
1866, having been thus forty-six years in coming
down from the point where the poor fellow ended
his life.

One may spend days at Chamounix and yet fail of a good view of Mont Blanc, this highest peak in Europe, the summit being so often enveloped in clouds. It costs, in fees to guides and other expenses, about fifty dollars to make the ascent, and about forty people go up every year. The view from the top is unsatisfactory, and there is nothing but the credit of having been there to compensate for the labor and expense. It requires three days' time.

The valley of Chamounix is a most charming place. The inhabitants are famous for their wood and ivory carvings, and souvenirs may be bought in great variety. No one who visits Europe should miss Chamounix. The hotels are admirable, while the grand mountain scenery, the pretty walks and rides, and the pure, invigorating air, render it one of the most delightful places imaginable.

A MOUNTAIN DILIGENCE.

CHAPTER XXI.

SWITZERLAND—A BEAUTIFUL RIDE—GENEVA—LAUSANNE—FREI-
BURG—BERN—BALE—THE SWISS REPUBLIC.

E leave Chamounix for Geneva by diligence, one of rather different construction from that in which we crossed the
Simplon. This has a coupe in front under the
driver's seat, but at the back of the coupe is a
large compartment for baggage, and over the
whole is the banquette. The latter has five seats
extending across the vehicle, each holding four or
five persons. The level of the seats is nine or ten
feet from the ground, and we climb to them by
ladders. When once up, there is no way of getting down, till a stopping place is reached and a
ladder is raised. Over all is a canvas cover with
side curtains for use in bad weather. The ponderous vehicle is drawn by five horses (three
leaders abreast) and, under the liberal cracking of
the whip, we bowl along at the rate of seven miles
an hour. The horses are changed every eight or
ten miles.

The road to Geneva, fifty-three and a half miles,
is intensely interesting and beautiful, and never
did seven and a half hours pass more swiftly. It

is macadamized, as smooth as a floor, and with
few or no heavy grades. It follows the valley of
the Arve all the way, that river joining the Rhone
at Geneva. As we leave Chamounix we wind
our way through deep mountain gorges, galleries
being cut for the road in the sides of the rocks.
In one place we pass through a tunnel of considerable length. Snow-covered mountains are in
sight at every turn. After twelve or fourteen
miles of this wild mountain scenery, the valley
widens and the road for the rest of the way is
lined with trees—a beautiful avenue the whole
distance, and much of the way an avenue of pear
trees. The fields and meadows are filled with
such a profusion of wild flowers as is never seen in
our own country; and many varieties are included
that are found with us only in cultivated gardens,
such as geraniums, pansies, etc.

We pass one beautiful cataract, said almost to
rival the famous Staubbach, in which the water
falls from such a height as to be entirely converted into spray before reaching the rocks below.
The reader can hardly fancy anything more beautiful than the dashes of water chasing one another
through the air, and quickly vanishing into a thin
mist. But this Alpine country is full of charming waterfalls.

At Sallanches, fourteen miles from Chamounix,
where we get out into the open valley, we have on

looking back a fine view of Mont Blanc towering above all the intervening mountains. It is indeed a much better view than any we can get in the valley of Chamounix. Though so far away we seem to be at its very foot, and the effect of the sun shining upon the great beds of snow and ice that constantly envelop its upper half is very grand.

The last part of the journey lies through a highly cultivated district, with numerous villages and chateaux, and picturesque old avenues of limes, elms and poplars. And so, without a thought of fatigue, we reach Geneva.

Geneva, the largest city in Switzerland (we get into Swiss territory again just before reaching it), has a population of about forty thousand souls. It is situated at the point where Lake Geneva empties into the lower Rhone, and is famous chiefly for the great men it has been the birth-place or home of. These include John Calvin the reformer, Jean Jacques Rousseau the philosopher, Jean Baptiste Say the political economist, Jean Charles Sismondi the historian, James Necker the financier, his daughter, Madame de Stael, and many others. Calvin's house may still be seen. Geneva also has always been the seat of advanced social and political thought and agitation. It is to-day mainly noted as the principal mart for the delicate wood-carving and ingenious mechanism for which the Swiss are so famous. Almost every other store is either an emporium for carved wood work, jewelry, watches or musical boxes—in the last two articles of manufacture Switzerland leading the world. It is quite a sight to see the great variety of pretty things with which these stores are filled.

Geneva is like an old house with a new modern front. Seen from the lake it is quite Parisian in its elegance—magnificent quays and bridges, beautiful public gardens adorned with monuments, and imposing five or six story buildings alone meeting the eye—but back of these the streets are narrow, crooked and filled with old-fashioned and often unsightly edifices. It is peculiarly deficient in towers and spires, the cathedral dome alone breaking the monotony of ugly roofs. The cathedral, finished in 1224, is a fine gothic church, disfigured by the bad taste of the seventeenth century, which gave it a Grecian facade. At the reformation it became a protestant church, and is still so used. It looks odd, after leaving the imposing high altars of the catholic churches of Italy, to see the beautiful choir or chancel of this church filled with seats facing the pulpit in the nave. Under the pulpit stands a chair formerly used by John Calvin. The church is now in process of being restored.

The reader may remember the wealthy but

eccentric Duke of Brunswick, who died in 1873, leaving the bulk of his property, including the finest collection of diamonds in Europe, to the city of Geneva. The city showed its gratitude by erecting in one of its public squares fronting the lake, a magnificent monument to the old Duke —a gorgeous sarcophagus, with marble canopy surmounted by a huge equestrian statue.

At Geneva we passed a new house in course of erection, and were amused at the method of conveying the brick and stone from the ground to the masons above. A long ladder reached to the top of the wall, and on this stood as many men as could find room on it, each standing with his back to the ladder and face to the street, one above the other. A stone would be handed to the first one who would quickly lift as far as he could reach over his head, where it would be taken by the next man and by him be passed on in like manner to the third, and so on to the top. In this way two or three stones would be constantly in process of passing up the ladder and they would be delivered in a steady supply at the summit.

Geneva is quickly seen, unless one has money to spend, when it will take him days to examine all the pretty things that are offered in the shops, and which would be very cheap if one could get them home without those detestable customs

inspections and extortions.   So we take the boat
for a three hours' trip up the lake to Lausanne.

Lausanne is a little city of about twenty-seven
thousand inhabitants, situated on the north bank
of Lake Geneva, about two-thirds its length
above the city of Geneva.   It is interesting
chiefly as having been the residence of Edward
Gibbon for the greater part of the time during
which he was engaged in writing his history of
the Decline and Fall of the Roman Empire.
Indeed, the hotel we stop at occupies the site of
the chalet or Swiss cottage that Gibbon lived in,
and our dining-room overlooks the garden where
one summer evening in 1787 he finally completed
his ponderous work.   Aside from this association, and a small but interesting Gothic cathedral
of the thirteenth century, now, like the one at
Geneva, used as a Calvinistic church, Lausanne
has but few attractions.   The town sits high
above the lake, and is reached by an inclined
plane railway.   The conveniences for transferring
baggage are very poor, and charges for every
service excessively high.   The trip up the lake
by steamer is comparatively an uninteresting one.
The scenery is tame, and the single object of
interest I noted on the way up was the chateau
at Coppet in which the great financier Necker
and his daughter, the eminent litterateur Madam
de Stael, lived and died.

Freiburg, Switzerland (there is another Freiburg in Germany), is two hours ride by rail north of Lausanne. It is a small place of ten thousand inhabitants, and is famous chiefly for the organ in its cathedral, which is said to be one of the largest in Europe. We were fortunate enough to be present at an organ concert, such concerts being given almost daily at an admission fee of a franc. Unlike the cathedrals of Geneva, Lausanne and Bern, that at Freiburg is still a Roman Catholic church. Over the main door is a rude but curious piece of relief sculpture representing the judgment day, according to fourteenth century ideas. The Almighty is represented with an apron full of saved souls, and a group of others, all naked, are wending their way to Paradise. The Virgin Mary holds the balances in her hand, in which she is weighing another batch, and Satan is hanging to the scale containing the weights in the vain attempt to make the poor fellows in the other appear of light weight, and so gain them for himself. Another demon with the head of a hog is leading away a party of unfortunates by a rope, and just beyond, still other demons are boiling a kettle full of sinners over a brisk fire, stirring them up meanwhile with three-pronged pitchforks.

Another hour brings us to Bern, the capital of of the Swiss republic. It is built on a high promontory, surrounded on three sides by the river Aar, one of the principal tributaries of the Rhine. Probably no city can compare with it for the beautiful views it commands. Across the river are delightful green hills, interspersed with picturesque houses and forests. In the far distance, looking south, we have one of the finest panoramas of the Alps anywhere obtainable. The houses are high and quaint, with arcades covering the sidewalks. The roadways of the streets are flanked by lines of heavy buttresses, connected by arches which support the front walls of the houses. The latter are usually four or five stories high, and all have roofs projecting several feet into the street. The arcades are low and rather dark, but the sidewalks under them smooth and very clean. There are a great many fountains and monuments in the middle of the streets, and nearly all are ornamented with bears, the emblem of the city. Wherever we turn we see a sculptured bear—walking bears, climbing bears, equestrian bears, crouching bears, sleeping bears, hugging bears, and bears in every other possible act and position, in bronze, stone, and wood.

We reached Bern one Saturday evening. On awaking next morning, the cathedral chimes were ringing most joyously, the sun shone brightly, the air was cool and refreshing, the view from our bedroom window most charming. Well was the hotel named Bellevue. At our feet lay the delightful hotel garden, with its neat gravel walks, its shady horse chestnuts and its bright flowers. Just beyond, the swift-flowing, winding river, with the gentle roar of its waters as they glided over the stone dam. Still beyond, a beautiful hill covered with bright green fields and groves of pines, and in the far distance the chain of snowy Alps. The streets were quiet as Sunday in any New England village. We went down to breakfast. Americans at home little know what good bread and butter are; and as for honey, our bees should take lessons in Switzerland. Every sense was gratified, and no cumbering care obtruded itself to mar the perfect enjoyment of the day. And so we sauntered to church.

The cathedral of Bern, a very good Gothic structure, was completed about the time of the Reformation, and, of course, was speedily reformed by this protestant community into a Calvinistic church. In sharp contrast with most of the catholic churches in Italy every seat in this large edifice was filled. Men and women sat apart, the former occupying the aisles and chancel, the latter the nave. On the higher seats in the chancel sat the elders. The minister wore a black gown and bands and timed his sermon by an hour-glass. Every soul stood during the prayers. The music consisted of plain, simple chorals similar to our Dundee and Old Hundred. After the sermon most of the congregation were dismissed, but what any American pastor would call a full house stayed to communion. In conducting the latter service, first there was a prayer from the pulpit situated half way down the nave. Then the minister removed to the table on which the bread and wine were placed at the entrance to the chancel. Holding up a piece of bread in his hand he said a few words standing, then ate the bread ; and so proceeded with the wine. The elders then came forward and partook of the elements at the hands of the pastor. Then came the turn of the congregation. The men first marched up, a single file from each side of the church. The pastor and one elder each held in his hand a strip of bread from which he broke off a piece and gave to each communicant as he passed. Farther to the rear, back in the chancel, stood two other elders serving the wine to the two processions, and between them still other officials were kept busy wiping out with napkins and refilling the goblets as they were rapidly emptied. Passing out through doors in the chancel the two processions filed back to their seats. Then followed the women in like order. The whole proceeding reminded us forcibly of a vote by tellers in our national House of

Representatives. While it was going on, alternately a young man in the pulpit read a chapter from the scriptures and the choir sang a hymn.

At a later hour Church of England services were held in a small chapel formed by partitioning off one bay of the north aisle of the cathedral.

The Swiss republic is very similar to our own in many respects. It is composed of twenty-two cantons, each of which is a sovereign power so far as its internal government is concerned. The regulation of foreign relations, the post-office, the currency, the army, and some other things is vested in the confederacy. There are two houses in the national legislature, the lower house consisting of one member for every twenty thousand of population, the upper of two members from each canton. The pay of the members is twenty francs (four dollars) per day, and there are two sessions each year, in June and December. The executive power is vested in a Council of seven, elected by the legislative body and serving for three years. One of the seven acts as President of the Council, and receives thirteen thousand francs per year (two thousand six hundred dollars); the other members receive twelve thousand francs each. The whole population of Switzerland is about equal to that of Ohio, while its territory is considerably less than half that of the

Buckeye state. About seventy per cent. of the people use the German language, twenty-five per cent. the French, and five per cent. the Italian. About three-fifths of the population are protestant and two-fifths catholics.

Three hours' ride northward from Bern brings us to Bale, or Basel, an important Swiss town near the German frontier. It is situated on the Rhine, and is in great part a well-built modern city. The principal object of interest is its cathedral, an interesting old Gothic structure built in the fourteenth century to replace an older one destroyed by an earthquake, some portions of which, however, still remain. It is now used as a Calvinist church.

Once, a long time ago, a jealousy existed between Great Bale and Little Bale, the two sections separated by the Rhine, and, to show their contempt for their neighbors, the inhabitants of the larger city, on the west bank, set up the figure of a human head on a tower just at the threshold of the bridge connecting the two places, the head being provided with great goggle eyes and a red tongue six or eight inches long, and the whole being so operated by clock-work that at intervals of a minute or so it would roll its great, fierce eyes and stick out and wag its long tongue, in a most insulting way, in the direction of Little Bale. The head is now exhibited among other curiosities in a room belonging to the cathedral.

Another curiosity in the same collection is a breech-loading gun, not very unlike some of our modern breech-loaders, yet the invention of two hundred and fifty years ago.

In another of the rooms belonging to the cathedral sat the famous council of Bale, convened in 1431 to reform errors and abuses already, at that early date, acknowledged to have crept into the church. The members talked and disputed for seventeen long years, when the reigning pope put an end to the muddle by excommunicating the whole lot. This was a sort of prelude to the reformation which culminated under Luther and Calvin a century later.

Among the monuments in the cathedral of Bale is that of the eminent reformer and brilliant scholar Erasmus, who was a resident of the place.

Northern Switzerland is not very mountainous, though rather more hilly than our own western country. It is well cultivated and a very pretty region to ride through. The castles of Switzerland are generally of the French chateau style, with round, extinguisher-topped, towers and turrets—more picturesque than the massive keeps of the German castles.

The railway carriages of Switzerland more nearly resemble our American cars than any others I saw in Europe. They have generally eight

wheels, and have an aisle and two rows of seats,
like our own, instead of compartments. They
approach ours in another respect: On none of
the other railways in Europe are the cars provided with water closets, but the trains stop every
few hours for ten or fifteen minutes for the passengers to get off at stations where accommodations are provided. The Swiss roads, however,
have a notice in every car that a water closet will
be found in the " Gepackwagen " or baggage
car.

The Swiss peasant costume, worn by a large
per centage of the women one meets, is very picturesque. It consists of a short, full skirt, with
tight-fitting black bodice, ornamented with silver
chains suspended from the points of the shoulder
blades and passing under the arms to the breast,
and tight sleeves with a sort of broad, white,
stiff-starched epaulet extending from the shoulder to the elbow.

Switzerland is especially famous for the excellence of its hotels. It is also a cheap, pleasant
and healthful country in which to make a pro-
tracted sojourn, though it affords fewer attractions in the realms of art and antiquity than the
other countries we have visited.

Throughout Switzerland a peculiar sort of public fountain is common. It consists of a stone

pillar with four pipes projecting from it horizontally, from which four streams of water are perpetually flowing. A large deep stone basin below catches the water and is the common wash tub and watering trough of the neighborhood.

A SWISS FOUNTAIN.

CHAPTER XXII.

INTO GERMANY AGAIN—BORDER CUSTOMS EXTORTIONS—STRASS-
BURG—ITS STORKS—THE CATHEDRAL—A GHASTLY EXHI-
BITION.

EAVING Bale we entered German territory,
and were once more subjected to that
abhorrence of travelers, a customs inspection. Most of our baggage was promptly chalked
upon our representation that we were going
through to Paris; but spying one small parcel
done up in paper, without any inquiry as to the
nature of its contents, an inspector snatched it
from us, threw it on the scales and demanded
forty pfennigs (10 cents) duty. In vain I told
the inspector it was only a little wood carving of
trifling value, and that I was on my way home to
America, and was taking it with me as a little
present. The only reply was, "You must pay."
Then I put myself on my dignity and pulled out
my passport. The obtuse individual looked it
over, turned up his nose at the great seal of the
United States and James G. Blaine's official autograph that had cost me five dollars, and reiter-
ated, "You must pay." Then I became annoyed
and told him he might keep the bauble as I

would *not* pay, as he had no right to charge duty
on the property of an American citizen that
would not be twenty-four hours in the country.
He seemed entirely indifferent, and as I saw
that I should lose my train if I parleyed any
longer, I at last gave him the half franc and left,
protesting that I would report him to Prince
Bismarck. Neither did that seem to affect him.
I doubt very much if he had ever heard of such a
man, and I am quite certain the imperial treasury will never see a cent of my contribution. In
fact I am convinced that this is the way these
fellows get their "trinkgeld," as they call it,
otherwise beer money. England and Switzerland
are the only two countries where travelers are not
annoyed by these official extortionists.

I had had a previous experience of this character: Passing through Austria (the Tyrol), to save
trouble, I registered my baggage through from
Munich in Germany to Verona in Italy, thinking
I should thus only have the Italian inspection to
undergo. But, to my surprise, when we reached
the Austrian frontier there was my baggage
thrown off on the platform. I explained to the
official that it was in the hands of the railway
company and out of my possession, and would
not be delivered to me except on Italian soil.
Nothing would do but it must be examined. Of
course the examination was all a farce. It con-

tained nothing dutiable, but the inspectors would
have been none the wiser if it had, from the indifferent way in which they did their work. Then
came a demand for twenty-five kreutzers for the
trouble of handling the baggage, the same being
preferred by the porter, who, of course "whacked
up," as the boys say, with the inspector, and
each got his beer at my expense. Free trade
would be a great promoter of honesty in every
country.

Two hours' ride from Bale brings us to Strassburg. This is a city of considerable commercial
importance. It was formerly a free city of the
German empire. Then it was captured by
France, and remained a French city with Ger-
man-speaking population down to 1870, a period
of about two centuries, when the Franco-Prussian
war reunited it with Germany. It is a curious
place, different from any other city we had seen.
The houses are tall, and all have their eaves
towards the street, with very steep tile roofs, the
latter usually containing three or four tiers of
dormer windows, making seven or eight floors in
all to every house.

On the tops of the chimneys of the taller houses
are numerous storks' nests, generally with three
or four young storks about the size of small geese
lazily rolling about in them. Looking down from
the tower of the cathedral we were able to count

STORKS NESTS ON THE CHIMNEYS AT STRASSBURG.

fifteen or twenty of these great nests with their black and white occupants. It is also a common sight in Strassburg to see an old brown stork perched on one leg on the summit of a tall chimney, and stand there for hours as immovable as a bronze statue. They are regarded as lucky birds, and are never driven off.

Strassburg is famous chiefly for two things—its cathedral and its *pates de foies gras*, or goose-liver pies, which latter are the most costly edible known, being sold at the manufactories at from one to eight dollars apiece. They are exported hence to all parts of the world.

The cathedral is notable as possessing the tallest spire in the world, it being four hundred and sixty-five feet high, or thirty feet higher than the summit of St. Peter's in Rome. It is moreover a beautiful spire, of light, open stone work, and it can be seen for miles away in every direction. For forty pfennigs (10 cents) one may ascend it, and the view from the summit well repays the fee and the labor of climbing, although, after all, we only ascend to a gallery about three-fourths the way to the top. The spire was badly damaged during the bombardment of the city by the Germans in the summer of 1871, and some shell marks still remain, though, in general, repairs have been fully made. The interior of the church is a noble piece of Gothic work, although built at different

periods and in varying styles, and so lacking in
perfect symmetry.

The famous clock of Strassburg Cathedral every
one is familiar with. It is situated in the south
transept, and is adjusted to record everything in
the almanac line for about a thousand years to
come. At each quarter hour a small figure steps
forward and strikes a bell, and at noon each day
there is a grand procession of the twelve apos-
tles, and a cock flaps his wings and crows loud
enough to be heard all over the great church.
We were surprised to see how much of an attraction this clock is, even to the natives of Strassburg. As the hour of twelve approaches, people
are seen running from all directions to the cathedral, and the crowd becomes so great that one
can scarce approach within a dozen yards of the
transept door, especially if he be a little late.

Another very ancient church—over one thous-
and years old—is that of St. Thomas, now a
Lutheran place of worship. It is visited for a
somewhat famous monument erected by Louis
XIII. to Marshal Saxe; but a more sensational
exhibit is that of the half-preserved bodies of the
Duke of Nassau, killed during the Thirty Years
War, 1618–1648, and his daughter. They are in
coffins with glass tops, and are horrible things to
look at, though evidently people enjoy seeing
them, or they would be buried out of sight.

There is also in St. Thomas' Church the monument of Jeremiah James Oberlin, a professor of the University of Strassburg, and a brother of the Swiss Pastor Oberlin, after whom Oberlin College, Ohio, was named.

The Alsatian costume (Strassburg is the capital of Alsace) is noticeable chiefly in the head dress of the women. Instead of wearing bonnets or hats in the street, the head is dressed simply with an enormous black Alsatian bow. It is peculiar rather than pretty.

CHAPTER XXIII.

THE trip from Strassburg to Paris is rather a dull and tedious one, and there are no points of any considerable interest at which the journey may be broken. The same, I think, applies generally to traveling through France. The country, compared with Italy and Switzerland, is very level; the railroad itself is no more interesting as an engineering work than any of our western roads, and the scenery is quite monotonous, France appearing to the traveler one vast farm, of which every acre is utilized.

Every station is marked with the number of kilometers to Paris, and as the number diminishes the stations grow more frequent, the houses begin to thicken, and evidences multiply that we are drawing near a large city. Then we catch a glimpse, in passing through them, of the walls of Paris—a long line of earthworks faced on the outside with masonry and a ditch. Inside the walls the view from the car window is just what might strike one in entering any large American city—long lines of freight cars, railway shops, ragged walls, new buildings in progress, etc. The train slows up, and finally stops in a magnificent station. As a rule, by the way, all the railway stations on the continent are very much superior in size and elegance to our American depots. We are met on the platform by porters who relieve us of our hand baggage, and an official with the word "Interpreter" on his cap is quick to note where his services are required. We name our hotel, and he conducts us to one of the small omnibuses, holding about six persons, and belonging to the railway company, which are in waiting outside; the fare by which to any hotel is one franc (20 cents). The interpreter inquires, "Have you any registered baggage?" We produce our receipts. They give receipts, or, rather, paper checks, for baggage, on the continental railways, a number being pasted on each article, and the traveler holding a receipt for so many pieces marked with that number. Our baggage coming from a station in Germany, has, of course, to be inspected by the customs officers. We explain to the interpreter that we are going through to London; that we have nothing that we shall leave

14

in Paris, and no tobacco, spirits or tea in any quantities, and by his assistance the inspection is soon over, only one piece of baggage being opened for form's sake. A franc satisfies the interpreter, half a franc the porter, and we bowl away through the grand streets and boulevards of Paris.

The hotel we had selected, though higher in price than any we had before patronized since setting foot on the continent, we found not satisfactory, so after putting up with it for a day we started out to find something better, and finally settled down on a very quiet, orderly, comfortable place in the Rue de Rivoli, overlooking the gardens of the Tuileries. Here everything was beautifully clean, and the attendance most efficient. The landlord was an agreeable gentleman, and one who gave his personal attention to every detail. Every one in the house spoke English, and the guests seemed to be almost exclusively English. The charges were less than three dollars a day, being five francs each for room, two for breakfast, six for dinner, and one for attendance. Candles, extra, according to what we burned.

Being comfortably settled for a fortnight, we began seriously the work of seeing Paris, and armed with a pocket map, very quickly "got the hang of the place."

Paris was, of course, some centuries ago, much smaller than at present. Like all mediæval cities, it was surrounded with fortifications. As it outgrew these limits, new defenses had to be erected beyond, and the old, being now useless, were removed, and on their site broad streets were opened. These were the original boulevards of Paris. A second general enlargement gave another series. From the circumstances of their construction, they of course encircle the center of the city. In their method of improvement they differ in no respect from ordinary streets. There is a broad roadway and two wide sidewalks; the latter in some cases are forty or fifty feet wide. There are also usually rows of trees on either side. Instead of the streets radiating from the center of the city being the main business thoroughfares, as with us, the encircling boulevards have attained this distinction, from their roominess, which makes them popular places of resort. Inside the boulevards, the city, a century ago, was an intricate net-work of narrow, crooked streets. The successive usurping governments of Napoleon I., Louis Philippe, and Napoleon III., found it necessary to bolster up their popularity with elaborate public improvements, and also to find work for the large population which otherwise were ready at a wink for riot and revolution. The political circumstances of the century have

hence contributed prominently to the beautifying
of Paris, until it has become without doubt the
finest city in the world. The old streets have
been widened and straightened at great expense,
and new and magnificent thoroughfares opened
between important centers.

Where a new street has been laid out or an old
one widened, the buildings have usually been
erected on a uniform plan, and on several of the
best streets the Italian fashion of arcaded sidewalks has been successfully adopted. On hot
days every one flocks to the shade of the arcades,
and on rainy days to the shelter they afford, and
this has made them very popular with shopkeepers. I saw one day hundreds of ladies out shopping in a rainstorm that would have soaked them
through in two minutes but for the friendly shelter of the arcades.

.The streets are very clean for so large a city.
Men are constantly employed with hose, sprink-
ling and washing them. Sweeping machines are
used in connection with this washing, also men
with stout brooms and rubber scrapers, and all
the slush is swept into the sewers. I even noticed
a man with rags and brushes cleaning the lamp
posts. This cleanliness is one of the things that
makes Paris so attractive, and draws so many
visitors to it, and I doubt not that in various
ways it well repays the cost.

The buildings of Paris are generally high—
often six stories, besides a mansard roof containing one or two more. These mansards are usually
covered with metal. The building material is
almost exclusively stone. A brick structure is
very exceptional, and there is probably not a
wooden house in all Paris. The cheaper buildings are constructed of rubble stone, and finished
with stucco; the better class are built of squared
stone in large blocks the full thickness of the
wall. Stone is abundant and easily worked.
The ornamentation is all cut after the building is
up, and so is the smoothing of the walls, which is
done with a sort of plane. The floors are constructed with five or six-inch iron beams, filled in
between with Portland cement concrete. To support this concrete, iron cross-bars are suspended
from the beams on a level with their lower edges,
and upon these rest other longitudinal bars, forming a sort of gridiron, which becomes imbedded in
the cement. The filling between the beams is put
in as the building progresses, and it is done by
means of a platform of boards temporarily constructed on the lower side of the beams, on which
the cement is poured. Practically, Paris buildings are completely fire proof.

Paris, the second city in the world in point of
population, is situated on both sides of the river
Seine, in the northeastern part of France. It is

somewhat oblong in form, with rounded corners, and its greatest length extends east and west. It is about seven miles long and five and a-half wide, and its walls are over twenty miles in circuit. The Seine flows through it from east to west, and forms in its course very nearly a semicircle, entering the city at its southeasterly corner, and leaving it at its southwesterly.

Near the center of the city, on the north bank of the Seine, with one end towards the river and fronting west, stand the ruins of the palace of the Tuileries, built by Catherine de Medici about three hundred years ago. The Tuileries was the residence of all the great Bourbon kings, of Napoleon I., Louis Philippe and Napoleon III., and was finally burned down by the commune in 1871. The walls stand just as the fire left them, and it is probable that sooner or later they will be pulled down and the site be used for other public buildings. It is sad to see the darkness and desolation that reign where once all was so gay and brilliant.

In front of the Tuileries extending westward lie the gardens belonging to the palace, now used as a public park. They are about half a mile in length and about a third as wide as long. They terminate in an immense open square called the Place de la Concorde. In the center of this square, stood the famous guillotine of the French revolu-

tion, upon which the unfortunate Louis XVI.
and his wife, Marie Antoinette, lost their heads.
The spot is now marked by the obelisk of Luxor,
a granite monolith from Egypt, similar to the one
recently set up in Central Park, New York. The
river forms the south boundary of the garden of
the Tuileries and the Place de la Concorde, and
just across the river, fronting the latter, stands
the Chamber of Deputies, a fine edifice, formerly
known as the Palais Bourbon.

Still further west is a very broad boulevard
lined with spacious parks and gardens known as
the Champs Elysees (pronounced *Shonseleeze*),
and this terminates in the famous Arch of Triumph, erected by Napoleon I. to commemorate
his victories. We thus have a continuous park
for about two miles, the Tuileries occupying one
end, the Arc de Triomphe the other. The arch is
a magnificent structure of massive stonework, one
hundred and fifty-two feet high, with a main
archway through it, forty-five feet wide and ninety high. There is also a transverse arch, fifty-
seven feet high, extending through it from north
to south. The exterior is ornamented with bold
relief sculptures, and the inside is inscribed with
the names of ninety-six of Napoleon's battles and
the names of his principal generals. It cost the
French nation over two million dollars.

Intersecting the Place de la Concorde, and at

right angles with the Champs Elysees, is the broad and busy Rue Royale (*Rue* is the French for street), and at the head of it, looking south, and directly facing the Chamber of Deputies, is the church of The Madeleine, one of the landmarks of Paris. The Madeleine, or church of St. Mary Magdalene, is an immense stone building modeled after a Grecian temple and conveying from its appearance anything but the idea of a Christian church. It was begun in 1764 and completed under Napoleon I., who contemplated changing its use from a church to a temple of fame, or place for the tombs and monuments of the great men of the nation—something like, perhaps, what Westminister Abbey is to England. His successor, however, changed the destination of the structure, and it is again an ordinary Roman Catholic church.

Parallel with the Rue Royale and one block east is the Rue Castiglione, which, a short distance up, widens into a square called the Place Vendome, from the Vendome Column occupying the center of it. This famous column is one hundred and thirty-five feet high and twelve feet in diameter, and is modeled after Trajan's Column at Rome. It is entirely covered with plates of bronze, cast from captured cannon, and bearing reliefs representing various scenes in Napoleon's campaigns. It was erected by Napoleon I., in

1805, to commemorate his achievements, and is surmounted by a statue of the emperor.   During the communist sway in 1871 the column was leveled with the ground, under the direction of the eminent French painter Courbet, but fortunately the fragments were preserved and it has since been restored, all Courbet's pictures being confiscated to help defray the expense.

A little north of the Madeleine and Column Vendome, and forming an equilateral triangle with them, is the Grand Opera House, the largest and most elegant theatre in the world.   It was begun under the auspices of Napoleon III., but was not completed till after his fall.   It cost nearly ten million dollars, and instead of paying rent for it the manager has a subsidy of one hundred and sixty thousand dollars a year from government to keep it running.   It is opened every Monday, Wednesday and Friday, admission from one dollar and forty cents to three dollars.   The other principal Parisian theatres are likewise subsidized by government, but to a less extent.   The Grand Opera House looks down a beautiful broad avenue running diagonally to the southeast, and terminating near the Louvre, known as the Avenue de l'Opera.

Just east of the palace of the Tuileries, and separated from it by a large open square flanked by public offices on its two sides, is the palace of the Louvre, the famous art gallery of Paris. The building was begun three centuries and a half ago, but was only finally completed by Napoleon III. East of the Louvre is the interesting old church of St. Germain l'Auxerrois, whose bells, on the memorable 23d of August, 1572, tolled the signal for the massacre of St. Bartholomew. A few blocks still further east and also near the river bank, stood the Hotel de Ville, the seat of the municipal government of Paris, burned by the communists in 1871, when they found themselves unable any longer to hold the city against the government troops. It will be remembered that on the occasion a great number of communists perished in the flames they had themselves kindled. A new building on the site of the old one is now well advanced towards completion. When finished it will be one of the finest municipal structures in the world. In the open space in front of the Hotel de Ville, criminals were formerly executed, and here, in 1610, Ravaillac was torn to pieces alive by horses attached to his several limbs, for the murder of King Henry IV., husband of Marie de Medici referred to in a former chapter.

Opposite the Hotel de Ville is a large island in the Seine, upon which stands the cathedral church of Paris, Notre Dame. The latter is a large and very excellent specimen of Gothic

architecture, the work of the thirteenth century.
Lower down on the island stands the Palace of
Justice, in a part of which, known as the Conciergerie, fronting the Louvre, Marie Antoinette
was confined prior to her execution, and later
Robespierre himself. Opposite the garden of the
Tuileries, on the south bank of the river, stand
the walls of the massive and beautiful building
known as the Palace of the Council of State, also
burned by the communists in 1871.

About three-quarters of a mile east of the Hotel
de Ville and at that point half a mile back from
the river is the site of the old castle known as the
Bastile, destroyed by the mob in July, 1789, the
event being the first step in the memorable French
revolution.   The outline of the fortress is marked
in the pavement by strips of smooth stone inlaid
among the paving stones and asphalt.   In the
center stands a bronze column erected as a
memorial of the subsequent revolution of 1830,
which drove the Bourbons from the throne and
installed Louis Philippe as king, who in turn was
himself deposed by the revolution of 1848.

A mile still further eastward, or bearing slightly to the north, is the cemetery of Pere la Chaise,
the famous resting place of a great number of the
eminent men and women of France.

South from the Place de la Bastile, and just
across the river, is the celebrated Jardin des

Plantes, or zoological and botanical garden of
Paris. It was founded by Louis XIII., and is
perhaps the most complete institution of natural
history in the world. It comprises over sixty
acres, and besides the very extensive botanical
and zoological collections, embraces a very large
library of works on natural history, very extensive museums, and an amphitheatre, in which
free lectures are periodically given on the various
branches of the science. It is all open free to
the public, and is a very interesting place to
spend an afternoon.

About three-quarters of a mile south of the
Louvre, and of course on the south side of the
Seine, is the palace of the Luxembourg, built by
Marie de Medici, and long used as a royal palace, but now occupied in part for the sittings of
the French Senate and in part as a gallery for
modern works of art, the property of the nation.

Half a mile south of the river, at a point a little
west of the Place de la Concorde, is the soldiers'
home, known as the Invalides, a very large edifice built by Louis XIV., but which at present
contains but about five hundred inmates. The
chapel or church connected with this institution
contains the tomb of Napoleon I. This church is
a large and elegant one, built by the famous
architect Mansard, the inventor of the mansard
roof, and completed in 1706. The tomb, com-

pleted in 1861, at a cost of one million eight
hundred thousand dollars, was constructed by
taking up the pavement of a large circular space
under the dome so as to expose the crypt below.
In the sort of circular well thus formed stands
the sarcophagus containing the remains of the
emperor, and it is looked down upon from the
gallery which the remainder of the old pavement
now forms. The floor of the well or pit is richly
laid in mosaic and the sides are ornamented with
statuary. In the center stands the sarcophagus
of porphyry, which weighs sixty-seven tons, and
took sixteen years to polish. With its base and
cover it is thirteen and-a-half feet high. A more
imposing tomb could hardly have been devised.

In chapels adjoining are the marble sarcophagi
of Napoleon's brothers Joseph, king of Spain,
and Jerome, king of Westphalia; also monuments to Vauban and Turenne, two eminent
French generals of Louis XIV's time, and here
also are collected the flags captured by the
French armies in the various battles of the past
two or three centuries.

West of the Invalides a short distance is the
Champ de Mars, a large open space extending
from the military school to the river, upon which
the international exhibitions of 1867 and 1878
were held. It is now in a state of disorder from
the buildings of the last exhibition having only
recently been removed.

It will be seen from the above that almost all the buildings and localities of historic interest are embraced in a belt extending across the city from east to west.

ARC DE TRIOMPHE.

CHAPTER XXIV.

THE history of France is so intimately inter-
woven with the history and associations of
Paris, that a review of the successive
reigns and revolutions for three centuries past is
almost essential to an intelligent description of
the modern French capital.

As school children we were all familiar with
Macauley's spirited poem, "Ivry," beginning—

Now glory to the Lord of Hosts, from whom all glories are!
And glory to our Sovereign Liege, King Henry of Navarre!

and in which the prowess of the white-plumed
knight, King Henry of Navarre, is immortalized.
This Henry was the champion of the protestant
forces in the religious war which wasted France
in the latter half of the sixteenth century. Peace
was finally restored by the accession of Henry to
the throne in 1589, under the title of Henry IV.,
and by his returning to the bosom of the Roman
Catholic church, while, however, he still continued to protect his old allies the Huguenots, or

French protestants.   One of the most popular
pictures in the Louvre, with engravers and copy-
ists, is Gerard's "Entry of Henry IV. into
Paris."   Henry married Marie de Medici, an able
princess of the famous Florentine family, and
became the first of the great line of Bourbon
kings, which ruled France for more than two centuries.   We often hear obtuse and bigoted people
compared to the Bourbons, but really for a century and a half the Bourbons were great and able
princes, and under their rule France enjoyed her
golden era.   Henry married the Italian princess
in 1600.   In the picture gallery of the Louvre one
of the loudest, if not most meritorious, exhib-
its, is a series of mammoth paintings by Rubens,
fulsomely adulatory of Marie de Medici.   They
are remarkable for their size and disgusting flat-
tery, perhaps, even more than for their artistic
excellences.   Henry IV. was a brave soldier and
popular ruler, but he did not get on comfortably
with his Italian wife, and in 1610 was stabbed to
death while riding in the Rue St. Honore—the
next street to that our hotel was on—by one
Ravaillac, whose horrible punishment by being
torn in pieces by horses was alluded to in the last
chapter.   At the lower end of the island in the
Seine upon which stands the Cathedral of Notre
Dame, is a fine bronze equestrian statue of Henry
IV.   At his death his widow, Marie de Medici,

governed France as regent during the minority of their son, Louis XIII. The famous Cardinal Richelieu (born 1585, died 1642) was her prime minister. Both queen and cardinal were ambitious, unscrupulous and intriguing, and soon an active contest for the supreme power sprang up between them, in which the long-headed cardinal was ultimately victorious. The queen erected for her royal residence the splendid palace of the Luxembourg. The cardinal built the very much more extensive and elegant palace now known as the Palais Royal. The queen was, by the machinations of Richelieu, finally deposed and made a prisoner in 1631. Then she became a wanderer without home or country, and finally died in great poverty in Cologne in 1642—the precise year that her unrelenting antagonist himself departed this life. Her heart lies buried in the choir of Cologne Cathedral.

Louis XIII., surnamed "the Just," proved himself an excellent prince. It was he who founded the French Academy and the Jardin des Plantes, and who built the Chateau of Versailles, which his successor enlarged into the present palace. He reigned for thirty-three years, and was cotemporary with James I. and Charles I. of England.

He was succeeded by his son, Louis XIV., surnamed "le Grande," or "the Great," who reigned

15

for the long period of seventy-two years, being cotemporary with the Commonwealth and with the reigns of Charles II., James II., William and Mary, and Anne, in English history. He died one year after the accession of George I. of England. Under the great military engineer, Vauban, and the famous marshal Turenne, whose tombs help to grace the sepulchre of Napoleon I., the military prestige of France under Louis XIV. was very great. By this monarch the city was very much enlarged, the quays of the Seine faced with stone, the Champs Elysees laid out, the Invalides founded, also the Astronomical Observatory and other important public institutions. The wealth of France was so great at that time, and the rage for luxury so excessive, that Louis is reported to have spent $240,000,000 upon the palace and grounds of Versailles alone. Every one has heard of the famous fountains of Versailles. Their magnificence may be judged from the fact that it costs about one hundred dollars per minute to supply the water for them. Such was the scale of Louis's extravagance, and such the preparation for the national exhaustion which precipitated the revolution of 1789.

He was followed by his great-grandson, Louis XV., who reigned fifty-nine years, or from 1715 to 1774, and did much for the improvement and adornment of Paris. He in turn was succeeded by his grandson, the unfortunate Louis XVI, a man of excellent character and disposition, but powerless to mitigate the evils into which the state had now fallen by the luxury and extravagance of more than a century. Driven to desperation, the people rose in insurrection, and their first achievement was the capture and destruction of the Bastile. At Sevres is to be seen a model of the old fortress. It was nearly rectangular in form, with a round tower at each corner and others midway the length of each side—six in all—and the building was very high in proportion to its width. It formed part of the ancient wall at the eastern extremity of the city, but the enlargement of the city had left it far inside the walls. Other relics of the ancient walls are found in the old gateways known as Porte St. Denis and Porte St. Martin, which are still left standing in the Boulevard St. Martin, some distance north of the Bastile. Their success in capturing the Bastile on July 14th, 1789, gave the people a confidence which nothing could now withstand. The royal family were soon prisoners. One of the most noticeable buildings on the south bank of the Seine is the Conciergerie, with its two feudal towers, where the beautiful queen, Marie Antoinnette, was confined. The Temple, the other prison of the royal family, has been long since destroyed. An organized attempt of the other

European powers in 1793 to reinstate Louis on the throne by force, precipitated both his and his queen's destruction by the fatal guillotine. Their bodies were obscurely interred in the church yard of the Madeleine, situated a little distance north of the church itself. Here they remained till royalty was restored in France, when their bones were exhumed and reburied in the Church of St. Denis, the resting place of a long line of kings. A chapel, known as the Chapel of the Expiation, was erected over their former graves, a sarcophagus in the crypt below occupying the exact spot where their bodies were laid. The present Church of the Madeleine, by the way, was begun by Louis XVI., who inherited the fondness for building of his ancestors.

Like most republics, but far sooner than some, the French republic of the eighteenth century in time degenerated into an empire. Napoleon Bonaparte was crowned emperor in 1804, and during his twelve years' reign upwards of $20,000,000 was expended in public buildings in Paris. Among the reminders of this epoch are the magnificent Arc de Triomphe, mentioned in a former chapter; a smaller triumphal arch in front of the Tuileries, upon which the four antique bronze horses stolen by Napoleon from St. Mark's in Venice stood, until restored to Venice in 1814; the Madeleine in its completed form; the Vendome Column; the magnificent Bourse, or stock exchange, and various other useful and ornamental structures. Napoleon was finally defeated and sent to St. Helena in 1815, and Louis XVIII., a younger brother of Louis XVI., came to the throne. (Louis XVII., son of Louis XVI., reigned only in a Pickwickian sense, and died before the restoration of his family.) He was followed ten years later by a still younger brother, Charles X., a corpulent old gentleman, more given to religion than statesmanship.

The country was still in a bad state, and even a much abler man would have found it difficult to pilot the nation through the existing hard times. And so, on the 27th of July, 1830, another revolution broke out. For three days there was considerable fighting and then King Charles betook himself to flight and left the government once more in the hands of the populace. This revolution is commemorated by a bronze column in the Place de la Bastile, known as the Column of July, and inscribed all over with the names of the men who fell in the three days fighting. The " Rue du 29 Juliet," which leads out of the Rue de Rivoli, also perpetuates the memory of this compact little revolution. This time the French people did not attempt a republic, but, by acclamation elected as king, the Duke of Orleans, a descendant of a younger brother of Louis XIV., a man of some popularity, but no doubt a good deal of a demagogue. He accepted the crown as Louis Philippe I. It was during his reign of eighteen years that the obelisk of Luxor was erected in the Place de la Concorde, and that the palace of Versailles, which had been sacked by the mob in the first revolution, and had since been in a ruinous condition, was partially restored at the king's private expense and converted into a gallery of historical paintings. Louis Philippe was rich, and though miserly, he spent three million dollars on this work.

Louis Philippe went out on the revolution of 1848, retired to England and died there a few years later. He was succeeded by the second republic, which even sooner than the first, became stranded in imperialism. Then came the era of Napoleon III., the public buildings of which period are ostentatiously marked with a capital N. The blackened ruins of the Tuileries and the funeral wreaths that fill the lap of the statue of Strassburg, one of eight colossal figures, symbolic of eight principal cities of France, which grace the Place de la Concorde, are the sad reminders of the gloomy ending of the brilliant but unstable regime of the grandson of the Empress Josephine. It seems strange that so mild, good-natured and polite a people as all the French seem to be, should ever have become aroused to such deeds of horror and destruction as characterized the reign of the commune of 1871. The third republic seems to have settled down into a successful permanence.

One thing that particularly strikes a stranger in Paris is the legend "Liberté, Egalité, Fraternité," carved or painted upon every public building, even the churches. I don't know how the Roman ecclesiastics like this conversion of sacred edifices into political signboards, but they cannot help themselves, for the ultra-democratic watchword is in most cases indelibly cut in the stone and usually in the most conspicuous place about the edifice.

Everybody has heard of the Bois de Boulogne. It is a tract of about two thousand acres lying just outside the walls, to the southwest of the city, and is the property of the municipality. A few years ago it was a forest of fine large trees, but the exigences of the war of 1870 compelled their destruction, and now it is for the most part a jungle of young trees and underbrush, intersected in every direction by splendid carriage drives. It has a lake, a cascade, places for refreshment, and some lawns and flower beds; but it is mainly what its name signifies, "the forest" of Boulogne. It is the favorite drive of the Parisians.

Père la Chaise, the principal cemetery in Paris,

is situated on rising ground in the eastern part of
the city, and is one of the least interesting cemeteries that I have ever visited. The carriage
roads are paved with rough blocks of stone, there
are few trees or flowers, no grass, and a surprising paucity of sculpture and artistic monuments.
All along the carriage ways, on both sides, are
continuous lines of sepulchral chapels, each' usually three or four feet wide, six or eight feet deep,
and high enough for a person to stand in conveniently. Each has a grated door in front and a
little altar in the interior, with the names of the
deceased cut in marble slabs above. Throughout,
the cemetery is very much crowded. The monuments are of ordinary stone and display little of
the good taste upon which Paris prides itself. To
the right of the entrance is the Jewish section,
and here is conspicuous the tomb of Rachel, one
of the greatest actresses the world has yet produced. Her tomb is noticeable for being penciled
over with hundreds of autographs—I might
almost say thousands. A little beyond is the
famous tomb of Abelard, the learned monk, and
his inamorata, Heloise, the love of whom has
been so celebrated for over seven centuries. The
tomb is a simple rectangular structure, surmounted by recumbent effigies of the deceased, side by
side, the whole being crowned by an open Gothic
canopy of considerable size. It is amusing to

observe the romance of the Parisians, who, notwithstanding the fact that the naughty couple
have been dead a matter of seven hundred and
forty years, still testify their admiration for them
by huge heaps of bouquets and funeral wreaths
strewn upon the grave.

In a small inclosure, unmarked by any stone,
but cultivated as a flower-bed, lie the remains of
Marshal Ney, one of Napoleon's most gallant
officers. When Napoleon was banished to Elba
in 1814, Ney gave in his allegiance to the restored
Bourbon government of Louis XVIII., and was
rewarded with the chief command of the French
army. When, a few months later, Napoleon suddenly returned to France from Elba, Ney proved
unfaithful to his trust, and hastened to join his
old master, taking the entire army with him.
For this act of treachery, after the defeat of
Waterloo in June, 1815, he was tried by court-mar-
tial and shot. A little farther on, in one enclosure,
are the tombs of Molière, the French dramatist,
and La Fontaine, the well known author of the
fables. The tomb of Bernardin St. Pierre, the
delightful author of Paul and Virginia, is also
in the same vicinity, and without much difficulty may be found the tombs of Chopin, Rossini,
Cherubini, Talma, Eugene Scribe, Racine, Beran-
ger, David, Arago, La Place, Marshals Kel-
lerman, Suchet, Macdonald, Massina, and many

other eminent men. Frequently in passing through the cemetery, we see tombs marked with an inscription indicating a perpetual right to the ground. Where this perpetual right is not obtained, the bodies are dug up after a certain term of years, and the grave is resold to a new occupant. The bones in such cases are deposited in the catacombs, or subterranean galleries that underlie much of Paris.

One of the most commendable things about Paris is its splendid omnibus system. Street railways are only partially introduced. The omnibuses are ponderous vehicles, carrying sixteen to eighteen inside, and as many on top, and drawn by three horses driven abreast. On the fine, smooth pavements they roll along beautifully, though severe on the horses on first starting, and on ascending hills. A splendid general idea of Paris can be gained from the top of an omnibus, and as it is easily reached by spiral stairs from a platform in the rear, ladies can enjoy an outside ride as well as the other sex. The fare uniformly is thirty centimes inside and fifteen out (6 and 3 cents), and for these sums you can ride astonishingly long distances.

Everything in the way of fancy articles is displayed with wonderful prodigality in the shop windows of Paris. The jewelry stores, picture stores, toy shops, and every other branch of fancy and art dealing, are numbered by the legion, and the prices marked are astonishingly low; but give the Parisian shopkeepers an opportunity to make a special charge, and Paris becomes the dearest city in the world. A pair of the best kid gloves can be bought for sixty or seventy cents, but if a button is lost they will charge you twenty cents for sewing one on again. So everything made to order is probably quite as expensive as at home.

Two favorite places with the ladies are the Magazins de Louvre and the Bon Marche, two extensive dry goods stores, each covering an entire block, and each overloaded with stock and swarming with customers. The extent of their business may be judged from the fact that at the latter place there are cashiers numbered from one to sixty-four, and perhaps even higher, and all are as busy as bees in taking in money and recording the amounts. The building contains three stories, all connected by a dozen large wells, with skylights above, and innumerable staircases. Such a lively scene as is here witnessed can probably nowhere else be found.

Another famous resort is the Palais Royale. The Orleans family, to whom it belonged in the last century, became financially embarrassed, and to replenish their exchequer they converted the ground floor of this spacious palace of Riche-

lieu into stores, which open upon the gardens
which the palace incloses. These stores are occupied mainly by jewelers, and there must be over
a hundred of them here congregated. Their windows are resplendent with gold and gems in every
possible style of ornament. The Palais Royale
is situated a little north of and facing the Louvre.

Paris sadly needs a visit from Anthony Com-
stock. Judging by their titles, the most dis-
graceful class of books are publicly exposed for
sale; and that too in respectable shops and on the
best streets. Nude pictures are seen in the shop
windows by tens of thousands, and pictures without the least affectation of modesty, such as is
usually given by artists to nude statuary. Paris
may be no more immoral than other cities, but it
will take the palm for indelicacy.

In Paris again we find the "continental Sunday." Builders are at work just as on other
days, and the streets are equally as cumbered
with great trucks with their immense loads of
squared stone, drawn by five or six horses. Fully
two-thirds of the shops are open, and apparently
as much business is done in the aggregate as on
any other day. But, while a large share of the
population thus toil, a still larger share would
seem to throng the cafés, the seats in the public
parks and the picture galleries; and, from the
amount of riding on the Champs Elysees, one

would think there was not an idle horse in all
Paris. At night the Champs Elysees is brilliantly
illuminated and all sorts of shows and amuse-
ments are in full blast.

Paris is very gay and brilliant every fine evening. The streets are well lighted, the Avenue de
l'Opera being lighted with the electric light for
its entire length, and the sidewalks thronged
with a gay and careless crowd till well into the
night.

Paris churches, excepting perhaps Notre Dame
which is pure Gothic, and the Madeleine which
is pure Grecian, are of a style peculiar to Paris,
in which there is a happy blending of many features of both the Gothic and Italian styles such
as I had not seen elsewhere.

In Paris the fuel used is chiefly wood and char-
coal. Both are sold by weight, and not in great
wood yards like ours, but in little shops scattered
all over the city, each of which is frescoed all
over its front with representations of piles of
stove wood. Much of the wood burned is mere
twigs smaller than your finger, such as we in
America consume in brush heaps and are glad to
get rid of. Every splinter, however, is saved in
thrifty France.

The Palace of Justice swarms with lawyers, all
in black gowns, white bands, and little stiff four-
cornered caps, and every one with a morocco

portfolio under his arm — a very gentlemanly looking lot of men. By the way, they have a system in France which we might do well to copy. Before any action at law can be brought the case must come before an official arbitrator, who uses his best efforts to bring about a settlement between the parties without the formality of a trial. Such a system with us would certainly diminish litigation one-half.

One day we strolled into the fine palace devoted to the national archives. The papers of the government are admirably kept, either bound up into volumes or packed in paste-board boxes of uniform size, and all properly labeled and ranged on shelves extending from floor to ceiling through a great multitude of rooms. Our city clerks, if not our state officers, could take a useful lesson from the perfect order with which the multifarious documents of two hundred years of government are here maintained. The more interesting and valuable documents, such as treaties, letters of royal personages, etc., are arranged in vertical glass cases so that they can be easily examined, a curtain covering the case to prevent any injurious effects of the light. These cases fill a number of large rooms and are chronologically arranged. Some of the instruments bear the signature of Charlemagne himself, and every king since is more or less represented. Among the curious papers are the will of Louis XVI.; the last letter written by Marie Antoinette; various papers in the handwriting of Robespierre; a letter of Charlotte Corday, written from the prison where she was confined for the assassination of Marat; Livingston's commission as minister to France, signed by Thomas Jefferson, and a host of other interesting autographs.

CHAPTER XXV.

PARIS probably ranks first among the cities of Europe as an art center. It has a very extensive school of the fine arts, liberally supported by the government. This school has three professors of painting, three of sculpture, three of architecture, one of line engraving and one of die sinking—eleven in all. Liberal prizes are given for the greatest advancement made by the students, the chief prize each year being a scholarship for four years' study in Italy, with all expenses paid. The effect of this school has been to give France a surprising number of capable artists, as is evinced by the fact that the annual Salon for the present year (1881) had no fewer than two thousand five hundred pictures and eight hundred pieces of statuary entered in competition for the various prizes. It should be understood that the Salon is an annual exhibition under government auspices, open to all French artists, and the principal prizes awarded at it are highly esteemed. The best works are pur-

THE FRENCH SALON. 241

chased from time to time by the government and deposited in the gallery of the Luxembourg. When an artist becomes very famous, his works are promoted to places in the gallery of the Louvre, where they hang in the company of the old masters. Thus the Salon represents the current year's productions in art, the Luxembourg gallery the *chefs d'ouvre* of living or recent French artists, and the Louvre the works of the most famous painters and sculptors of all ages and countries.

The Salon is held in the building facing the Champs Elysees, constructed for the great international exposition of 1855. It was afterwards purchased by the government and christened the Palace of Industry.

The Luxembourg is open free to the public. It contains about three hundred paintings and one hundred pieces of sculpture, and is a very interesting gallery to visit, as the works are carefully selected and are all comparatively modern and not dimmed by age. Among the most notable painters represented are Rosa Bonheur, the famous horse and cattle painter; Bouguereau, the greatest living French artist; Courbet, the communist of Column Vendome notoriety, who died in 1877; Lefebvre, one of the greatest living painters of the nude; Meissonier, whose works are reputed to command the highest prices paid

16

to any living artist; Gustave Dore, Bertrand, Corot (died 1875), Giraud, Giroux, Goupil, Millet (died 1875), and others.

The Louvre is probably the most extensive museum of art in the world. It occupies four stories of an immense range of buildings forming the four sides of one large quadrangle and a portion of another. It embraces in its scope much more than galleries of painting. No country has a finer collection of Egyptian antiquities than France, and these occupy a portion of the Louvre. Then there are Assyrian, Grecian and Roman antiquities, Chinese and Japanese curiosities, a very extensive general ethnological museum, several rooms filled with naval models, relief models of the Suez Canal and of the various harbors of France, an immense collection of porcelain, ancient and modern, and many rooms filled with drawings and designs. Simply to walk through the different rooms without giving much time to examination and study, is alone the work of several days.

In the number of its oil paintings the gallery of the Louvre is probably unsurpassed by any other collection in Europe, but in sculpture it is secondary to the galleries of the Vatican. It contains, however, one object of priceless value and incomparable beauty in the Venus of Milo, an antique statue found some years ago in one of the islands of the Grecian archipelago, and which, though mutilated, both arms being wanting, possesses a symmetry and grace that cannot fail to strike even the least cultivated eye. It is peculiarly the gem of the statuary galleries of the Louvre.

The picture galleries are really tiresome in their extent. All the various schools are represented, but naturally the French predominates. The most famous of the older French painters are Nicholas Poussin (1594–1665), Gaspar Poussin (1613–1675), and Claude Lorraine (1600–1682). Their pictures differ from those of the Italian masters in making the landscape a principal feature, whereas the Italians rarely gave any attention to anything but the figures. Claude's pictures are very numerous and can easily be picked out without the aid of a catalogue. They have a dreamy arcadian sort of air, peculiar to themselves. Greuze (1725–1805) was really a beautiful painter. His works in the Louvre are not numerous but are, every one, gems of art. The contrast between Greuze and any one of the old Italian masters is very striking, and I am sure nine out of ten of my readers would prefer the French artist. David (1748–1825) is also highly esteemed. Among the more renowned later artists are Robert, Delaroche, Vernet, Delacroix and others.

Twelve miles south of Paris lies the city of

Versailles. When the principal seat of the court
of France, a century ago, it was a place of a
hundred thousand inhabitants, but it has now
scarcely a third as many. Its principal attraction is an immense palace, built by Louis XIV.,
with a large park, adorned with magnificent avenues of trees and the finest fountains in the
world. The palace itself has a frontage of a
quarter of a mile, and commands a splendid view
to the southward. The amount of money said to
have been spent on this palace, staggers belief.
For a century it was the principal residence of
the kings of France; then it was sacked, and in
great measure destroyed, by the revolutionists of
1789, and later was converted into a gun factory.
Napoleon I. thought of restoring it for his
Imperial residence, but the estimated cost, ten
million dollars, frightened him, and the property
remained a ruin up to the time of Louis Philippe.
That king spent a large sum from his private
resources in a partial restoration, and collected
there some five thousand modern pictures illustra-
tive of French history. The historical scenes are
arranged by reigns, from Charlemagne down to
Louis Philippe, and many of these are large and
spirited pictures by the most eminent artists of
the century. Another series of rooms is devoted
to pictures illustrating the part France took in
the Crusades. Another salon, extending nearly

half the length of the building, is filled with large pictures, representing the great battles in which France has been victorious, from the days of King Clovis down to the era of Napoleon. Still other rooms contain many hundreds of portraits of the public men, not of France alone, but of the whole civilized world. Here are pictures of Washington, Franklin, Adams, Jackson, Polk, Webster, and various other American statesmen; numerous members of the English royal family, and English statesmen and men of eminence for a hundred years past, and, of course, a very rich collection of French celebrities. The number of rooms seems almost interminable. We begin an afternoon's inspection by looking at each picture, and end, when the attendants evince an anxiety to close up and go home, by simply glancing down long vistas of rooms still unvisited. The whole forms an exceedingly interesting collection. Besides the pictures, there are to be seen at Versailles the bed upon which Louis XIV. slept and died, a suite of rooms occupied by the unfortunate Marie Antoinette, and many other objects of rare historic interest.

The park of Versailles is famous for its magnificent avenues of large forest trees, in some cases more than a mile in length, and so trained as most perfectly to shade the intervening roadway. Much, too, of the Versailles park, is left in a state

of perfect wildness, but is intersected in every
direction by pleasant roads and foot-paths, a
light lath fence hedging in these ways. The
result is a delightful solitude for a stroll, and a
park melodious with the songs of the birds which
seek a home in the dense foliage.

Four miles north of Paris is the village of St.
Denis, famous for a beautiful Gothic abbey
church which, since the days of King Dagobert,
thirteen hundred years ago, has been the burial
place of the French kings. At the revolution in
the last century, the National Assembly passed
an edict ordering all the royal tombs destroyed,
and in October, 1793, the work was carried out.
The bodies, including that of Louis XIV., which
was found in good preservation, were reburied in
a common grave, the lead coffins were melted up
for bullets, and it was only with great difficulty
that some of the fine sculptured tombs were
saved by being deposited in a national museum in
Paris as specimens of French art. The building
was stripped of its roof, and its entire destruction meditated, but fortunately not determined
on. Under Napoleon I. it was restored, and the
tombs replaced, but all of date prior to 1790 are, of
course, only cenotaphs—empty sepulchres. Upon
the restoration of the Bourbons, in 1814, the bones
of Louis XVI. and Marie Antoinette were removed
to St. Denis, and now rest with those of later

kings in leaden coffins in the royal vaults under the choir of the church.

St. Denis is on the river Seine, two hours by boat below Paris, although only four miles by wagon road. The current of the Seine is very rapid. Navigation as far up as Paris is inconsiderable, and the river at that point is filled mainly with floating baths. There must be dozens of them— some exclusively for women. In some the fee for a bath is as low as three cents of our money. A crookeder river than the Seine it would be hard to find. It leaves Paris at its south-west corner, flows south to Sevres, six miles, bends around to the north, passes the city only a short distance from the walls, touches St. Denis four miles north of Paris, and so continues its way to the sea, taking about four miles to go one. One of the prettiest excursions imaginable is a trip down the Seine to St. Denis by steamer. The scenery on every side is most beautiful. In that short distance the boat passes through a lock of six or eight feet, so rapid is the fall of the river. Just beyond Sevres we pass the old royal park and palace of St. Cloud, the latter now in ruins, having been destroyed during the siege of Paris in 1870, partly by the French guns, and partly by the Prussians who occupied the town.

At Sevres the French government have long maintained a manufactory for the finest porce-

lain, and Sevres china is known by reputation
the world over. The manufactory is carried on
at a considerable expense over and above the revenue derived from it, as a department of the fine
arts, which France makes it her special care to
foster and encourage. Armed with a ticket from
the "Direction des Beaux Arts" we visited this
celebrated factory. The porcelain is made of a
very pure white clay known as kaolin, and
brought from Limoges, in the southwest of
France. The process of manufacture is probably
similar to that of porcelain made elsewhere, but
the designs are peculiarly artistic, and the manip-
ulations probably finer than elsewhere. We were
particularly interested in the process of making
the very delicate China tea cups, the substance of
which is scarcely thicker than a piece of card-
board. These cups are not turned in a lathe nor
pressed into moulds, but a matrix of porous clay
is carefully prepared of the size and shape of the
outside of the cup or other vessel, as the case may
be, which matrix being perfectly dry is filled with
a solution of the kaolin of about the consistency
of good rich milk. The porous mould quickly
absorbs a quantity of the water, and the kaolin is
deposited in a thin layer uniformly over the interior of the mould. When sufficient thickness is
attained, the remainder of the solution is emptied
out, and the mould allowed to dry, when the cup,

fragile as a wafer, easily slips out. The decorating is done after the article is burned. The pattern, if it is to be in gilt, is first engraved upon a steel plate. From this plate an impression is taken on the finest paper by means of an ordinary copper-plate printer's press, but with, of course, a peculiar kind of ink. From this paper the pattern is transferred to the porcelain by placing the paper, face down, upon it and rubbing it over for some time with a small roller. Powdered gold bronze is then applied with a camel's hair brush, and by another burning the gilding is firmly fixed. Flowers and other ornamentations in several colors are painted by hand, and then burned in.

If the visitor hopes to bring away a specimen of Sevres china, he will probably be appalled to to find that the cheapest article costs more than he cares to invest. The cheapest tea set made is sold at about two hundred dollars, and from that sum the prices run up indefinitely. A pair of ordinary sized mantle vases were marked eight hundred francs ($160), but perhaps not one person in ten would recognise them as any choicer than a set that could be bought for sixteen dollars at any large china store. But the gem of the whole establishment is a series of framed porcelain pictures, copies of the great masters, and more exquisitely beautiful than the originals ever could

have been, painted in oils.   Unless the reader has
seen some really fine paintings on porcelain, he
can have little idea of the possibilities in this
branch of the fine arts.   We saw some very beautiful specimens of porcelain painting at Munich,
in the New Pinakothek, but the productions of
the Sevres manufactory are incomparably superior, and the adjective fails to suggest itself that
will do justice to their exquisite beauty.

CHAPTER XXVI.

THE journey from Paris to Dieppe lies in great part along the valley of the Seine, which is a much more beautiful and interesting part of France than that between Strassburg and Paris. We break the journey at Rouen, a large and important place, well built, but interesting chiefly for several old churches and other buildings which have not been spoiled by modern restoration. We were charmed with the simplicity of this old Norman city. The churches were all open, and we were dunned for no fees by omnivorous vergers. The shops were clean and inviting, and the nicest pastry was obtainable at ridiculously cheap prices. The charge for taking care of our baggage at the station was one cent per piece; this including the giving of a written receipt for the same. The people all seemed so polite and good natured that we were quite charmed with Rouen.

The cathedral of Rouen is a fine specimen of Gothic architecture, very richly ornamented. It contains the tomb of Richard I. of England, who, though of the fourth generation from William the Conqueror, still loved Normandy better than England, and had his bones laid there.

Dieppe, though less famous, is well worthy a few hours' inspection. It has two nice old Gothic churches incomparably more interesting than many of the grand churches of Italy. Dieppe, strange as it may seem in a fishing town so far away from the center of art, is also famous for its ivory carvings. Here we take a steamer for New-haven, on the English coast. The sea, though broader here than at Dover, is much smoother, and the steamers are larger and better fitted up.

During our stay in France, and indeed on the entire continent, it was a matter of remark that we did not encounter a single case of drunkenness. Our observation in this respect would seem to bear out the claims of those who argue that the general use of light wines is rather promotive of temperance than otherwise, for wine is cheap and the quantity consumed enormous. At a table d'hote dinner a whole or half bottle is seen at almost every plate, and about that quantity is actually drunk by each person. The usual table wine is a harmless beverage, and costs from forty to sixty cents per quart bottle.

In France, notwithstanding the youthfulness of the republic, there is already great complaint of the low state of political morals. As in our own country, the offices are regarded as prizes, to be sought at the sacrifice of all sentiments of patriotism and public spirit, and a mean selfishness is said everywhere to pervade the public service. The better class of people are disgusted, and in this lies the danger of the failure of the republic, as the Frenchman's only notion of reform is by revolution.

The money of account of France, like that of Belgium, Italy and Switzerland, is the franc, of a value of a trifle under twenty cents of our own money. The franc is supposed to be divided into one hundred centimes, but very few of that coin are in circulation, or even of the two centime piece. Practically the sou, or five centime piece, is the coin of minimum value. The other coins are the ten centime in copper, equal to two cents of our money, the half franc, franc, two franc and five franc in silver, and five franc, ten franc and twenty franc piece in gold. For larger sums Bank of France notes are used, the smallest denomination being one hundred francs.

One can travel very conveniently without any knowledge of the European languages, but in that case his sources of information will be confined mainly to his own powers of observation. His tour will hence be only half as instructive as if he could ask questions.

CHAPTER XXVII.

E land at Newhaven and after our two months ramble among foreigners thoroughly enjoy the novelty of again being in a land where the language is familiar to us, and where we can understand everything that is said by those around us. We pass off the steamer without inspection of our baggage, upon our simple assurance that neither tea, tobacco nor spirits is contained therein. How much better this than the insulting and humiliating tumbling over of one's clean shirts and pocket-handkerchiefs by a coarse and insolent official, as one experiences in countries like ours, where a tariff is laid on a hundred different articles easy of being smuggled.

Brighton, a few miles down the coast from Newhaven and fifty-two miles from London, is a city about the size of Rochester, Detroit or Milwaukee, and is supported almost entirely by its position as the principal seaside watering place for the British metropolis. It extends for three miles along the beach, has hundreds of hotels,

254

and its grand parade on a pleasant evening is a
rare scene of outdoor enjoyment. Aside from its
fashion and gaiety there is nothing at Brighton
of especial interest to the traveler.

A ride of a little more than an hour brings us
again to the British metropolis. Compared with
the continental cities, London presents a gloomy
appearance and by comparison its streets are
abominably dirty, though contrasted with those
of any American city they would be regarded as
very creditable to the municipality: The atmosphere is filled with soot, and it is impossible to
keep one's linen clean for more than a few hours.
Old buildings, as St. Paul's for instance, are to a
great extent incrusted with a rough black deposit
of soot, which has become as hard as the stone
itself, and in protected places is often an inch or
two thick.

When an American arrives in London the first
thing he does is to register at the American
Exchange, and the next thing is to subscribe for
the privileges of the Exchange for the time he
will remain in Europe. It costs but the trifle of a
dollar and a quarter per month, and for this small
sum he has the free use of the rooms, which are
situated at Charing Cross, the very heart of London, and the common focus from which every
part can be reached by rail or omnibus. Here
he can receive his mail, read all the American

papers, see bulletins of the latest American news, meet all the fresh arrivals from his own country, write his letters, and for a very moderate fee can store any superfluous baggage that he may not want to carry with him. When he goes on the continent his letters will be forwarded to him to whatever address he may indicate from day to day, and throughout his travels he will receive his mails with a promptness that would be impossible were letters mailed to him direct from America. These are only a few of the conveniences offered to American travelers by the Exchange, and no one can for a moment afford to neglect availing himself of them. It may be added that Mr. Henry F. Gillig, the managing proprietor, is an affable gentleman, and is constantly on the alert to assist in all ways his numerous patrons.

One coming from the continent is struck with the pre-eminence of London over all other European cities as a general mart for the products of the whole world. In paintings, the specialty of Italy, Rome and Florence sink out of sight in comparison with London in the number of shops devoted to their sale, the magnitude of the stocks they carry, and the comparative cheapness at which they can be purchased. In engravings, one of the specialties of Paris, London offers twenty times the inducements to buyers. In fact any article can be purchased quite as advantageously here as at the home of its production, be it anywhere in the wide world. So much for free trade and a well developed commerce.

The manufacturers of England complain bitterly of our American protective tariff, which is ruining many branches of their trade; but the disinterested, thinking men say nothing, for they see that what England loses in manufactures by our American policy she more than makes up in the commerce that we by the same policy foolishly throw into her hands, so that on the whole she loses nothing by it, if indeed she be not the gainer. Great Britain never was richer, and on the whole more prosperous than at the present moment. And this notwithstanding the fact that the country is vastly over-populated and that the relation between wages and the cost of living is steadily widening. Clerks' and bookkeepers' salaries in London range from five dollars to fifteen dollars a week, the latter being considered rather a high figure, and on this income scores of thousands are supporting in attempted respectability the large families that seem to be the invariable rule with the wage class in that country.

One is struck on entering any place of business with the great number of clerks, and immense amount of bookkeeping, that seems inseparable from business operations in England. Old-fashioned and cumbrous ways of doing things prevail,

17

much in contrast with our American common-sense
habits of simplifying everything to the utmost.

Our hotel windows overlooked Covent Garden
market, the great central wholesale vegetable
emporium of London.   It was amusing to see the
great number of people constantly employed
there, and the circumlocutory way in which
everything was done. Loads of lettuce would
arrive as large as loads of hay at home, and in
unloading every head would be handled separately. They would be thrown into baskets to be
carried to other parts of the market, and men
would stand holding their baskets on their heads
all the time they were being filled. Articles
would be piled up in one place, and directly after
removed to another, and everything done as
slowly and deliberately as if the sole object were
to kill as much time as possible. A smart American, I am sure, would do all the work with a
third the number of hands. And it was laugh-
able to see how busy they all seemed to think
themselves over what, to a Yankee, looked so
much like child's play. But perhaps it is for the
best, for if they did things after our fashion, half
the people of England would find nothing to do.
As another illustration, I noticed a large barge
load of grain being unloaded into a great flouring
mill on the banks of the Thames, and each sack
was drawn up separately by a rope into the fifth

or sixth story—a long and tedious process to accomplish what an American miller would have appliances for doing in an hour or two.

As we begin to look about us, we are struck with the immensity of London, the world's metropolis. What is called "greater London" contains fully five million souls, or about eight times the population of Chicago. During 1880 no fewer than twenty-five thousand new houses were built, and seventy miles of new streets created. The ordinary police force numbers eleven thousand men, or a force equal to nearly half the entire standing army of the United States. But these immense figures give no appreciable idea of the enormous aggregation of human life that calls its home London. A better idea may be gained by taking a train at one of the central railway stations (for there are about a dozen of them) and riding out eight or ten miles. Not until that distance is reached can we at all feel that we have even reached the suburbs. From the railroads, generally elevated on massive brick viaducts high above the streets, we look out upon a wilderness of roofs and chimney tops as far as the eye can reach. People living in one section of London are as much strangers to other sections as though hundreds of miles intervened. Even cabmen, when required to drive any distance from their own stands, not infrequently are forced to stop

and inquire of policemen or others, "Do you
know any such-and-such street in this vicinity?"
and this, too, notwithstanding that commission-
ers have been for years engaged in the simplifying and harmonizing of street nomenclature. It
is a wonderful city in its size and populousness.
More properly speaking, it is a collection of cities
which have each grown so extensive as to amal-
gamate the one with another, until all traces of
intervening country have been lost. It, the aggregation, is known as London, but strictly the City
of London embraces only the comparatively small
district extending from Temple Bar in the west
to Aldgate in the east—perhaps a twenty minutes' walk—and lies wholly north of the Thames.
Over this portion alone, embracing a population
of less than two hundred thousand, the Lord
Mayor and aldermen exercise jurisdiction. The
remainder has a complex government divided
between the vestries of the several parishes and
various metropolitan boards appointed immediately by the national government. Practically,
therefore, the government of London outside of
the city proper, devolves on the nation at large.
While there can be no question of the desirable-
ness and efficiency of self-government in the case
of nations, it may be questioned if the system be
equally adapted for large cities, and if the control
of these abnormal aggregrations of population—

wens on the body politic, I think some famous
writer called them—should not largely devolve
on the state or nation.

It is certain, at least, that this vast aggregation
of people embraced in the metropolitan district
or greater London is admirably governed. No
complaints are heard of extravagance in the use
of the public funds, of oppressive taxation, of
dishonest rings or swindling schemes of jobbery,
and there are certainly no petty contests over the
allotment of trivial offices periodically recurring,
nor disgusting personal bickerings among the
highest officials. With the men who share in the
government of London it is a life business and a
road to the highest honor, and the government is
hence conducted as a great business should be
and not as a political bagatelle. I am hardly
prepared to recommend this undemocratic system
for adoption in America, but I may be permitted
to record the fact for what it is worth that there
is far less scandal in the conduct of the government of London than in that of any one of our
western cities of less than one-twentieth its population. So satisfactory is it in fact that the subject is more or less agitated of procuring the
repeal of the charter of the City of London proper and bringing it also under the control of the
Metropolitan Board of Works, for the management of the affairs of the old central municipality

is less satisfactory. But the corporation is so rich and enjoys so many special privileges that it will be difficult to compel it to relinquish its franchises, and it certainly never will give them up voluntarily. Practically the "City of London" is governed by a lot of mediæval guilds or trades unions, all now close corporations and immensely wealthy. Every alderman must be a member of one of these guilds, and the Lord Mayor is chosen by the guilds from among the members of the Board of Aldermen. Of the revenues and expenditures of the various guilds and of the city itself the public knows very little, but as both guilds and city own valuable landed estates and enjoy various lucrative monopolies, the amounts they handle must be very great. It is certain that very large sums are spent annually in feasting and display and in the entertainment of distinguished visitors.

Seen from a distance London is noticeable for the great number of church towers and spires it presents. In the midst of all rises conspicuously the great dome of St. Paul's. On the river Thames, which flows through London from west to east, at the eastern extremity of the original city, stands the Tower of London, an ancient fortress with a great square tower surmounted by a turret at each corner, and which forms a conspicuous landmark. Midway between the Tower and St.

Paul's stand in a group the Bank of England, the Royal Exchange and the Mansion House, the latter the official residence of the Lord Mayor. This locality, popularly known as "the Bank," is regarded as the business center of London, and the lines of omnibuses that make it a starting point are almost innumerable.   The main thoroughfare connecting the Bank with St. Paul's is the historic Cheapside, perhaps the busiest street to be found anywhere.   A little north of Cheapside, and at the head of a short street opening into it, stands Guildhall, the city hall of London, the great banqueting hall of which is a fine old Gothic edifice of about the fourteenth century. At St. Paul's the great artery of travel divides into two, the most southerly, or that lying nearest the river being known in successive sections as Ludgate Hill, Fleet Street and the Strand. The dividing line between Fleet street and the Strand was formerly marked by Temple Bar, a stone gateway, originally one of the gates of the city, but which was pulled down a year or two ago as a useless incumbrance.   Between the site of Temple Bar and the river lie the extensive range of buildings occupied exclusively by lawyers, known as the Temple, and just across the street is an immense structure just being completed for the Law Courts, which will be here concentrated.

The Strand terminates westwardly in Charing
Cross, a business centre second only in importance to the Bank.   Here is located the American
Exchange, before referred to, important railway
stations, and several large hotels.   A few rods
still further west is Trafalgar Square, with the
Nelson column in its midst, the north side of the
square being bounded by the National gallery,
the great picture gallery of the British nation.
From this point a street known as Whitehall
leads southwesterly to Westminister Abbey and
the Houses of Parliament on the banks of the
Thames, and another street continuing more westerly, and known as Pall Mall, contains most of the
famous clubs of London.   But the main current of
travel does not follow Whitehall or Pall Mall,
but continues westward on Piccadilly, a street a
few blocks farther north.   Then we come to the
parks—Hyde park, Green park and St. James's,
about which cluster the fashion and aristocracy
of London.   At the western extremity of St.
James's park stands Buckingham palace, the
Queen's London residence, and around the park
are the residences of the Prince of Wales and the
offices of the war, navy and foreign departments
of the British government.

What some of the fashionable thoroughfares of
our northern cities are in times of good sleighing,
such, for a crowd of pleasure drivers, is Hyde

Park every afternoon in the year. All the aristocracy turn out for an hour or two after four o'clock, and the drives are one mass of horses and carriages, numbering many hundreds, if not thousands. The more stylish have their coachman with curled wig and footmen with powdered hair, all in livery to match the upholstering of the carriage. About five o'clock the word is given by the police, and a way is opened through the crowd of vehicles, for the carriage of the Princess of Wales, who, usually accompanied by her little family, makes a few turns around the park. The Princess is beautiful and popular, and her daily ride is a continuous ovation.

The other thoroughfare westward from St. Paul's first passes the General Postoffice, then Christ's Hospital, or the Bluecoat school, a public school founded some three hundred years ago, and the pupils of which still dress in the peculiar costume of the period of its establishlishment—long blue gowns and yellow stockings, with no hats, whence the popular name of the school—then Newgate prison, beyond which the street is known as Holborn, and still further westward as Oxford street, one of the principal retail business streets of London. At the extremity of Oxford street formerly existed the locality known as Tyburn, where so many hundreds of people used to be hanged for offenses that in the present day are condoned by a few months' imprisonment. A few blocks north of Newgate is the great central meat market of London, Smithfield, the place where protestant heretics were roasted at the stake in Queen Mary's reign, three hundred and thirty years ago.

Running north and south, and intersecting Oxford street and Piccadilly, is fashionable Regent street, where the best of everything can be purchased at about double Oxford street prices.

Above Westminster, on the north bank of the Thames, is Chelsea, the late home of Thomas Carlyle and many other literary celebrities. Opposite Westminster is Lambeth palace, the residence of the Archbishop of Canterbury; and still farther down, on the south side of the river, the populous section of London known as Southwark.

The Thames is crossed by a number of fine stone and iron bridges, that lowest down the river, London Bridge, being located about midway between the Tower and St. Paul's. Below this are the several extensive dock yards and all the shipping trade, for only small barges and omnibus steamers pass above London Bridge.

CHAPTER XXVIII.

ONDONERS are apt to laugh when one talks of visiting the Tower of London, affecting to regard the old castle as only a sort of show place for children. But they do it injustice. The castle itself, as an old Norman structure of the time of William the Conqueror —eight centuries old—and as the scene of the imprisonment and tragic death of Anne Boleyn, Lady Jane Grey and many other notable characters in history, is certainly an object of interest; but besides this, it contains one of the most complete museums of ancient arms and armor that can perhaps be found anywhere, and which well repays a visit. Here also may be seen the royal crown and other crown jewels of England, the whole valued at a fabulous amount. A great improvement has been introduced since my last visit, in permitting visitors to go about unattended by guides, and to stay as long as they choose. Formerly they were conducted through in parties, and given no time for the careful examination of anything.

In connection with Guildhall, the municipal headquarters of the city of London, there is a large free library and a very interesting museum, the latter comprising solely London antiquities. Here are sculptures, mosaics, ornaments, tools, pottery, household utensils, and even shoes, of the Roman period, all found at different times in excavations made in the city. Of their Roman origin there can be no doubt, but it is remarkable how many of the articles, as knives, spoons, nails, tweezers, and other manufactures of metal, resemble those of the present day. In a former chapter was mentioned a breech-loading gun, seen in a museum at Bale, and quite like a modern gun in its construction, yet made two hundred and fifty years ago. In the museum connected with the London Free Library is a copy of the London Farthing Post, of January 15, 1739, and yet it is popularly supposed that the cheap press is a product wholly of the present generation. But, more wonderful yet, there are seen in the same museum safety pins precisely such as are now in general use by ladies and infants, but made and used by the Romans near two thousand years ago. Truly, there is nothing new under the sun.

After seeing St. Peter's at Rome, St. Paul's, which is in great measure modeled after it, loses greatly in interest. Exteriorly I think it the superior of St. Peter's, but within it is not nearly so imposing. It is, nevertheless, claimed to be the largest Protestant church in the world. In the churchyard may be seen some remains of old St. Paul's, a large Norman or Gothic church built under William the Conqueror, and destroyed in the great fire of London in 1666. Six years later Sir Christopher Wren was employed to rebuild the structure, which he completed in 1710, and it is no doubt his most meritorious achievement.

While Westminster Abbey contains principally the monuments of England's literati and statesmen, St. Paul's is more particularly devoted to the tombs of her artists and warriors. In the crypt lie the remains of Nelson, Wellington, and Sir John Moore, with a great number of less distinguished naval and military officers, together with those of Sir Christopher Wren, the architect, Joshua Reynolds, J. M. W. Turner, Benjamin West, Edwin Landseer, and other noted painters, besides those of Dr. Samuel Johnson, Bishop Heber, the author of

"From Greenland's Icy Mountains,"

Dean Milman, the historian, Howard, the philanthropist, etc. The monuments, chiefly of white marble, are ruined by the dust and smoke that defiles them, and are anything but objects of beauty. For sixpence we descend to the crypt, where is to be seen Wellington's funeral car, constructed wholly from captured brass cannon, and weighing several tons. Ascending to the base of the dome, we find ourselves in what is known as the whispering gallery, so called because, when all is quiet outside, the faintest whisper uttered on one side of the immense circular structure is distinctly heard at the other, one hundred and forty feet away. We still ascend higher to the summit of the dome, where a gallery, known as the golden gallery, two hundred and ninety feet from the ground, commands the finest birds-eye view of London obtainable. St. Paul's is too well known to the average reader from the prints of it, which are so common, to require any more minute description here.

Among the finest of the public improvements effected by the Metropolitan Board of Works is the well-known Thames Embankment. The river Thames rises and falls with the tides some twelve or fifteen feet. At low water there were formerly on each side of the river great beds of mud, hundreds of feet in width, but which were entirely covered at high water. Now, heavy stone walls have been built at the line of the low water channel, and the space at the back has been filled up and improved as a park. The houses that formerly bordered the river now stand one or two hundred yards inland, and look down upon brilliant flower beds, green shrubbery, neat gravel walks, and statues of eminent personages. The Egyptian obelisk, brought to England a few years ago at so much cost, is also one of the adornments of the Thames Embankment.

Starting out for a walk on the Embankment one evening, I turned down Craven street from the Strand, when on one of the houses, No. 7, a circular tablet caught my eye. It bore this inscription:

HERE LIVED
BENJAMIN FRANKLIN,
PRINTER.
Born 1706.
Died 1790.

Parton, in his life of Franklin, mentions his residing at No. 7 Craven street in 1757, when on a mission from the colony of Pennsylvania to the Penn family and the British government of that day. "His landlady," says Parton, "was Mrs. Margaret Stevenson, one of the most amiable of women, with whom and her daughter he soon contracted a friendship which was warmly cherished on both sides as long as he lived. At Mrs. Stevenson's house he enjoyed, during his long exile, all of a home which can be enjoyed away from home." He lived in considerable style in London, and finding the hackney coaches dilapidated and inconvenient he set up a modest chariot of his own. His son William, who was with him, entered the Middle Temple as a student of law. One can hardly turn anywhere in London without stumbling upon some such historic locality.

Relics of the olden times are very numerous. On some of the fashionable streets in the "West End" almost every house still retains the posts or brackets and frames which once held the oil lamps with which the doorways were lighted before the discovery of gas. More curious still are the great iron extinguishers which project from the porticoes or iron fences in front of the houses, and which were used for the putting out of the torches of the link boys who walked before and lighted the way for the sedan chairs, in which our ancestors went out to balls and parties before the paving of the streets made the use of carriages practicable. No one seems to think of destroying these things because they cease to be useful. Another old-time relic is an occasional plank elevated about four feet from the sidewalk on iron posts on the line of the curbstone, its humane object being the affording of a resting place for burdens carried by men and boys, before the days of trucks and express wagons.

I alluded above to Whitehall, a thoroughfare connecting Charing Cross with Westminster. This is a notable street. On the left we first pass Scotland Yard, the headquarters of the London detective police. A little further on is the Banqueting House, the only remaining portion of Whitehall palace, the principal London residence of the Stuarts. From one of the windows of this Banqueting House Charles I. was led out to execution two hundred and thirty-two years ago. The building is now used as one of the royal chapels. Its interior is plain and old-fashioned, with high pews, and one especially large one surmounted by a canopy and gilded crown for the use of the royal family. The audience on the occasion of our visit was thin and the services not particularly imposing.

Nearly opposite is the Admiralty, or navy department, an old-fashioned building with a court yard. Just beyond are the Horse Guards or military headquarters, in front of which two cavalry soldiers in full dress, with steel breastplates and helmets, constantly stand guard, both men and horses so motionless as almost to lead one to believe they are equestrian statues. Still further on a short street branches to the right, separating the treasury department from the immense and imposing pile of buildings erected a few years ago for the foreign and home departments. This is the famous Downing street, which we see so often referred to in English despatches in connection with diplomatic affairs Another block and the Houses of Parliament, or, more

18

correctly speaking, the Palace of Westminster, is reached. One wonders to what purpose such extensive premises can be put, especially in view of the very small and inadequate quarters that are allotted to the two legislative bodies. Our Congress would not put up with such accommodations for a single session. Most of our western state legislatures are incomparably better housed. The chambers are small, gloomy and inconvenient, notwithstanding that a sum equal to $15,-000,000 was spent upon them. There are scarcely seats sufficient for half the members, and none are provided with desks of any sort. The galleries, too, are very small, and only a very limited number of visitors can be accommodated to listen to even the most important debates. Nothing could be more absurdly inconvenient and unadapted to its purpose.

Viewed from the exterior the building is very large, imposing and rich in its ornamentations. In fact it is so large that it has entirely dwarfed and spoiled the effect of Westminster Abbey, which it almost adjoins. Although it has not yet been completed for forty years, the finely carved stone work is showing seriously the effect of decay, and already in places the work of restoration has begun.

On each Saturday the public are admitted to the principal rooms in the building. The first large room we enter contains a gilded throne and is known as the Queen's Robing Room. From this we pass to the Royal Gallery, a long room through which the Queen passes in state to the House of Lords to open or prorogue parliament. Then another large ante-room called the Prince's Chamber. The next room of the suite is the House of Lords, which is ninety feet long by forty-five wide. At one end is the royal throne, in the middle the seats for the members, and at the other end a small space beyond the bar for the members of the House of Commons who are summoned hither when the queen attends for the purposes mentioned above. No seats are provided for the Commons, and the space allotted them will certainly not accommodate a fourth of their number. Continuing our walk, we pass to the Peers' Lobby, from which, at one side, the Peers' Robing Room opens, in which is a famous fresco painting of Moses giving the law to the Israelites, the peculiarity of it being that the painter, Mr. J. R. Herbert, with true British fidelity, visited Arabia and made sketches from Mount Sinai itself from which to paint his mountain; and all the characters in the picture, both in feature and dress, are equally exact representations of the people of that region. This is true art.

Continuing on in a right line we pass from the

Peers' Lobby to the Peers' Corridor, and from this to the great central octagonal hall of the building. From this we pass to the Commons' Corridor, Commons' Lobby, and House of Commons, which latter is a sixth smaller than the House of Lords. All these rooms are rich with carved oak, stained windows, and frescoes, the pictures being portraits of the kings and queens of England and notable scenes in English history. It is all rich and costly, but is dingy and unimposing. From the Central Hall we pass through St. Stephen's Hall, a building occupying the exact site of the old St. Stephen's Chapel, in which Parliament sat up to the time of its destruction by fire in 1834. This brings us to what is really the finest part of the entire structure, old Westminster Hall, built nearly eight hundred years ago, and long regarded as the finest old mediæval hall in Europe. In it have taken place most of the famous state trials, and in other ways it is peculiarly identified with English history.

Just across the street is Westminster Abbey, one of the most famous churches in Europe. It was built by King Edward the Confessor, about eight hundred and fifty years ago, and rebuilt by Henry III. at the period when Gothic architecture was at the zenith of its purity and excellence. It is not one of the larger churches of England, being only three hundred and seventy-five feet long, but it is very lofty and imposing. Its chief interest, however, attaches to its being the burial place of a large number of the English kings, together with the great men in literature and statesmanship through a long period of England's history. The earlier tombs are, of course, in a decayed and ruinous condition, and few possess any artistic beauty. Fifteen English monarchs are interred here, including Edward the Confessor, Richard II., Henry III., Henry V. and Henry VII., Edward I., Edward III. and Edward VI., Mary, Elizabeth, James I., Charles II., William III., Anne, and George II. Oliver Cromwell was formerly buried here, but his remains were exhumed and destroyed at the Restoration. Mary Queen of Scots also sleeps here in a tomb equal in elegance to that of her rival, Elizabeth. Here lie also two of Henry VIII.'s six wives, Jane Seymour and Anne of Cleves.

These royal tombs are mostly in the chapels which surround the choir. The south transept is known as Poet's Corner, and here are monuments to Chaucer, the earliest English poet, Spenser, Shakspeare, Ben Jonson, Milton, Addison, Dr. Watts, the hymn writer, Garrick, the actor, John and Charles Wesley, Gray, Southey, Campbell, Sheridan the dramatist, Dr. Johnson, Thomson, Goldsmith, Dickens, Macaulay, Wordsworth,

Thackeray, and many other famous poets and authors, most of whom are actually buried here.

In the north transept are collected most of the monuments of the statesmen buried in the abbey, which include William Pitt, Earl of Chatham, the friend of America at our Revolutionary period, William Pitt the younger, whose statesmanship proved more than a match for Napoleon's military genius, Charles James Fox, Spencer Percival, the prime minister who was assassinated in 1812, Warren Hastings, George Canning, Lord Palmerston, Lord Mansfield, the eminent jurist, Richard Cobden, the father of English free trade, William Wilberforce and Thomas Fowell Buxton the leaders in the movement which abolished slavery in the British colonies, and others less widely known. Among other interesting monuments scattered over the abbey are those of the Duke of Buckingham, the favorite of James I.; Gen. Monck, who, as commander of the army, abolished the Cromwellian republic and restored the monarchy by placing Charles II. on the throne; James Watt, the perfecter of the steam engine; Gen. Wolfe, the hero of Quebec; Mrs. Siddons, the great actress; Sir John Franklin, who was lost in the Arctic regions; Admiral Kempenfelt, who went down with the British man-of-war, the Royal George, with her crew of nearly nine hundred men off Spithead in 1782—a similar case to the Eurydice of a year or two ago ; Isaac Newton ; Herschel, the astronomer ; Robert Stevenson, the engineer who built the Victoria bridge at Montreal ; Major Andre, the British spy hanged by Washington ; and the musical composers, Handel, John Blow, and William Croft.

Some of the abbey monuments are old-fashioned and ugly tablets fastened upon the wall. Some of the more modern consist of statuary portraits of the deceased. Those of the period of the Stuarts are often of stone, painted in various bright colors, and the more pretentious royal tombs generally have an effigy of the deceased with an elaborate stone canopy overhead, supported by marble columns. All look very dingy.

In Westminster Abbey all the sovereigns of England are crowned ; and here is seen the shabby old chair which for nearly six hundred years has done duty on such occasions. The sovereigns of Scotland for an even longer period were crowned sitting on a stone, reputed to be the veritable one on which Jacob rested his head when he had his famous vision of angels ascending and descending from heaven at Bethel. When the two kingdoms were united the stone was fitted into the seat of the coronation chair, so that both stone and chair have since been simultaneously occupied.

The visitor to the abbey must not pass by the Chapter House, formerly the council room of

the authorities of the abbey, but for three hundred years used for the sittings of the British
House of Commons.   In 1547 the Commons were
removed to St. Stephen's Chapel, alluded to
above, and since then down to a recent period the
Chapter House has been used for the storage of
public documents.   It has lately been entirely
restored and now serves as a museum of antiquities connected with the abbey.   It is octagonal in
form with a stone vaulted ceiling, in common, in
this respect, with every other part of the abbey.

On Mondays every part of the church is open
free to the public, but on other days sixpence is
charged for admission to the chapels.   As in all
cathedrals full choral services are held twice each
day, at ten and three o'clock.   On Sunday evenings there is also a service in the nave at which
sermons are delivered by the ablest preachers in
the kingdom to immense crowds.

THE TOWER OF LONDON.

CHAPTER XXIX.

LONDON AND ART—THE BRITISH MUSEUM—THE NATIONAL GAL-
LERY—THE GREAT FLEMISH, DUTCH AND GERMAN MASTERS
—THE SOUTH KENSINGTON MUSEUM.

A FAMOUS institution is the British Museum.
It began in 1753 with a large collection of
curiosities and antiquities brought together
during his lifetime by Sir Hans Sloane, and purchased after his death by the government. To
this collection additions were rapidly made by
purchase and donation. Among the larger gifts
was that of the extensive library collected during
his long lifetime by King George III., and which
his pleasure-loving successor, George IV., having
no use for, got rid of by presenting it to the
museum. When a nucleus is once formed for
such a collection is is astonishing how rapidly
accumulation goes on. Forty years ago it was
found necessary to rebuild on a much larger
scale the premises occupied by the museum, and
these becoming again overcrowded, the later policy
has been to transfer to other museums certain
portions of the collection, so as to leave this institution almost purely a museum of antiquities and
library of books. The latest removal has been

that of the extensive natural history collection, which has been transferred to a building erected especially for its reception at South Kensington, in the west end of London. Under the operation of the copyright law a copy of every new book published in Great Britain must be deposited in the British Museum, and this, with the large resources of the management, which enables them to be constantly on the search for rare and valuable books, has resulted in making the library of the museum, with but one exception, the largest in the world. And this magnificent library is open free to everybody, the only requirement being the recommendation of a householder or person whose name is found in the city directory of London. No books are allowed to be taken from the library, but every convenience is afforded for reading and copying on the premises. The library is very rich also in manuscripts, containing, among other rare treasures, one of the three oldest manuscript copies of the bible in existence, the Codex Alexandrinus, written on vellum nearly fifteen hundred years ago. It is preserved in a glass case. There is also a copy of the Latin Vulgate of nearly eleven centuries antiquity. Here also may be seen in glass cases a rich collection of Egyptian papyri and ancient and oriental books, some written on sheets of gold, some on cloth, ivory, birch bark, palm leaves,

etc., in a great variety of forms. In other cases
are mediæval books beautifully written on parchment or vellum, and adorned with brilliant water
color paintings and illuminations. In still other
cases are autograph letters of a great number of
eminent men, including Luther, Calvin, Cranmer,
Wolsey, Knox, Raleigh, Bacon, Hampden, Penn,
Newton, Durer, Rubens, Galileo, Voltaire, Swift,
Addison, Burke, Pitt, Fox, Washington, Franklin, Wellington, Nelson, Whitefield, Goethe, Shelley, Handel and a great many more, all arranged
so that they may be easily read and examined.
In this autographic collection most of the kings
and queens of England are represented, and if
Queen Mary saw the letter of Lady Jane Grey
here exhibited it is not to be wondered at that
she took off her head, for in it she alludes to the
"Lady Marye, bastard daughter to our great
uncle Henry th' eight."

In this library there has also been collected a
great number of maps, drawings and prints illustrating the changes that have taken place in the
geography and architecture of London, beginning
at a very early period. This suggests that in
every city collections of such maps, plans, drawings and photographs should be preserved.

In another room of the library are exhibited
early printed books, from the period when an
entire page used to be engraved on a single block

of wood, these being known as block books, down
to the perfection of the art by Gutenburg, with
specimens of his work, as well as that of Faust,
Schoeffer and Caxton.

In another department of the British Museum
there are collected copies of every known print or
engraving that has ever been published, the work
of any artist of note. Some of these when very
rare have been acquired at fabulous cost. They
are all carefully mounted on thick paper of uniform size, properly classified and arranged, and
preserved in portfolios for the use of artists or
connoisseurs who may wish to examine them.

But the department of the museum that is most
visited by the general public is that of the antiquities. In Assyrian and Babylonian remains no
other museum contains anything like so rich a collection; as the researches in the valleys of the
Tigris and Euphrates have been carried on mainly
by English explorers, and to a large extent in
direct behalf of the British Museum. It is wonderful how much may be learned of the very earliest civilization from these resurrected sculptures,
inscriptions, pictures and implements. The
Egyptian collection is perhaps somewhat inferior
to that of the Louvre in Paris, as the French did
for Egypt what England has done for Assyria;
but the British Museum nevertheless contains the
richest prize known to Egyptology in the Rosetta

stone, the sole key to the deciphering of the Egyptian hieroglyphic records. It is a slab of stone about the size of the top of a small table with an inscription upon it in three different languages, Egyptian hieroglyphic, Coptic and Greek. The Greek being of course understood, the hieroglyphics were easily unraveled.

Passing to the Grecian department we again find the rarest treasures in the sculptures which formerly adorned the pediments of the famous Parthenon at Athens, and which are believed to be the work of Phidias, the greatest of ancient sculptors. These are known as the Elgin marbles, because brought to England by Lord Elgin while minister to Turkey. They are esteemed as priceless treasures. There are also to be seen here many sculptured fragments from the famous tomb of Mausolus, reckoned by the ancients one of the seven wonders of the world.

In Roman antiquities, of course the galleries at Rome are superior in extent and richness, but, taken altogether, the British Museum is quite the peer of the Louvre and the Vatican in the interesting character of its antique treasures.

This leads me to remark, by way of generalizing, that the museums and galleries of London are, as a rule, more satisfactory to visitors than those found on the continent, because more carefully selected and better arranged, and less overloaded with rubbish. And all the great English galleries and museums are entirely free to the public. Thus, of all the galleries of old paintings I have seen, I like the National Gallery the best, for these reasons: 1. It is not so extensive, the pictures are more carefully selected, and one has not to search among a score of very ordinary pictures for every one worth examination. 2. Most of the pictures are exhibited under glass, by which means they are kept clean and bright; and every picture is labeled, both with the subject and the name of the artist, with the years of his . birth and death. 3. The rooms, having been constructed especially for the purpose they are used for, are much better lighted, and the pictures every way seen to better advantage, than in any gallery in Rome, Florence, or Paris. 4. As a rule, all the great painters are represented by excellent specimens of their work. 5. The catalogues contain satisfactory sketches of the lives of the painters, and, where necessary, descriptions of the pictures. Altogether one derives in London a more intelligent and satisfactory introduction to the great masters, with less wearisome labor, than anywhere else.

The National Gallery was founded in 1824, and now contains about eleven hundred choice paintings in oil. Of these over four hundred are of the British school, and are as a rule a delightful lot of pictures. Instead of tortured martyrs, bloody heads of Medusa, or simpering nude figures such as have been so much affected by the continental painters, here we have delicious rural landscapes, glorious marine views, wonderfully life-like animals, and charming genre pictures, displaying more real genius than all the saints and madonnas of the old masters put together.

Four of the so-called British painters here represented were really Americans, viz: Benjamin West, died 1820, J. S. Copley, 1815, Gilbert Stuart, 1828, and C. R. Leslie, 1859. The picture of West's exhibited at our Centennial was very far from being one of his best. In "Christ Healing the Sick," in the National Gallery, his Christ, for softness and beauty, is quite worthy of Murillo.

For quiet landscapes Patrick Nasmyth, who died in 1831, leads all others, though John Constable, 1834, is perhaps quite as famous. For marine views none can approach Clarkson Stanfield, who himself began life as a sailor. He died in 1867. The best genre painters—by which we mean delineators of ordinary scenes in every day life—are Sir David Wilkie, 1841, and Wm. Mulready, 1863. As animal painters I can hardly choose between Sir Edwin Landseer, who died in 1873, and Sir T. Sidney Cooper, who is still living. Leslie, alluded to above, seems to have excelled in his character delineations.

But the most famous painter in this gallery is J. M. W. Turner, who died in 1851, and left his large collection of paintings to the British nation. At a first glance Turner's pictures are noticeable for their brilliancy. Inspected more closely, one hardly knows what to make of them, and almost doubts if their hanging there be not a huge joke. He looks at one closely, and finds it only a mass of white paint thickly laid on, with little daubs of color here and there. Likeness of anything, in either heaven above or in the earth beneath, it is impossible to distinguish. He crosses the room and takes a distant view of it, but it is no more a picture than before. It expresses nothing but a great uncertainty. And this is the general character of all the later pictures of this remarkable artist, whose works are so much prized. Of course all his paintings are not equally obscure. Turner made his reputation in the first instance upon the great care and fidelity with which his pictures were worked up. Then he began in later life to sacrifice careful drawing to brilliancy of coloring, and toward the close of his career he seems to have aimed at seeing how little of representation of anything he could produce and still have it pass for a picture. The connoisseur of course pretends to think his works very beautiful, but I am quite sure that nine hundred and ninety-nine out of every one thousand of my

readers would pronounce Turner an arrant hum-
bug. Still, it is interesting to sit down for an
hour and examine pictures that are so highly
valued. What is a picture? Webster says, "a
resemblance in color." The nearer the resemblance, therefore, of course the better the picture,
and I am unable to see how any amount of skill
in laying on the color can compensate for defi-
ciencies in delineation. The nearer the approach
to nature, common sense would dictate, the more
meritorious the art. A picture that requires cultivation to understand cannot by this rule be a
picture of the highest merit, though no doubt
people may work themselves up to a high esteem
for it, just as they do for ugly old porcelain and
rubbishing old furniture. I fancy there is very
much of this factitious taste in the admiration
that is expressed for the works of Turner as
well as for those of Titian and others of the old
masters. But I prefer pictures that everybody
can appreciate.

It may not be out of place to mention here the
names of some of the great German, Dutch and
Flemish masters, as those of France and Italy
have already been summed up in former chapters.
Perhaps the most famous of all is the Flemish or
Belgian painter, Peter Paul Rubens, who was
born in 1577 and died in 1640. His pictures in
the various galleries of northern Europe are very

19

numerous and his style so well defined that one soon learns to pick out his works with tolerable certainty. His subjects are almost exclusively historical scenes painted on large expanses of canvas, with figures often life size, generally spirited but frequently gross and indelicate and lacking in grace and dignity. The next most eminent Flemish painter is Van Dyke (1599–1641). He was particularly famous for his portraits. Then comes David Teniers the elder (1582–1649) and David Teniers the younger (1610–1690), both of Antwerp, whose pictures are almost invariably home-like country or village scenes, in which a great number of figures are introduced. Unlike those of Rubens the Teniers pictures are almost invariably of comparatively small size. They, too, are easily identified.

Of the Dutch or Holland masters, there are Rembrandt (1606–1674), whose paintings are remarkable chiefly for having most of their surface very dark and obscure but some particular portion brought out very strongly in high lights; Paul Potter (1625–1654) and Albert Cuyp (1605–1691), both famous animal painters, particularly of domestic cattle; Ruysdaal (1630–1681) and Hobbima (1629–1670), both delightful landscape artists; Gerard Dow (1613–1680), a celebrated genre painter; Wm. Van de Veldt (1633–1707), a splendid marine painter; Wouwerman (1619–

1668), an admirable delineator of horses and battle scenes, and others almost equally noted.

The German school numbers Jan Van Eyck (1390–1441), the inventor of oil colors; Albert Durer (1471–1533), a masterly painter, but more famous as an engraver, and Hans Holbein (1497–1554), a painter chiefly of portraits.

What the Salon is to Paris the exhibition of the Royal Academy is to London. The exhibition, which continues through the months of May, June and July each year, last year (1881) numbered about fifteen hundred pictures, all, of course, new ones. While less extensive than the French Salon, this exhibition is scarcely less interesting, the modern British painters having developed a high degree of perfection in certain fields. Thus they seem particularly to excel as animal painters, as I have nowhere else seen such life-like productions as in this country of Landseer. Landscapes, marine views, quiet genre pictures, and perhaps I may add historical paintings, seem to be also the forte of English artists. Nudities, which French painters seem to regard as the highest achievement of art and in which they certainly excel, the English painters do not at all affect. I think there was scarcely one nude figure in the entire catalogue of the Academy. The French, I fancy, also excel in battle pieces; the English more in subjects that will admit of a faithful reproduction of nature.

In statuary the French are no doubt incomparably ahead of the English. Sculpture seems to find its best development in the warm countries of southern Europe, while painting and architecture improve as we advance northward. I think there is a more painstaking fidelity to nature in northern painters, and better conceptions of effect in northern architects. The Italian painters of all ages seem more to have cultivated the imaginative, and their architects to have sacrificed everything to immensity, in their productions.

Picture galleries are terribly wearisome places for the legs, the standing for hours together being the most tiring of occupations, but they may nevertheless be made very interesting even to the merest tyros in art. There is cultivation in merely determining in one's own mind which is the best picture in a room full, and comparing results with the conclusions of one's companions. This tends no doubt to develop a critical observation. The peculiarities of painters may also soon be learned, so that one with a little practice may pretty safely venture to name the artist without referring to his catalogue. Of course this does not apply to all painters, but the pictures of Andrea del Sarto, Fra Angelico, Canaletto, Murillo, Claude Loraine, Vernet, Teniers, and some others, we soon learn to tell almost at a glance.

One of the outgrowths of the great international exposition held in London in 1851 was the South Kensington Museum. The exhibition itself proved a stimulus to art-culture, and the profits accruing from it formed a nucleus fund for the establishment of this grand museum of arts and sciences. The latter has grown with wonderful rapidity, and provision is made for still immense expansion in the future. The museum occupies twelve acres of land in the west end of London, upon which very extensive buildings—some permanent, others only temporary—have from time to time been erected. The scope of the museum is mainly in the direction of art culture. It embraces a large collection of models of famous architectural works and casts of architectural details, a very large collection of ceramics, a great variety and endless number of miscellaneous objects of an art character, ancient and modern, including bronzes, furniture, glassware, jewelry, carved work, etc., and a very large collection of drawings and paintings by British artists. The large museum of East Indian curiosities formerly belonging to the East India Company, also occupies a suite of rooms at South Kensington, and there are also extensive libraries of works on educational and art topics. To carefully examine everything would take a week's time at the very least.

We first enter the National Portrait Gallery, which contains several hundred portraits and busts of English celebrities from the earliest periods, and which very much resembles in character the great gallery of portraits at Versailles, described in a former chapter. These great portrait galleries are very interesting, and it is high time that an American collection were begun at our national capital, state collections at each state capital, and local galleries at every important point. Retiring governors, mayors and members of Congress ought to present their portraits to such galleries, and search should be made for old paintings, sketches, engravings and photographs of the men who in the past have been identified in any way with the history of the commonwealth.

The gallery of miscellaneous pictures in the South Kensington Museum is very extensive and interesting. It is composed mainly of private collections that have been bequeathed or presented to the museum, and of pictures loaned to it. Among the latter are the seven famous cartoons of Raphael, which long hung in Hampton Court palace, and of which prints are so common. There are also a number of choice pictures belonging to the Royal Academy, some of the best selected from the annual exhibitions, and purchased from a fund provided for the purpose.

The bequests and donations include an immense
number of water colors and drawings by eminent
artists, and their examination is very enjoyable.
Besides pictures, some of these bequests include
valuable collections of autograph letters, notably
the Forster collection, which contains the original
manuscripts of several of Charles Dickens's most
important works, including David Copperfield,
Martin Chuzzlewit, Oliver Twist, and the Old
Curiosity Shop. These autograph collections are
of rare interest to all who are fond of history and
literature.

Connected with the South Kensington Museum
are art schools open to every one at the trifling
fee of about five dollars per month.

Near the South Kensington Museum is the new
Natural History Museum, the branch of the British Museum alluded to above. It is a very large
and beautiful building, with both inside and outside walls of terra cotta, and with much original-
ity in its design. It will probably be the com-
pletest thing of the kind in the world when open
in all its branches, and, as in the South Kensington Museum, everything is so nicely labeled and
described that it is a pleasure to go through it.
I should have mentioned that all these museums
and galleries, that of the Royal Academy alone
excepted, are open free to the public, and thousands visit them daily.

CHAPTER XXX.

ONE of the standard sights of London is Madame Tussaud's exhibition of wax works in Baker street. The founder, Madame Tussaud, was a Swiss artist, patronized by the court of Louis XVI. of France. She was one of the sufferers by the French revolution, and ultimately took refuge in England, where she devoted her artistic talents to the modeling of a series of portrait figures in wax of the celebrities of her day. At first her show was of the traveling order, but it soon outgrew the capacity of the means of conveyance of that period, and for nearly half a century has been permanently located in London. New figures are added from time to time, and those which have lost interest with the public, are removed to make room for them. Conspicuous among the collection to-day are the figure of the late President Garfield, those of all the members of the royal family of England, with the boyish-looking Marquis of Lorne, Mr. Gladstone, the principal participants in the

Afghan war, the members of the famous Congress
of Berlin, and a great number of other public
characters, including Spurgeon, Baroness Bur-
dett-Coutts, John Bright, H. M. Stanley, Parnell,
the claimant in the Tichborne case, Bradlaugh,
etc., etc. But of fully equal interest is a fine
collection of all the kings of England and the
great men of past ages, as Wyckliffe, Wolsey,
Luther, Regent Murray, Calvin, Knox and many
others. Two entire rooms are devoted to the
Napoleon family and relics connected therewith,
including the veritable carriages that Napoleon I.
used at Waterloo, and that Napoleon III. was
captured in at Sedan. But one of the most interesting objects exhibited is the knife of the original
guillotine used during the French revolution and
which took off the heads of Louis XVI., Marie
Antoinette, Madame Roland, Robespierre and
thousands of other famous and unknown French
men and women.

By the way, I admire the guillotine as a mode
of execution. It is instantaneous in its operation,
and blundering on the part of the executioner
is impossible. In each of the two upright posts
of the instrument there are two parallel grooves.
In the first is fitted the collar that encircles the
neck of the victim—the same being a board with
a round hole in it, cut into two sections, the
upper of which slides up in the grove to admit

the head. In the other groove slides the heavy knife with diagonal blade, which nicely shaves off the head close to the wooden collar. Nothing could be more neat and satisfactory, and, if we must perpetuate capital punishment, it will be a great step in advance when we abolish the old and barbarous gallows and adopt the product of the higher French civilization, the guillotine.

My older readers will remember the great international industrial exhibition held in Hyde Park, London, in 1851, the pioneer exhibition of the kind. The building in which it was held, constructed wholly of iron and glass, was in its day unique. It covered a dozen or more acres of ground, and when the exhibition was over was purchased by some of the railway companies, in connection with other capitalists, and removed to a high hill at Sydenham, seven miles south of London where, with two hundred acres of ground attached to it, it was opened in 1854 as the Crystal Palace, a grand place of public amusement. Two railways run into stations directly connected with the building, and the traffic this palace creates is immense. A good share of the space in the structure is rented out to tradesmen for the exhibition and sale of their wares, and to restaurateurs, confectioners, beer sellers and others, who supply refreshments to the multitudes of visitors. Then there are casts of all the most famous statuary in the world, casts of rare and beautiful pieces of architectural ornament from all countries, a winter garden, ferneries, an aquarium, theater, concert hall, great organ and other permanent attractions. Besides these, temporary exhibitions of all kinds are on from time to time. At the time of our visit the specialties were a rose show, and a display of woolen manufacturing machinery in full operation. In a few weeks these would be replaced by other novelties. There are also in the building a great number of extra shows, to which additional admission fees are charged, and these change as their popularity declines. The grounds outside are laid out in magnificent terraces and gardens, with lakes and fountains, and plenty of open space suitable for any outdoor exhibitions that may be required. On each Thursday evening during the summer season a grand display of fireworks is given, and these far surpass any of our Fourth of July exhibitions at home. Besides enormous set pieces of artistic design, the other fireworks embrace many kinds wholly unknown to us and some of surpassing beauty. One set piece in particular enlisted our admiration. It was a huge willow tree, fifty feet high, the trunk and branches of which were outlined in white light, while the drooping leaves and smaller branches were represented by showers of green sparks. The effect can be imagined, and this illustrates the perfection to which pyrotechny has been brought in England. The railroads sell round trip tickets to the Crystal Palace, with admission included, for about two shillings, or forty-eight cents.

There are many other things in London worthy of a visit, but which must be passed over briefly here. Among these are the Regent's Park, Zoological Gardens, the finest in the world; Kensington Palace, where Queen Victoria was born, and Buckingham Palace, where she lives when in London; Hampton Court, a palace erected by Cardinal Wolsey; Chelsea Hospital, "the Invalides" of London; Greenwich Hospital, formerly a palace, now an asylum for decayed seamen; the Botanical Gardens at Kew, some miles up the Thames; the immense docks of London, the system of underground railways, the new law courts in the Strand, the quaint old Inns of Court, and many interesting churches, monuments, picture galleries, and places of historic association.

Sunday evening services in the churches are usually held at half-past six or seven o'clock, instead of half-past seven or eight, as with us. In hot summer evenings it is far preferable, as thereby the use of gas is dispensed with, and people have a long evening at home after church.

Owing to the much higher latitude, the summer days in England are noticeably longer than with

us. In July it is light enough to read at nine
o'clock in the evening and it is near ten before it
is fairly dark. Of course in the winter the days
are correspondingly short. If the reader has
never had his attention attracted to the fact, it
may surprise him to know that London in the
southern part of England is in a latitude higher
than any point in the United States, Alaska, of
course, excepted, being on about the parallel of
the northern edge of the Province of Manitoba.
Paris is in about the latitude of the northern
edge of Minnesota, Florence in about that
of Green Bay, Wis., and Rome about that of
Chicago.

A friend showed me one day a bill that a lawyer had rendered for services in transferring a
lease of some property in London, the amount
being something over forty pounds sterling, or
about two hundred dollars—an amount very
nearly equaling the value of the lease itself. So
it is apparent that the legal profession is much
the same all the world over. The lawyers enjoy
the oyster, the clients must be content with the
shells.

Still, it is said, there is no such overplus of
lawyers in England as exists in America. Greater
restrictions are thrown about an entry at the bar
than with us. Instead of a couple of terms at a
law school putting a young snob on an equal

footing with the old members of the profession, a five years' apprenticeship in the office of a practicing lawyer is required, and for the privilege of thus learning, a premium of from one thousand to two thousand dollars has to be paid to the said lawyer, besides a stamp tax of about four hundred dollars to the government. The student during this five years receives no compensation for anything he may do, nor can he practice on his own account till fully out of his time. Only those, therefore, who can afford an immediate payment of fifteen hundred to twenty-five hundred dollars, and who can afford to spend five years wholly without remuneration, can aspire to the legal profession. During the five years, the unworthy and incompetent are naturally culled out, so that the English bar ranks far above ours in both ability and respectability.

When out of his time the young lawyer is licensed as a solicitor, and in this capacity is qualified to advise clients, prepare cases for trial, draw papers and perform other such functions; but the solicitor never appears in court. When he has a case ready for trial it is turned over to a barrister, a lawyer of a higher grade, who alone is empowered to conduct trials. In the selection of barristers there is, of course, another weeding out, and thus the purity of the English bar is maintained. Barristers of the highest repute are

in due time promoted to the rank of queen's
counsel, and become benchers in the inns of court.
There is thus a constant avenue for advancement
open to every lawyer, and no one can afford to
jeopardize his future by shystering practice unless
he be a confirmed Quirk, Gammon or Snap.

Land tenure in England presents some curious
features. Originally all the land was assumed to
belong to the king, who granted it to his favorites, but who exacted an acknowledgment of his
feudal ownership in the shape of fines to be paid
every time the property changed occupants by
descent or otherwise. In like manner these ten-
ants-in-chief granted lands in smaller subdivisions
to their retainers, exacting similar fines at each
transfer of ownership. And this system very
largely continues to the present day, the title
under it being known as "copyhold." Gradually, however, a "freehold" system like our own
is becoming more general.

All over England there are large tracts of wood
land known as royal forests, originally the hunting grounds of the kings of England. The title
to the soil in these forests has been particularly
involved. The crown seems to have exercised
only hunting rights. Other rights, as of cutting
timber, digging gravel, etc., were enjoyed by the
so-called lord of the manor, but he had no right
to inclose. Then all persons whose homesteads

adjoined the forests possessed by long usage the
right of pasturing stock in them and of cropping
the timber for firewood.   Just northeast of London is a famous old forest ten or twelve miles
long, by two or three wide, known as Epping
Forest.   As London spread out in that direction,
land in the vicinity became immensely valuable,
and the idea, worthy of an American speculator,
suggested itself to some one to gain possession of
the immense property and cut it up into building
lots; and the scheme well nigh succeeded.   First
the lord of the manor, by some influence at court,
purchased for a song the royal hunting privileges.
This it was thought would remove all obstacle to
inclosing the property; but the land grabbers
were too fast.   No sooner was their scheme apparent than the commoners, as those enjoying pasture rights were called, flew to the courts for
injunctions, and a hot fight was inaugurated, the
result of which would have been very doubtful,
in view of the immense stake for which the spec-
ulators played, had not the corporation of the
city of London, with its great resources, taken
up the cause of the commoners.   By virtue of
owning a piece of cemetery land adjoining the
forest, the city of London was itself one of the
commoners, and right heartily did it stand up for
its rights.   The litigation ended at last in the
triumph of the people, and the subsequent pur-

chase by the city, for one hundred and fifty thousand dollars, of all the royal and manorial rights. An act of Parliament was then procured establishing the forest as a public park for all time to come, and cutting off the rights of the commoners to crop the trees. There will now be a chance for the stunted beeches with which it is covered to expand into large trees, but beyond the preservation of the property it is not the intention to immediately embark in any extensive improvements of it. .

In England, when a person acquires sufficient wealth to enable him to live comfortably on the interest of his means, he almost invariably retires from active business and gives other men a chance—a practice which ought to be more common in America. But with us, usually the more a man is worth, the deeper he dips in, and the more he seeks to monopolize all the trade of his locality.

Frequently men get out of business by converting their establishments into limited liability companies. Such companies are very common in England in every field of commercial enterprise. They are very popular, and no doubt useful, though it must be acknowledged that the system is often abused. Sometimes rotten concerns are unloaded upon such corporations; sometimes they are made the instruments of swindlers to secure

20

them the handling of other people's money;
sometimes the rights of minorities are overridden
by dishonest majority stockholders; and sometimes the interests of all are neglected by incompetent and inefficient directors. But often it
happens that a capable man possesses the elements of success, and when backed with capital,
is able greatly to benefit himself, and at the same
time make large profits for his backers. In such
cases these companies find their legitimate use.
They prove safe and profitable investments for
capitalists, and enable capable men to advance
themselves who otherwise would have to be content merely with the wages of humble employes.

For fifteen or twenty years the English barbers
have been brushing hair by machinery, and I
wonder the idea has never been adopted in America. A line of shafting, usually driven by a small
steam engine, runs along the ceiling of the shop,
upon which there is a grooved pulley over each
chair. From each pulley is suspended an elastic
rubber belt. The brush is cylindrical, with a
pulley at one end, and a loose axle with a handle
at each end running through it. The pulley is
slipped into the rubber belt, when the brush
begins rapidly to revolve. It is held by the two
handles, and is moved rapidly about over the
customer's head. The sensation is delightful,
and such a thorough brushing is impossible by
mere hand work.

The friends of temperance will be glad to know that the use of wine and beer on the table is greatly declining in England. From what I have observed and been informed, it is now the exception rather than the rule, and in families, too, where the use of such beverages was formerly habitual.

I was struck, too, with the small amount of profanity one hears in that country compared with America. In all my railroad, omnibus and steamboat travel, I cannot call to mind a single oath. I was reminded of this from overhearing one day a fierce quarrel between two hucksters in Covent Garden market, whose wagons in the crush had become locked together. The war of words went on for some time, with the most emphatic assurances on the part of each that the other was to blame, and must be at the pains of unloading, but throughout all the name of the Deity was not once mentioned. I conclude that the rank and file of the English are not a swearing people.

CHAPTER XXXI.

GENEALOGICAL RESEARCH—AN OLD ENGLISH CATHEDRAL TOWN
—PARISH RECORDS OF TWO HUNDRED AND FIFTY YEARS AGO
—HOW SURNAMES BECOME CHANGED AND CORRUPTED—THE
HERALDS' OFFICE.

AS there are very many people in this country interested in genealogical studies and
research, the story of my experience in this
direction may be worth devoting a chapter to, as
affording a general idea of the sources of information, the means of gaining access to them and
the character of knowledge to be gained. Being,
while in London, within sixty-seven miles of Ely,
the birthplace of an ancestor who emigrated to
America nearly one hundred years ago, I felt
some curiosity to see the place and, if possible,
find out something more of the family origin and
ancestry. A pleasant two hours' ride through a
level but beautiful country brought us to the old
cathedral city of Ely.

Like most cathedral cities it is a sleepy old
place. It occupies rising ground in the midst of
a vast flat plain, known as the Fens, which before
the days of drainage was an almost impenetrable
marsh; it is now, however, a highly cultivated

and fruitful district. Ely, also called from its
originally moist inaccessibility the Isle of Ely,
was the last place in England to hold out against
the Norman invader, William the Conqueror.
The place was founded as a religious community
by the Saxon queen Etheldreda, a little over
twelve hundred years ago, the good queen herself
retiring from her throne to become the abbess of
the new establishment. Soon after the conquest
the Norman ecclesiastics who obtained control of
the property, began the erection of the present
cathedral, one of the largest in England, and now
nearly eight hundred years old. It was originally a pure Norman structure, very massive and
imposing. Early in the fourteenth century the
central tower which had been overloaded with a
tall spire, fell with a crash and destroyed in its
fall the choir or eastern end of the structure.
This was then rebuilt in the Decorated Gothic
style of the period, of which it is one of the most
beautiful specimens to be found. Where the
central tower formerly stood a large octagon was
constructed, with a wooden vaulted roof surmounted by an immense lantern, the whole forming something entirely unique in Gothic architecture, and, now that it has been fully restored
and redecorated, a work of exceeding beauty.
At a later period chapels were added to the
cathedral in the Perpendicular Gothic style, so

that the building to-day illustrates every form
of architecture from the earliest Norman to the
latest Gothic, which makes it a peculiarly interesting edifice.

Dean Merivale, the eminent historian, is the
dean of the cathedral. I caught a glimpse of him
in the cathedral library poring over the old
books, a fine, healthy, but intellectual looking
old gentleman. Services are held in the cathedral at ten and four o'clock every day, and the
music is very superior.

The cathedral is surrounded by an extensive
park filled with beautiful shade trees, and around
and overlooking the park are the various subordinate buildings connected with the cathedral, as
the dean's residence, the residences of some of
the canons, the school attached to the establishment, the muniment room, vergers' residences,
etc., all very old and picturesque, and all originally part of the old monastic establishment
founded by Etheldreda.

Lying entirely around the cathedral precincts
is the city—a clean, rather pretty place of eight
thousand inhabitants, with little or no trade
beyond what the cathedral creates. The houses
are brick, usually two stories high, and mostly
of the poorer class, with many a pretty garden
and a noticeably rustic air.

The hotel we put up at is called the Lamb Inn.

ELY CATHEDRAL, ENGLAND.

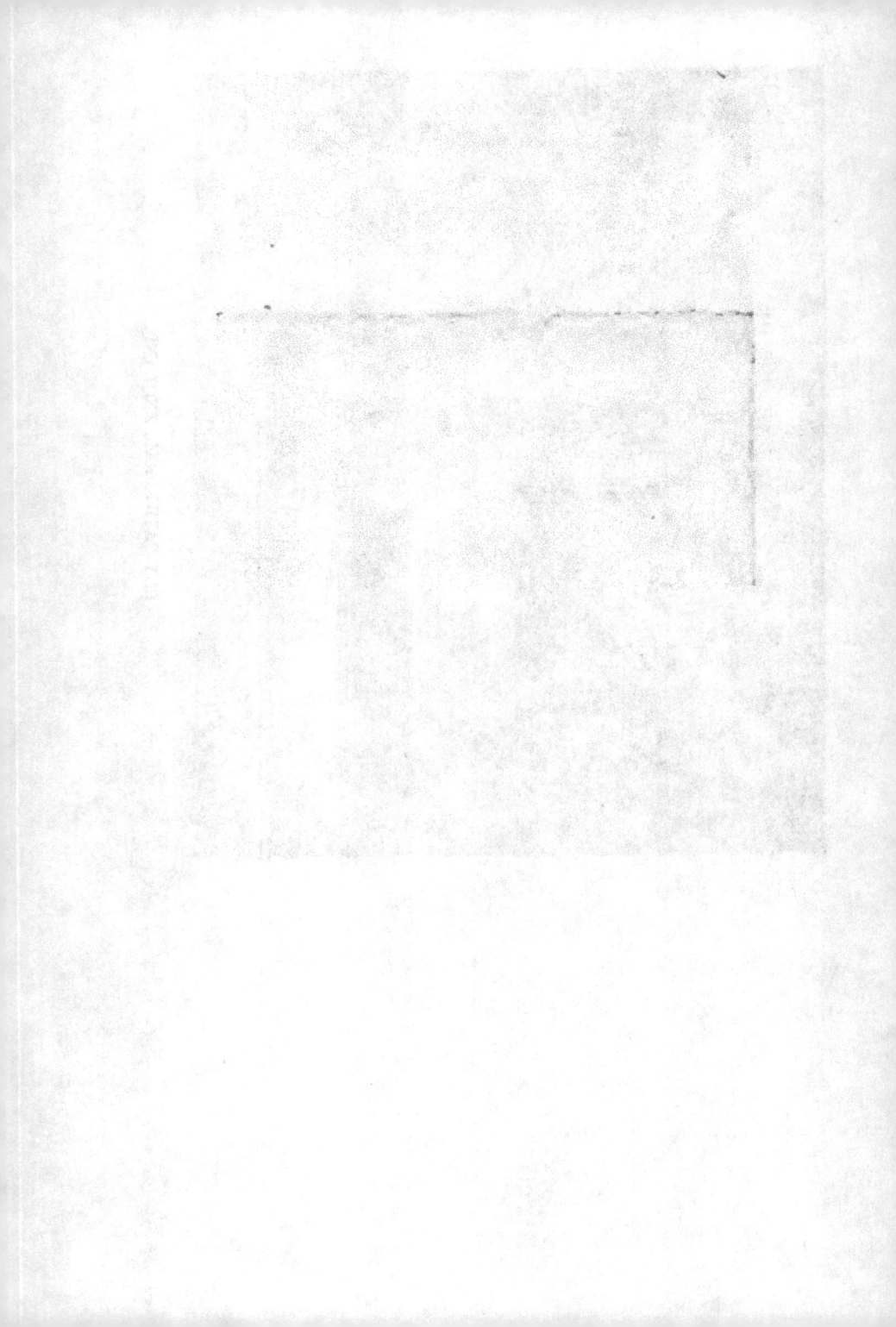

The entrance hall is paved with flag stones. A genial landlady and a ponderous theological looking waiter receive us. We partake of a nicely cooked dinner of mutton cutlets, hot and tender, American cheese, bitter ale, and gooseberry pie with cream—everything clean and nice. For supper, or tea as it is called, we have tea, toast and butter, the teapot and cups and saucers being brought in on a tray and set before the lady of the party who presides at the table just as she would at her own house. The coffee-room, in which the meals are served, is a pleasant home-like room, Brussels carpet, curtained windows and good engravings on the walls. The chambers are of good size but unpretending, and scrupulously neat and clean. Mine is furnished with an old-fashioned, carved mahogany, four-posted bedstead, hung with white curtains. There are lace curtains on the window and the dressing table is hung with a white vallance. A print of John the Baptist after Murillo, the original in the Royal Museum at Madrid, adorns the wall, and the religious leanings of the country stand out in a card over the mantle-piece, reading "Believe in the Lord Jesus Christ and thou shalt be saved." The English hotels contrast with the American in being less pretentious and more home-like, greater attention being given to little comforts and elegancies. But to my mission.

I find there are two parishes in Ely, in each of which records of christenings, marriages and burials have been kept for over three hundred years. The keeping of such records was made imperative by law in Queen Elizabeth's reign. I apply to the rectors of the respective parishes for permission to examine the registers, and rather hesitatingly am accorded the same, for the records are jealously guarded and can only be seen in the presence of the rector or one of his curates. We proceed to the parish church, and enter the gloomy little vestry all hung around with surplices and stoles. An old-fashioned iron "strong box" is opened and a series of long, musty, parchment covered books is brought out. They are of different sizes and shapes and have been kept with varying degrees of neatness, correctness and legibility, but in all the leaves are of parchment, the one side yellow and greasy, the other white and dry like paper. I begin back about a century, and soon find the record of the burial of Susannah, the mother of the first Scripps to settle in the new world, but the name is spelled Scrips. Then I come to the births of other members of the family, with whose existence and dates I was before acquainted, all still spelled with a single p. The baptisms are very numerous, but infantile deaths almost equally so, and I begin to see how it was that, prior to the present enlightened cen-

tury, population in England increased so slowly.
Bad ventilation, ignorant medical treatment
and other causes, carried off in childhood—I
might almost confine it to babyhood—fully three-
fourths of all the children brought into the world.
Prior to 1699 the handwriting of the registers
assumes a sort of text character, difficult at first
to read. The letter c takes the form of a small
cross easily mistaken for a t, and a person casu-
ally opening the registers at this period would
easily mistake the name Scrips for Strips, Scott
for Stott, etc. During the period of the Commonwealth it was clear that the family were puritans,
and no doubt approved the taking off of Charles
I., for the Roundhead names Moses and Faith
appeared. In 1633, during the lifetime of two
generations of Thomases, the name suffered an
important transmutation. Prior to that year it
had been written Crips. How naturally it became corrupted to Scrips, will be seen by attempt-
ing to repeat quickly the name Thomas Crips,
and it was while the principal head of the family
bore the name Thomas that the change in writing
the surname occurred. The change probably
occurred with the incoming of a new rector or
clerk, who wrote the name from sound. It was
made so abruptly that some infants who a few
months before had been baptized as Cripses, were
buried just after as Scripses. The change, the

result purely of ignorance or carelessness, illustrates the transmutations that have no doubt taken place in hosts of other surnames.

The registers of Trinity parish, Ely, were generally well kept, and, considering their age, have been remarkably well preserved, but back of the year 1600 the writing becomes small and close, and more difficult of deciphering, and having accomplished what I desired, viz., the establishing of the origin of the name, I there concluded my researches. From other sources I satisfied myself that the first to spell his name with two p's was one William Scripps, about 1757, who, by the way, was a builder and had an important part in the reconstruction of the lantern of the cathedral.

At an early period the abbots, and later the bishops of Ely, had conferred upon them by royal charter an autocratic civil jurisdiction over the territory known as the Isle of Ely. No other law but their mandates existed, and they exercised a sway as absolute even as that of the Czar of Russia. A dwelling house was pointed out to me, which was formerly the jail in which their prisoners were confined, and, as an old gentleman of antiquarian tastes who rendered me valuable services in my investigations, remarked, the bishops appointed both judges and executioners. That they wielded their power of life and death

with a sturdy hand is apparent from a tablet on
the exterior wall of St. Mary's church, which
reads thus :

> Here lye Interred in one grave
> the Bodies of
> WILLIAM BEAMISS,
> GEORGE CROW,
> JOHN DENNIS,
> ISAAC HARLEY
> and
> THOMAS SOUTH,
> Who were all executed at Ely on the 28th Day of June, 1816,
> having been convicted at the special assizes holden
> there of divers Robberies during the Riots
> at Ely and Littleport in the month
> of May in that year.
> May their awful fate be a warning to others.

This civil power of the Bishop of Ely continued
down to 1836, when it was abolished by act of
parliament.

Upon returning to London I visited the college
of Heralds, a sort of record office of genealogies
and coats of arms. It is a quiet, old-fashioned,
highly respectable office in the heart of the city.
A fee of five shillings is charged for a search,
and an expert clerk then refers to indexes and
records filling thousands of volumes ranged on
shelves in an inner room. Here I simply ascertain
that the names Cripps and Crisp are identical in
their origin, that the family was originally located
in the south-eastern counties of England, and

that they boasted a coat of arms as far back as 1482—ten years before the discovery of America.

Thence I sought the government Record office in Fetter Lane, which is open free to the public, and where by running over indexes I discovered reference to a charter of some kind granted to one Roger Crisp, by King John, in 1199. Satisfied with this indication of antiquity, I went no further with my investigations.

CHAPTER XXXII.

THE ENGLISH CATHEDRALS, THEIR OFFICERS, SERVICES AND
ARCHITECTURE—THE RELIGIOUS CONDITION OF ENGLAND—
THE HIGH AND LOW CHURCH CONTROVERSY.

A CATHEDRAL is a bishop's church, and there is properly, of course, one cathedral to each diocese. A cathedral is usually very much larger than an ordinary parish church. Services in the English cathedrals are held regularly twice every day throughout the year, and are invariably choral, the singing being done by a dozen or twenty men and boys, wearing white surplices. The prayers are intoned, or chanted on a single note. Nothing is read but the lessons, all the rest of the service being musically rendered. The effect of an English cathedral service is very beautiful.

The clergyman at the head of a cathedral establishment is called a dean, and his assistants, usually four in number, are denominated canons. The director of the music is known as the precentor and is always a clergyman in orders. The burden of the daily services devolves on two subordinate ministers, known as minor canons. The dean of a cathedral is usually a man of some emi-

nence in literature or theology, the comfortable
salary with the comparatively insignificant duties,
rendering the position one peculiarly favorable to
the prosecution of study and research. Many of
the most famous writers and scholars of recent
times have been the deans of cathedral churches,
as, for instance, Dean Milman of St. Paul's, Dean
Alford of Canterbury, Dean Stanley of Westminster, Dean Trench of Dublin, Dean Merivale
of Ely, Dean Howson of Chester, and many
others. The canons are usually clergymen of
eminence or professors in the universities, as
Canon Farrar and Canon Liddon, for example,
their cathedral duties requiring their attendance
but perhaps a dozen times a year each. Often
they are at the same time rectors of parish
churches. The entire staff of a cathedral, including the chorister boys and vergers or sextons,
usually numbers twenty-five or thirty persons or
more. These are all paid from the endowments
of the church, which are usually quite ample.

Most of the cathedral churches of England were
formerly abbey churches, but they are by no
means an indication of the number of abbeys that
existed before the reformation. Very many of
these abbeys are now mere ruins and many more
are preserved as parish churches. An abbey in
mediæval times was a community of monks identical with what we now denominate a monastery.

Its chief officer was an abbot. The abbeys of England prior to the sixteenth century became very rich and much of their wealth was devoted to the erection of large and beautiful churches in connection with their establishments. No where was more beautiful and interesting architecture developed than by these English abbey monks.

Their churches were invariably cruciform or cross-shaped, the head of the cross always pointing to the east and the long arm consequently to the west. The transverse members pointing respectively to the north and south are known respectively as the north and south transepts. The principal front or façade is always at the west end, and the portion of the building west of the transepts is called the nave. That portion east of the transepts is the choir and corresponds to the chancel of a parish church. On either side of the nave, transepts and choir are aisles, usually of a lesser height. Under the choir there is often a cellar or basement called the crypt and which is often fitted up for worship. The buildings are invariably of stone, and usually a stone vaulting, relieved by stone ribs or groins, forms the ceiling. In Cologne Cathedral this vaulting is one hundred and fifty feet above the pavement, but in the English cathedrals from sixty to one hundred feet is the usual height. The space from one column to another is called a bay.

In the angle formed by the nave and one of the transepts are usually situated the Cloisters. The cloisters of an abbey or cathedral are a covered walk surrounding an open square, and were in the olden time the place of exercise and recreation of the monks. They form a quadrangle perhaps two or three hundred feet square. The open space in the center forms either a garden or lawn, or is used for burial purposes. The covered ambulatory or arcade is perhaps twelve or fifteen feet wide and about the same in height. It is paved with stone and has stone vaultings overhead. On one side is a blank wall, often used for memorial tablets, and stone benches; on the other an open arcade or range of windows with mullions but no glass. Sometimes the cloisters also contain stone writing desks, at which the monks could sit to write their letters. The cloisters are always quiet, secluded places, and pleasant resorts for study and reflection.

In the angle formed by the choir and one of the transepts usually stands the Chapter House. This was originally the hall in which the monks gathered for the transaction of the business of their abbey. It is generally round or polygonal in form, with a column in the center to support the stone vaulted ceiling, and with stone seats all around the sides. The chapter houses are often very beautiful pieces of architectural work.

Prominent among the other monastic buildings
is the Refectory or dining room of the monks.
This is usually a large rectangular hall with timber roof.   On one side is a niche in the wall,
forming a sort of stone pulpit, in which it used to
be the practice for one of the brothers to read
aloud from the Lives of the Saints, or some other
holy book, while the rest in silence ate their meals.
Another principal hall is the Hospitium or guest
chamber, in which visitors to the abbey were
lodged.

Most cathedrals have an extension of the choir
eastward, known as the Lady Chapel, from its
being dedicated to the Virgin Mary.

The earliest existing churches were built in the
eleventh century, and in the style known as
Norman.   They are very massive, but generally
of rude workmanship.   The predominating features of the Norman style are round columns
with very simple capitals, semi-circular arches,
and zigzag mouldings.   Very few of the Norman
churches have vaulted ceilings, the skill of the
period being hardly equal to their execution.
Perhaps in a majority of the old churches and
cathedrals of England more or less Norman work
is found.   Durham Cathedral presents one of the
best specimens of Norman work.

About the close of the thirteenth century the
Norman gave way to the Early English Gothic,

a simple, and even to this day a very beautiful style. In this the windows and arches are narrow and sharply pointed. The windows are without tracery, and there is very little ornamental stone work in the way of sculptured foliage or figures. The columns of this period are clustered—usually a large round pillar of common stone in the center, encircled by four or more smaller shafts of polished brown marble. Very often a church is seen, begun in the Norman style and finished in the Early English, the transition from one style to the other taking place during the progress of erection. The Early English is as light and graceful as the Norman is heavy and uncouth. Salisbury, Lincoln and Worcester cathedrals are good illustrations.

A century later English church architecture developed into what is known as the Decorated period. In this the windows are much enlarged, and are filled with elaborate tracery of stone work, and the capitals of the columns, the brackets and the bosses are richly sculptured. The severe plainness of the Early English is lost, but the ornamentation is not carried to excess as it was at a still later period. This is regarded as the golden age of Gothic architecture and many beautiful specimens are found, notably in the choirs of Ely and Lincoln cathedrals.

Still later the rage for ornament so overloaded

the churches that the more graceful forms of the earlier period were lost in excess of decoration. The arches became wider and flatter, the columns degenerated into piers, with the mouldings of the arches simply continued to the floor, and the vaulted ceilings were made to hang all over with stalactite-like pendants of stone. This is known as the Perpendicular period, and of all it is most open to criticism, though displaying wonderful skill in construction. The best specimen of this age is Henry VII.'s chapel connected with Westminster Abbey.

Within the past thirty or forty years there has been a great rage in England for restoring the old cathedrals, most of which had become almost ruinous with age and decay. Sir Gilbert Scott was of all the architects most prominent in this work. The weather-worn stones are removed and others substituted for them, and where, by the vandalism of the sixteenth and seventeenth centuries, rich ornamental work has been destroyed or incongruous repairs or alterations been made, the whole is put back to the condition of its highest perfection. The old cathedrals are thus all made to look like new churches and have been made very beautiful and artistic, though deprived of the charm of antiquity they formerly possessed.

England is essentially a religious country, as is evidenced by the quiet, orderly sabbaths, the

crowded churches, the deep interest that everyone seems to take in church matters, the orderly
and attentive crowds that gather around the
street preachers, the earnest zeal of the Salvation
Army followers, the bibles and religious books
that are so numerously found in the hotels and
railway stations, the demand for religious tracts
that makes their hawking on the public streets a
possibility, and, generally, by the respect that in
all quarters is shown to sacred things. The religious energy of the country is found at least in
full share in the established church. This is,
perhaps, the more remarkable, as the church of
England suffers from bitter internal dissension,
though it may still be possible that its apparent
vitality is in some sort a result of the earnest
rivalry between the contending high and low
church factions. The dissension, which began
nearly half a century ago, is still far from its cul-
mination. The high church party is a party of
reaction. It deems that at the Reformation the
work of reform was overdone, and that a great
deal that was harmless and even good in the old
Catholic church was done away by the excessive
zeal of the times, just as the beautiful architecture of the churches was ruthlessly marred and
defaced. With the restoration of the churches
came the desire to restore also all that was good
and beautiful in the ancient worship. A more

decorous respect for the church as a sacred place began to be inculcated, the beautiful harmonies of a choral service were revived, and by various little rites and observances it was sought to impress the religious sensibilities. All this the low church party have strongly condemned, as tending to an ultimate return to the bosom of the Roman church.

The low church is radically protestant, and will ally itself with dissenters far sooner than with the faction of the church of England that it regards as little better than renegade and apostate. Of course there are all grades of sentiment and feeling in both parties, from the broad churchman, who will concede liberally, even in points of doctrine, to preserve the unity of the church, up to the extremist who will prefer its disruption by far, to a church in which his views are not in the ascendant. All seem to feel that the struggle must some day be brought to a final issue, and the most prodigious exertions are being put forth on each side to create for that day a preponderance of strength and influence that shall decide it in its own favor. And hence it comes about that an amount of missionary work is being done in England such as probably was never before known. The high church party fills up its churches by the most beautiful and impressive musical service that perhaps the world has ever known, while, it furnishes employment for the more active minds in the duties and self-sacrifices, the faithful observance of which it earnestly teaches. That it reaches a very large number who could not be reached by mere intellectual argument is certain, and I cannot doubt that a good work is being done, for I hold that it is better far for one to cross himself before partaking of a meal, as is now common with the extreme section of the high church party, than to have no thought at all of the Giver of all Good in connection therewith.

Meanwhile the pulpits of the low church are being filled with intellectually strong and earnest evangelical men, who by their preaching powers draw large audiences, and who doubtless by their intelligent presentation of religious truths exert a great influence with the more thoughtful minds. Of course all the good preaching is not on the low church side, but practically that wing leans most heavily on the pulpit, as the other side does on the choir stalls. As there is nothing seriously objectionable in a musical service, it is not uncommon for the low church advocates to steal the thunder of their opponents by themselves employing more or less fully the choral service. In one church of well recognized evangelical standing, St. Martin's, Birmingham, a surpliced choir leads the devotions. The rector, Dr. Wilkinson, re-

frains from intoning the prayers, but the respon-
ses are in full choral style. The sermons are such
as would thoroughly please a Presbyterian or
Methodist hearer. At some other churches the
musical innovation is confined to the chanting of
the psalter, which was always formerly read
responsively, as in this country. The amount of
music in the service is hence in itself no criterion
of the position of the church on the great question under agitation. The eastward position
assumed in reciting the Apostle's Creed is the
first distinguishing indication of ritualistic leanings. Where such eastward position is not
assumed it may be taken for granted that the
church is evangelically inclined, even though the
whole service be musical.

There is nothing so beautiful as a well-conduct-
ed cathedral service in the Church of England.
No Roman Catholic services that it has been my
fortune to hear have possessed half the simple
beauty of the English service, musically rendered.

It seems strange that, while the Protestant
Episcopal church of the United States is essentially more high church in its views and practices
than even the conservative element in the church
of England, the choral service, which is not incon-
sistent with English evangelicism, should be so
utterly neglected here.

It only remains to add that the Queen, who by

the constitution is the head of the church, is very properly a broad church woman, sympathizing with neither extreme.   It is true some pretend to believe that her majesty was more or less impregnated with the German rationalistic views of her husband, the late Prince Albert, and that hence arises her indifference.   But in this they probably misrepresent her.   Her children make no disguise of their ritualistic preferences, and the Prince and Princess of Wales are frequent attendants at All Saints, Margaret street, one of the leading ritualistic churches of London.

While position on church affairs is in no wise conterminous with party politics, Mr. Gladstone is the *bete noir* of the low church radicals.   A Romanist in disguise, bent on the subversion of the Church of England, is what they delight to call him, on account of the many concessions he has made in the direction of religious toleration. Meanwhile the high churchmen are equally dissatisfied with the amount of interference with church matters that a secular parliament has indulged in, and do not hesitate to say that they would welcome disestablishment as a relief from such control.

Church rates, or the tax for the support of the church, having been abolished a few years since, the town churches are now dependent on the pew rents for their maintenance.   In the rural districts, however, the tithing system is still continued, by which the vicar may claim and recover by process of law a certain proportion, assumed to be a tenth, of the produce of all agricultural lands in his parish, and on these tithes the country parson grows fat in the midst of his handful of parishioners, while his metropolitan brother has to depend on his popularity alone for a decent maintenance.

The immediate management of the affairs of each parish devolves on the vestry. In the newer parishes, in which the vestry has no civil powers, that body is usually elected by the pew holders. In the old parishes, which, as the reader is aware, are civil subdivisions, the vestry has all the powers that a town meeting enjoys in this country. It manages the poor, the street paving and cleaning, the levying and collecting of taxes, etc. The mode of election of vestrymen in this case is not uniform, but one common method is for the vestry to elect each year a church warden inside or outside their own number, the vestry itself being composed of all the surviving ex-wardens, who may still be residents of the parish. It will be seen how great power is thus lodged in what is practically a close corporation, but such is the general sense of responsibility of Englishmen in public life, that it is rare that there is any abuse of the powers enjoyed.

CHAPTER XXXIII.

THE SUMMER ASPECT OF ENGLAND—WINDSOR CASTLE—THE
ALBERT MEMORIAL CHAPEL—BATH AND ITS ABBEY.

WE leave London via the Great Western
Railway, one of the pioneer lines of the
country, and the broadest gauge (seven
feet) ever constructed in any country. The main
line extends from London to Bristol, one hundred
and twenty miles, and the express trains make
the distance in two hours and thirty-six minutes,
including a stoppage of ten minutes at Swindon
for refreshments—a speed equal to fifty miles an
hour.

A ride through England in June or July is
most enchanting. The country is generally more
rolling than ours, and in cultivated portions there
are twenty trees where there is one in our country. The effect is to add greatly to the beauty of
the scenery. Trees line every roadway and every
field, and are often scattered promiscuously
through the fields. No doubt much land is
wasted by their shade, but it is a question if this
be not more than made up by the modification
they effect in the climate, and the increased fruit-
fulness of the remaining portions of the land.

Our American farmers should cultivate more trees. on their farms. A thousand years' experience has taught England that it pays. Besides the beautiful foliage, the country is full of picturesque old farm-houses with thatched roofs, with here and there the square tower of an old church peeping up through the trees. The little, narrow, winding country roads, so charmingly shaded, are also exceedingly pretty. We waste too much land in our American country roads. In England twenty-five or thirty feet suffices, and they have splendid roads, too.

Twenty miles from London we reach Windsor Castle, the principal residence of the Queen. It was built by Edward III. about the middle of the fourteenth century, and thoroughly restored by George IV. in the early part of the present century. It is situated on a considerable eminence on the south bank of the Thames, and is surrounded by a park seven miles across and twenty-five in circuit. The royal forest of Windsor adjoins the park, and the entire royal domain is fifty-six miles in circumference. The castle itself, the largest in England, covers seventeen acres. In the center rises the "keep," or great round tower, so familiar in all pictures of Windsor. The Queen's private apartments are confined to one tower situated at the southeastern corner of the castle, and commanding a most beautiful view

of the park and surrounding country. Adjoining
the private apartments of Her Majesty are the
state apartments.

As we enter the castle we first pass through a
large, irregular shaped court-yard, with the royal
chapel of St. George on one side, barracks for the
soldiers and houses for the castle attendants on
the other, and the great round tower at the
farther end. Beyond this is a second court-yard
on the crest of the hill, surrounded by the private
and state apartments above mentioned, When
the Queen is not at Windsor all the principal
buildings are thrown open to the public. We
first ascend to the summit of the round tower,
from which, in clear weather, the dome of St.
Paul's and the clock tower of Westminster palace
are distinctly visible, the tower commanding a
view of about twenty-five miles in every direction.
To the south we look up the Long Walk, a carriage drive of three miles leading directly away
from the castle through the park, with a bronze
statue of George III. at its farther extremity.
To the west is Clewer, the principal seat of an
important Protestant sisterhood resembling the
Catholic Sisters of Mercy of our own country.
Here is a church said to be twelve hundred years
old, and the oldest but one in England. The
churchyard where Gray's Elegy was written, and
the home of William Penn, are also objects of

interest within the range of vision. Just under the castle, to the north, lies Eton, with its famous college. The whole scene on a fine day is very beautiful.

St. George's Chapel, the chapel of the castle, is a large cruciform structure, almost worthy of being a cathedral. It is built in the late or Tudor Gothic style, with a beautiful stone vaulting ornamented with what is known as fan tracery. The nave contains a number of tombs, and an elaborate monument by the sculptor Chantrey to the memory of the popular Princess Charlotte, daughter of George IV. Daily services are held in the chapel, just as in a cathedral. Adjoining St. George's Chapel on the east is a smaller Gothic chapel, long known as Wolsey's Chapel. In the crypt under it the royal family for several generations past have been buried, instead of in Westminster Abbey. Within a few years the Queen has taken in hand the restoration and adornment of this chapel, as a memorial to her deceased husband, Prince Albert, and has changed the name to the Albert Memorial Chapel. It is certainly one of the most beautiful buildings I saw in all my travels. The stone ceiling is rich with gilding and mosaic, the floor of inlaid marbles is polished like a mirror, the windows are filled with the richest stained glass, and the walls are covered with etchings in marble, reliefs, medallions, mosaics and busts in elegant profusion. The large etched pictures are unique. Various light shades of marble are used for a groundwork, something after the manner of Florentine mosaics, and the pictures are then brought out strongly by black lines indelibly burned into the substance of the marble, after which the whole is highly polished. By this means both drawing and shading are very perfect, and the effect is novel and pleasing. At the upper end of the chapel stands an elaborate monument to the Prince Consort, though his remains are really interred at Frogmore, a locality in the royal park, a short distance outside the castle.

We continue our journey, and one hundred and eight miles west of London, we reach the city of Bath, a place of about fifty-two thousand inhabitants, beautifully situated on the hills skirting the river Avon. For nearly two thousand years Bath has been famous for its mineral springs and the high curative powers of its waters. In the last century it was to England what Saratoga is to the United States, the center of gaiety and fashion. But other places have more or less usurped, or at least divided its popularity, and Bath to-day looks regretfully back on the good old times of the past. It presents still rather an aristocratic air, from all the buildings being of dressed stone. In the center of the town is the

Pump Room, a large and stately hall where people gather to lounge away the time and drink the waters. Just behind the Pump Room is the Abbey church, to the stranger the chief object of interest in the place. The abbey was built some three hundred and fifty years ago, and was finished just in time to be made a protestant church by the Reformation. It is a fine structure of the Tudor style with ceiling of fan tracery all in stone. Its west front is curiously ornamented. On either side of the main doorway are carved in the stone walls two ladders extending quite to the roof, with angels climbing their rounds, the whole being intended to represent Jacob's dream at Bethel. Probably nowhere else is there so large a church so filled with memorial tablets. The walls up to the level of the windows are completely covered with them. The reason probably is, that Bath being a resort for invalids of the wealthier and more aristocratic class, a great many people of social position have died and been buried there. Judging from the inscriptions, no other place can boast such a lot of truly good people as have made it a point to die in Bath. Some of the tablets date back to the beginning of the seventeenth century, and many are very quaint in their expression. One speaks of the deceased in large capitals as "An excellent person." Another, dated 1698, has a stanza of poetry appended, "By Mr. Dryden." The spelling also is very eccentric, as "sonn" for son, "citty" for city, etc. Among the vast number of tablets, I stumbled upon that of the famous Beau Nash, the accomplished gentleman whose life business it was to lead the fashion at Bath, and who supported himself in luxury through a long career by his graceful manners alone. His epitaph reads:

Adeste O Cives, adeste lugentes
Hic silent leges
RICARDI NASH, armig:
Nihil amplius imperantis
Qui diu utilissime
Assumptus Bathoniæ
Elegantiæ arbiter
Eheu!
Morti (ultimo designatori)
Haud indecore succubuit
Ann Dom 1761. Æt suæ 87.
Beatus ille qui sibi imperiosus.

If social virtues make remembrance dear,
  Or manners pure on decent rule depend,
To his remains consign one grateful tear,
  Of youth the guardian and of All the friend.
Now sleeps Dominion here, no Bounty flows,
  Nor more avails the festive scene to grace:
Beneath that hand which no discernment shows,
  Untaught to honor or distinguish grace.—H. H.

But very much more interesting is the monument to Malthus, the political economist whose

advanced ideas of social science so shocked the
good people of England half a century ago.
It reads thus :

Sacred to the memory

Of the Rev. Thomas Robert Malthus, long known to the lettered
world by his admirable **writings on** the social branches
of political economy, **particularly by his**

Essay on Population.

One of the best **men and** truest philosophers of any age **or** country.

Raised by native **dignity of mind above** the misrepresentations
of the ignorant **and the** neglect of the great

He lived **a serene and happy life,** devoted to the pursuit and
communication of truth.

Supported by a firm but calm conviction of the usefulness of
his labors,

Content with the approbation **of the** wise and good.

His writings will be a lasting monument of the extent and **correctness** of his understanding.

The spotless integrity **of his** principles,

The equity and candour of his nature,

His sweetness of temper, urbanity of manners and **tenderness**
of heart,

His benevolence and his piety,

Are the still dearer recollections of his family and friends.

Born Feb. 14, 1766.   Died 29 Dec., 1834.

In another place is this tablet to an American :

Sacred

To the Honorable William Bingham, **a native and** senator **of the**
United States of America, **where his** knowledge of the
interests of his country and his **zeal for their**
advancement, the **marks of** patriotism
equally active and enlightened,
will be long and gratefully
remembered.

He died in this place on the 7th of Feb., 1804, aged 49 years.

22

Bath has a very pleasant park opened by the Princess Victoria before she became queen, and which is ornamented with a statue of her.

Lovers of Pickwick will recall Mr. Sam Weller's experiences at this celebrated place, and particularly his invitation to join the "select footmen of Bath" in partaking of a "friendly swarry consisting of a boiled leg of mutton," and how ignominiously the entertainment wound up.

CHAPTER XXXIV.

ONE of the most delightful experiences of my
whole trip was a two days' ramble in one of
the most beautiful and interesting portions
of England, viz., its southern tier of counties.
Let the reader glance at a map of England. The
long peninsula which forms its southwestern corner constitutes the county of Cornwall. East of
Cornwall, and extending from the English Channel on the south to the Bristol Channel on the
north, lies Devonshire. East of Devon, and lying
along the southern shore of the island, comes
Dorsetshire ; and north of Dorsetshire, Wiltshire,
of which Salisbury is the capital. Still east of
Dorset and Wilts, as they are popularly called,
lies Hampshire.

Our journey was first to Exeter, the capital of
Devon, and the principal scene of Judge Jeffreys'
atrocious cruelties in the reign of James II., when
he sent so many to the gallows without law or
justice that his holdings of court are known as
the Bloody Assizes. Exeter is now a quiet place

of about forty thousand inhabitants, and is
famous chiefly for its cathedral, though its location on the little river Exe, with a prospect of
green hills in every direction, is exceedingly beautiful. The oldest portions of the cathedral date
from the twelfth century, and are of Norman
architecture. About the middle of the thirteenth
century the church began to be rebuilt in the
Gothic style, and the two great Norman towers
were utilized as transepts—the only example in
England, I believe, where the towers are so placed.
The cathedral is not a large one, being only three
hundred and eighty-seven feet long, but it is an
imposing old structure, and quite worth a visit.
It was concerning the reredos or altar-piece of
this church, some years ago, that a memorable
litigation arose—one of the first appeals to law in
the famous dissensions between the high and low
church parties.

A short ride from Exeter brings us to Torquay,
a famous watering place and health resort on the
English Channel coast. The town lies on the
side of a rocky. hill, and commands from every
part a beautiful sea view. Just across the bay
(Torbay) is the village of Brixham, where William
of Orange landed in 1688, when he came over
from Holland to pick up the crown which his
father-in-law, James II., had run off and abandoned, the epoch being known as the English

Revolution. A little farther up the bay, and distinctly visible from Torquay, is the glittering dome of the magnificent residence that Isaac M. Singer built for himself when he had acquired his immense fortune in the manufacture and sale of his sewing machines. It was here that he died a few years ago.

We stop for the night at a clean and cozy little inn at Exeter, and bright and early next morning are up and on our way to Winchester, one hundred and eighteen miles distant. Winchester is the county seat, or capital, as they call it, of the county of Hampshire, from which our State of New Hampshire takes its name. To reach it we traverse the counties of Devonshire, Dorsetshire and Wiltshire, and the journey is a most interesting one. The country, particularly in Devonshire, is very beautiful—undulating, well settled, beautifully shaded with trees and hedges, watered with small trout rivers, and full of green lanes, picturesque old thatched and ivy-clad houses, and more picturesque square-towered churches. Devonshire is one of the best agricultural counties of England, and is the original home of the famous Devon cattle. The fields are small, and one wonders that so much land should be wasted in hedge-rows. The trees, from not being crowded, grow very wide-spreading and ornamental, and the whole country has quite the appearance of an immense park.

Soon we pass the town of Honiton, the place where the famous Honiton lace is made, and a little later Axminster, which has given its name to the well known Axminster carpets, the most costly variety usually found in our carpet stores.

In about five hours Winchester is reached. This old-time capital of England is a place of about eighteen thousand inhabitants, with quiet streets lined with old-fashioned two and three-storied houses in great variety of styles. We had but a short time to devote to it, and so hastened to the cathedral, the central object of attraction.

Winchester Cathedral is one of the largest and oldest in England. The first church on the site was built nearly seventeen hundred years ago. This and the succeeding ones were destroyed in the various Saxon and Danish wars, and the present structure was finished in 1093. It was built in the semi-circular-arched Norman style of the day, with walls of great strength, and the towers and transepts, which remain to the present, are to-day the most substantial part of the entire structure. A little more than a century later the choir was rebuilt in the Early English Gothic style, and in 1406 William of Wykeham, Bishop of Winchester, and a famous architect and builder, who was also the founder of New College, Oxford, and Winchester College, altered

the Norman work of the nave into what is known
as the late or Perpendicular Gothic. It was not
a rebuilding, but a substantial alteration, and this
nave, with its Norman skeleton, is consequently
one of the most massive to be found in any
Gothic church.

The cathedral is full of historic associations.
In a carved wooden box—one of several exposed
on the top of the screen that surrounds the
choir—are the remains of Egbert, the first king
of united England, who died A. D. 837, or more
than a thousand years ago. In the rear of
the altar is the tomb of William II., known as
William Rufus, son of the Conqueror, who, it will
be recollected by readers of English history, was
accidentally killed with an arrow while hunting
in the New Forest, near Winchester. In order to
corroborate the fact of this being his tomb the
sarcophagus was opened a few years ago, and
among the bones and gold tinsel of the robe in
which he was buried was found the arrow-head of
iron which had killed him. In the Lady Chapel,
or chapel in the rear of the main altar, Queen
Mary was married to the persecuting Philip II.,
of Spain, and the chair is still seen in which she
sat on the occasion—a chair, by the way, which
no American second-hand dealer would take as a
gift. Adjoining the chair is the tomb of Stephen
Gardiner, bishop of Winchester, the execrated

persecutor of the protestants in Mary's reign.
In the nave is the tomb of Bishop Wykeham, the
builder of the church, with a well preserved effigy
of the great man in marble reclining upon it.   In
the south transept stands a new and beautiful
monument of the late bishop of Winchester,
Samuel Wilberforce, son of the great English
abolitionist and philanthropist, William Wilberforce.   The bishop was a man of wonderful per-
suasive powers, and was popularly known as
Soapy Sam. He was killed in 1873 by being
thrown from his horse. He was widely known as
one of the staunchest supporters of modern ritu-
alism.   In the north aisle we observe a brass
tablet reading:

JANE AUSTEN.

Known to many by her writings, endeared to her family by the
varied charms of her character, and ennobled by christian faith and piety, was born at Steventon,
county of Hants (Hampshire), Dec. 16,
1775, and buried in this cathedral, July 24, 1817.

"She openeth her mouth with wisdom, and in her tongue is the
law of kindness."—Prov. xxxi, v. 26.

Miss Austen was the popular novelist of the
beginning of the present century. Her "Pride
and Prejudice," recently reprinted by the Har-
pers, is a capital story, and a good illustration of
the best style of fiction of her day.

Winchester Cathedral is one of the longest in

England, being five hundred and sixty feet in length inside the walls. Over the altar is a good painting by our Benjamin West, representing the raising of Lazarus. The old oaken stalls and furniture of the choir date from the thirteenth century.

Winchester has always been one of the richest and most desirable dioceses in England, and the story is told of one bishop who, being offered promotion to the archbishopric of Canterbury, the highest position in the English church, declined it, remarking "Canterbury is the greater honor, but Winchester has the deepest manger."

Near the cathedral is Winchester College, one of the famous ancient collegiate schools of England, of which those of Eton, Rugby and Harrow are among the other principal ones. Read Tom Brown's "School Days at Rugby," and a good idea will no doubt be gained of school life at Winchester.

Retracing our journey twenty-five miles we reach Salisbury, whose cathedral ranks as one of the best in England, and boasts the highest spire, its summit being four hundred feet from the pavement. Salisbury Cathedral has few tombs of world-wide celebrities, and fewer historical associations than .Winchester, but it is famous as being the only cathedral in England which is not an architectural patch-work, it having been begun

and (except the spire) completed under one architect. It is very large, being four hundred and
forty-nine feet in interior length and a full half
mile in exterior circuit. It was begun in the year
1220 and completed in 1258, the spire being added
a century later. Although over six hundred old,
it is kept so clean and in such good repair that it
seems quite like a modern church. It is in the
pure Early English Gothic style, with only narrow lancet windows without tracery. The columns, numbering, it is said, as many as there are
hours in the year, are clustered, the smaller ones
being of polished dark marble. The whole is
very symmetrical and elegant, and to any lover
of Gothic architecture well repays a visit.

Before the Reformation a curious custom pre-
vailed in this church. The choir boys annually
elected one of their number a bishop, and he
retained the honor for one year. On one day in
the year the cathedral authorities recognized the
farce, and received the urchin in the cathedral
with episcopal honors. If the lad died during
the year he was buried with all the pomp that
would attend the funeral of a real bishop. Thus
did our ancestors combine play with even the
graver duties of religion. A few years ago, in
making some repairs, the stone effigy which had
at one time ornamented the tomb of one of these
boy bishops was discovered, and it is now to be

seen among the other monuments in the nave of
the church.

The original Salisbury was a mile or two north
of the present city, and the locality is now known
as Old Sarum. It continued to be represented
by two members of parliament down to the period
of the Reform Bill of 1832, even though it had
long been entirely deserted of inhabitants. We
drove past it on our way to Stonehenge.

This is another object of especial interest in this
exceedingly interesting section of country. Just
north of Salisbury is a stretch of a dozen or
twenty miles of open country known as Salisbury
Plain. Who has not heard of Hannah More's
famous tract "The Shepherd of Salisbury Plain?"
This plain is naked of trees and nearly barren,
being composed of a thin turf lying almost immediately upon a vast bed of chalk. It is, however,
being gradually brought under cultivation. The
plain lies several hundred feet above the level of
the city of Salisbury, and is traversed by numerous fine roads. About ten miles north of Salisbury, as the road goes, are the remarkable pre-
historic remains known as Stonehenge, consisting
of a number of immense stones set up on end,
with others lying horizontally on top connecting
one with another. As we approach the locality a
great number of mounds or tumuli are seen scattered about the plain, and the first presumption

is that they have some connection with the stones, but we are assured by those who assume to know that the mounds are the remains of the Roman period, and that the outlines of an entire Roman military camp may be traced in the neighborhood.

Stonehenge stands out on the open plain with neither house, fence nor tree near it. It is surrounded by the remains of a low circular ditch and mound perhaps three hundred feet in diameter. The stones form a circle about one hundred feet across. Each upright stone is planted three or four feet in the ground and stands fifteen or twenty feet above the level of the turf. Each is five or six feet wide and two and-a-half or three thick, and they stand perhaps three feet apart in the clear. The connecting stones above may be a yard square and eight or ten feet long. The upright stones have each rude tenons on their upper ends about the size and shape of inverted three gallon kettles, and the transverse stones have corresponding mortises to receive them. Originally there was a complete circle of these upright and connected stones, but not more than half of them still remain in position. The rest lie prostrate on the ground in a more or less broken state. Within this outer circle is a second, composed of smaller stones set up like huge posts. Then comes another circle of large stones, with connecting lintels like the first, and

then another circle of smaller like the second,
thus making four in all. The two inner circles
are less perfect than the outer, and it is claimed
that they were intended to be of horseshoe rather
than circular shape, having the openings toward
the east. In front of this assumed opening, and
perhaps two hundred feet distant, is a large,
upright, single stone, rather pointed at its summit, to which significance is attached by archæologists. Such is Stonehenge as I saw it. Who
built it, when, and for what purpose, has always
been a profound mystery. The mystery is intensified when one views the immense blocks, estimated to weigh from fifteen to forty-five tons each,
that compose it, and reflects on the very rude
appliances that in the age of its construction
must have been available for the conveyance and
hoisting of such masses. And the wonder still
increases when we learn that there is no stone of
the kind in the vicinity, and of some of the pieces
none is known to exist in England. I am sorry
to say the digging that has been done about the
base of some of these stones, with the effects of
the frosts of many centuries of winters, is gradually leveling the structure with the ground. One
of the finest uprights in the inner circle leans ten
and-a-half feet from the perpendicular, and may
topple over at any time. Of course the presump-

tion is that Stonehenge is a Druidical temple—a sort of cathedral, perhaps, of the remotest period of England's antiquity.

We spend the night at Salisbury, and take an early train to Bath, and thence to Bristol, reaching the latter place after a most charming ride in time for a late breakfast.

CHAPTER XXXV.

BRISTOL, one hundred and twenty miles west of London, was formerly the second city in the kingdom. It now boasts about two hundred and forty thousand inhabitants. It is situated on the river Avon, a tributary of the Severn, at a point where the former river makes an abrupt turn in its course and enters a rocky defile, through which it flows northward six miles to its debouchure. In old times Bristol was a great commercial city, and largely interested in the West India trade. It was the first port in Europe to establish steam communication with America, but lost its advantages by the difficult navigation of its river and the superior dock facilities of Liverpool. In late years it has been making an effort to regain its commercial ascendency. Over $3,000,000 has been expended in deepening and straightening the river, and $3,500,000 more in constructing a commodious dockyard and warehouses at the mouth of the river, and a railroad connecting the same with the city. Simultaneously with these improvements, two lines of steamships, the Great Western and City of Bristol lines, have been established between Bristol and New York, and both are understood to be doing a profitable business, and to be gradually extending their operations. Bristol is several hours nearer New York than Liverpool, and with her present excellent facilities there is no reason why she should not become a great entrepot for American trade.

As the center of West India traffic, Bristol became a great sugar mart, and engaged heavily in the manufacture of refined sugars, but this trade has been absolutely ruined by French competition. England maintains a free trade system; France, like our own country, cherishes protection to her manufactures. In order to encourage the manufacture of sugar, the French government pays a bounty on every pound exported to England. The result is, loaf sugar is sold in England at about eight cents a pound, while in France the same cannot be bought for less than twelve cents. This pernicious interference with the natural laws of trade has been death to the sugar interests throughout England, but the people at large have been immensely the gainers by it, saving, as they do, two or three cents on every pound of sugar they consume. Meanwhile the French people pay the full value of the article for what they use, and moreover are taxed heavily to enable the English consumers to buy so much more cheaply than they do themselves. Thus, while free trade, as in England, may be injurious to the few, it is money in the pockets of the community at large; and while, as in France, protection no doubt benefits the few manufacturers, all the advantage they gain has to be paid for ultimately by the great body of tax payers and home consumers.

But while Bristol has lost her sugar refineries, she has built up very extensive interests in the manufacture of soap, leather, boots and shoes, and clothing. The city is spreading rapidly, and has all the outward signs of business prosperity.

Besides the improvement of the harbor, important public works have recently been carried out in the opening of new and broad thoroughfares in various parts of the city where formerly the traffic was confined to narrow, crooked streets, and a very complete system of street railways has been established. These railways, by the way, employ boys of fourteen and sixteen as conductors, in place of men, and by a system of checks find it quite' satisfactory, and much more economical.

Bristol is famous for many antiquities and historic associations. In the suburb of Clifton is still to be seen a well-defined Roman camp, probably nineteen centuries old.   In William the Conqueror's time there was a castle here, but no vestige of it now remains.   The chapter house of the cathedral, however, and a gateway to the once existing abbey of St. Augustine, date back to the Norman period.   So does the parish church of St. James, the main portion of which dates from the beginning of the twelfth century.   Of the same period is the curious old Temple church, erected in 1145 for the fraternity of Knights Templar, and noticeable for its tower, which leans five feet from the perpendicular.   In the rebellion of 1642 Bristol played an important part, her sympathies being with the parliamentary party and against King Charles I., and the remains of a fort then built on Brandon Hill are still visible.   Queen's Square is famous as the scene of a great riot in 1831, growing out of the reform bill agitation, in which all the buildings on two sides of the square, the Bishop's palace, and the various prisons of the city, were burned.   It cost the tax payers of Bristol about $350,000 to make good the losses of the two days' rioting.   Four of the rioters were hanged, and about eighty more transported.

   In Bristol William Tyndale, the translator of the bible, preached, and here some of his descendants still reside.   To Tyndale we owe much of the literary beauty of our English version of the bible, his translation having been largely followed by subsequent revisers. He met his death in Belgium, in 1536, under orders from the Emperor Charles V., being first strangled, and his body afterwards burned.

Admiral Penn, father of our William Penn, was also a native of Bristol, and his monument is still seen in Redcliff church. Joseph Butler, author of Butler's Analogy, one of the ablest theological works ever written, was Bishop of Bristol, and the witty Sidney Smith was a prebend of the cathedral, where he early began to make a sensation by his preaching. Here Lady Huntingdon established one of her chapels, the building now being in use by the Salvation army; here George Whitefield lived and preached, and opened for his services in 1752 a spacious tabernacle, still in existence; and here John Wesley also at one time labored, Bristol being peculiarly the cradle of Methodism. In the suburb of Westbury stands the chapel in which Adam Clarke, the commentator, preached his last sermon. Rev. Rowland Hill, having been refused ordination by six bishops, was at last ordained by the Bishop of Bristol, and here also began his earnest ministry. At Kingswood, another suburb, Wesley founded his college for the education of ministers, which has since been removed to Bath.

In one street in Bristol the former residence of the celebrated Baptist preacher Robert Hall is pointed out. By the way, it was concerning a baptist or congregational chapel in this city, the cellar of which was rented to a wine merchant, which suggested the old rhyme:

> There's a spirit above and a spirit below,
> A spirit of love and a spirit of woe;
> The spirit above is the spirit divine,
> The spirit below is the spirit of wine.

Here is a bridge with its romance. Some years ago a deserted infant was found upon it and taken to a public institution to be brought up. In the absence of a legitimate name he was called from the place of his discovery, Bridges, and, from his being found on the half of the bridge embraced in St. Thomas parish, Thomas was made his baptismal name. In due time Thomas Bridges developed ability, became a teacher, then a clergyman, and is now at the head of a flourishing mission in Patagonia. Rev. Thomas Bridges was recently in England superintending the printing of a translation of the scriptures he had made into the native language of his converts. His story will illustrate another phase of the origin of surnames.

S. T. Coleridge and Robert Southey at one time resided in Bristol, the latter being born here, and at St. Mary's Redcliff church the two poets married a pair of sisters, milliners of the place. David Hume, the historian, was here apprenticed in early life to a merchant, and was dismissed for presuming to correct his employer's grammar. Bristol was the birthplace and home of that talented but unfortunate genius, Thomas Chatterton. While only a boy of seventeen he produced imitations of ancient literature which deceived even the learned and astute Horace Walpole. When Walpole discovered the youth and humble position of his correspondent he treated him with such contempt that Chatterton's heart was broken. He went up to London to seek literary employment, struggled with starvation for four months, and then closed his sad career with poison in 1770. It was in the muniment room of Redcliff church that Chatterton professed to have found the Rowley manuscripts, which, however, were really the emanation of his own skillful pen. Had he lived Chatterton would have occupied a front rank in English literature. A fine monument to him adorns St. Mary's churchyard. On Park street the house is still standing in which Hannah More, the authoress, and her sisters, kept a school in the early part of this century, and in a populous district in the east end of Bristol is a chapel erected to her memory and known as the Hannah More Memorial Chapel.

Dr. Jenner, the discoverer of vaccination, was a resident of Bristol in the opening years of the present century. Thomas Lawrence, the eminent painter, was born here, and so, if I mistake not, was Sebastian Cabot. At all events the Cabots sailed from Bristol on their famous voyage in which Newfoundland was discovered and a foothold on American soil given to the English by right of discovery.

It was in Bristol that the first shot tower was erected, and, though nearly a century old, it still stands just opposite Redcliff church. The common shot, produced by permitting a shower of melted lead to fall from a great height, the drops assuming a globular form and cooling before they reach the bottom, was the invention of a Bristol plumber, one Wm. Watts, in 1782. His first experiments were from the tower of Redcliff church, which proving successful, led to the erection of the shot tower here alluded to, which earned for the inventor a large fortune. Like many other fortunate inventors he soon sunk his pile in an impracticable scheme and died miserably poor.

Of all the cities I visited in Europe Bristol is the most difficult for a stranger to learn the topography of. The crookedness of the river, the irregularity of the hills upon which a great part of the city is built, with the conformatory necessities of the old original walled city and the æsthetic tastes of the layers out of the newer residence portions, all combine to confuse and baffle the traveler. It is a city of curves, and threading its often narrow streets one is constantly coming out in the most unexpected places. Business is confined chiefly to the lower portions near the river. For residence, people seek the hill, which rises two or three hundred feet, and at the western extremity is known as the suburb of Clifton. The views obtained from many points in this upper portion of Bristol are very fine, in some places extending across the valley of the Avon for many miles. Back of the residence portion is an extensive down or open common which in late years has been secured to the public for a park. Stone is very abundant in Bristol, and the houses are mostly built of that material. One variety is a red sandstone, a wall of which has a very pleasing effect. It is this red stone that has given name to Redcliff parish, the church of which, St. Mary's, is quite cathedral-like in its proportions, and is claimed to be the finest parish church in England.

St. Mary's Redcliff is about six hundred years old. Having fallen into decay and been seriously damaged by the fall of its spire, it was rebuilt and restored in the fifteenth century by one Wm. Cannynge, the richest Bristol merchant of his day, and five times mayor of the city. It is told of this Cannynge that being visited by the king the latter set his heart on marrying his host to a favorite lady of the court. As the king's will could not be opposed, Cannynge, who was not inclined to matrimony, escaped by becoming a priest and assuming the abbacy of a convent he had founded at Westbury near by. Cannynge, or Canning as we should spell it nowadays, died in 1474. The spire of Redcliff church was never rebuilt until a few years ago, when two hundred and sixty-five thousand dollars was spent in a thorough restoration of the edifice. We visited the muniment room over the north porch and saw the old mediæval wooden chests in which Chatterton professed to have found his manuscripts. William of Wykeham, afterwards bishop of Winchester, alluded to in a former chapter, was vicar of Redcliff in 1356.

Bristol Cathedral was formerly the abbey church of St. Augustine. The abbey was founded in 1142, and the old Norman church was replaced by a Gothic one in the first half of the fourteenth century, but only the choir and transepts were completed. Within the past few years the enterprising citizens of Bristol have completed the structure, at a cost of $250,000, by the erection of a nave, comporting in style with the older portions of the building. Bristol Cathedral is one of the smallest in the kingdom, and is peculiar for its choir, nave and aisles being all of the same height; in other words, possessing no clerestory. It contains the tomb of Bishop Butler, alluded to above, who was born in 1692, died 1752.

In Bristol Cathedral I first noticed a deflection in the choir from a right line with the nave. Subsequently I observed it in other old churches, and in the ancient parish church of Henbury, near Bristol, it is very pronounced. The deflection of the chancel or choir is universally to the left, as seen from the nave. An authority in such matters informs me that it was designed by the symbol-loving builders to represent the drooping of the dead Saviour's head as he hung upon the cross.

Bristol has a famous school founded and endowed in 1706, by Edward Colston, another wealthy Bristol merchant. Under its original organization one hundred poor boys were fed, clothed and educated until fourteen years of age, when they were discharged with an apprenticeship fee of ten pounds each. The scope of the school is now considerably extended.

Everybody has heard of George Muller and his famous orphan houses. It will be remembered that Mr. Muller visited America a year or two ago and preached in many of our churches. He is a member of the sect known as the Plymouth Brethren, and began his ministerial labors in Bristol some forty-five years ago. Soon after settling there his warm christian heart led him to

take into his family a friendless orphan child,
then another and another, till his house was full,
and other houses had to be taken for their accommodation. For the support of his large family
he trusted solely to Providence, confidently
believing that being engaged in the Lord's work,
the Lord would provide the means for carrying it
on. When the larder was depleted he would
resort to prayer, and always, he assures us, with
signal success. Then he began to pray for means
wherewith to erect a larger and more suitable
home for his numerous dependents, and the means
were promptly forthcoming. He purchased a
tract of land on Ashley Down, a mile or two from
Bristol, and there built a large, plain, but substantial three story building with accommodations for about four hundred orphans. This was
speedily filled, and a second nearly similar building erected. From time to time the scope of his
operations has increased until to-day there are
five of these orphan houses with over two thousand inmates. The buildings and land have cost
nearly $560,000, the annual expense of main-
tenance is nearly $150,000, and the whole amount
collected and expended from the first by this
earnest man has been nearly three million dollars, and not a dollar of all this large sum has
been solicited from any one. The houses are finished in the plainest manner possible, and the

children, though kindly treated, are by no means pampered. That they are well taken care of is evident from the fact that out of two thousand two hundred and fifty inmates of the institution for the past year only twenty-two died —an extraordinary small percentage for children of these ages. They are all taught to work, and when old enough are sent out, the girls as domestic help, for which they have been especially trained, the boys as apprentices to useful trades. All receive in the schools sound religious training, and those who are capable of it no inconsiderable intellectual culture, as was evident from the rapid mental calculations made by boys of ten or twelve years, on the occasion of our visit.

CHAPTER XXXVI.

LEAVING Bristol, we cross the Severn, the
largest river in England, into Monmouth-
shire, originally one of the counties of
Wales, and lie over a few hours at Chepstow for
the purpose of visiting an old mediæval castle,
mostly in ruins, to be found there. It was a very
interesting experience to climb the turret stairs
and thread the passages in the walls of this old
structure. The floors and roofs have long since
disappeared, but much of the stone work is still
in good condition and well illustrates the arrange-
ment and accommodations of an ancient castle.
Chepstow castle was built immediately after the
Norman conquest, and for several centuries was
an important fortress on the western border of
England. During the great rebellion it stood a
long siege by the parliamentary army, and was
only at last starved into surrender. It then con-
stituted the prison of the holy and eloquent
Jeremy Taylor, who was too strong a royalist for
Cromwell to trust at large. After the restoration

it became, in turn, the prison of Henry Marten, one of the most active participants in the conviction and execution of Charles I., and who was kept here for twenty years, or until his death. The property now belongs to the Duke of Beaufort, and is being carefully preserved.

Four miles from Chepstow, on the banks of the Wye, an affluent of the Severn, stands the very fine ruin of Tintern Abbey. This religious house was instituted early in the Norman period and continued until the Reformation, when the abbey was dissolved and the buildings were permitted to go to ruin. The abbey church, which must have been a beautiful one in its day, was very substantially built, and, except part of its north wall, seems hardly to require more than a roof to fit it again for occupancy. It is two hundred and twenty-eight feet in length and was seventy feet in height to the vaulting, none of which now remains. The walls are largely overgrown with ivy, and present a very picturesque appearance. Besides the church there can be traced the remains of other monastic buildings, as the cloisters, chapter-house, sacristy, refectory, kitchen, guest-house, etc. The entire premises of the abbey embraced thirty-four acres. The grounds in and around the abbey are nicely sodded and well kept by the proprietor, the Duke of Beaufort, and to defray the expenses of protection and repairs a charge of sixpence each is made to all visitors.

On a commanding eminence overlooking for miles the valley of the Severn, is a tall monument to Tyndale, the reformer and translator of the scriptures.

Gloucester, thirty-seven miles north of Bristol, is a place of thirty thousand inhabitants, and is known to the younger portion of my readers as the place where, a trifle more than a century ago, Robert Raikes established the first Sunday school. It has a fine old cathedral, part of which was built in the ninth century. It was originally of Norman style and very massive, but in the fourteenth century was altered over in part to Perpendicular Gothic. The result is, though interesting, it has a patch-work look which detracts much from its elegance. It contains the tombs of Robert, Duke of Normandy, eldest son of William the Conqueror, and Edward II., who was murdered in Berkeley castle, not far distant, in 1327. A very common thing in old English churches is to see the tomb of the parents of a large family adorned with kneeling effigies in stone of all the children, the sons kneeling on one side, the daughters on the other, and all arranged in order of age, the eldest in the center of the tomb and the processions tapering away to the babies at the sides. In Gloucester Cathedral there is one such with this inscription:

John Bower had nyne soncs and seauen daughters by his wife Ann Bower.

John died in 1615. A statue of Dr. Edward Jenner, the discoverer of vaccination, stands in the nave, and another of Robert Raikes is to be added. The east window of the cathedral dates from 1350, and is reputed to be the largest in England.

Just west of the cathedral is the square where John Hooper, bishop of Gloucester, was burned at the stake February 9, 1555, for being a protestant. A fine monument to the martyr now occupies the site.

In one of the principal streets of the city stands the Bell Inn, modernized it is true, but the same inn where George Whitefield was born and passed his early life.

Passing on twenty-eight miles to Worcester we have on our right the Cotswold hills, whence the famous Cotswold breed of sheep take their name. On our left are the famed Malvern hills. Worcester is a comfortable old city of perhaps forty thousand inhabitants, situated on the Severn, which is here a small stream. It is memorable as being the scene of the last struggle between the royalists and the parliamentary forces under Cromwell, September, 3, 1651, when the royalists were utterly defeated. Worcester is also known all the world over by the Worcestershire table sauce manufactured there.

Worcester Cathedral is one of the most beautiful I have seen. It much resembles Salisbury, though in the crypt, chapter-house and portions of the nave, remains of the original Norman structure, destroyed by fire in 1113, are discoverable. The choir is very pure Early English Gothic of the twelfth and thirteenth century. The cloisters of a later period are among the best found in any of the cathedrals. The spandrils of the arches around the choir and transepts are filled with rude reliefs representing scriptural scenes, and some of them from their excessive realism are very amusing. Although almost entirely restored, Worcester Cathedral well illustrates the iconaclasm of the puritan regime. During Cromwell's rule, orders were sent down to all the cathedral churches to hew down the tabernacle work and deface the images inclosed, and then to whitewash the previously decorated walls. Scarcely a statue or effigy can be found in any church, of an earlier date than the Commonwealth, that has not at least its nose knocked off. In Worcester some of the more delicately carved stonework is shamefully hacked and battered. The whitewash of generations has now been carefully scraped off, and hundreds of polished brown marble columns have been brought to light.

Worcester Cathedral is not over-filled with tombs. The principal are those of King John, from whom Magna Charta was wrested by the barons, and who died A. D. 1216, and Prince Arthur, elder brother of Henry VIII., who died A. D. 1502. His widow, Katharine of Aragon, it will be recollected, Henry married, and the neglect of the Pope to divorce him when the illegality of the marriage began to prey on his conscience, precipitated the Reformation in England. Besides these the most noticeable is a monumental brass in the south transept to the memory of Rev. Wm. H. Havergal, the musical composer, and the father of Frances Ridley Havergal, the poet and author. Mr. Havergal, who was a canon of Worcester Cathedral, died in 1870, his daughter in 1879. A popular hymn tune of his composing, and called by his name, is found in most of our American tune books.

There are also several tombs of Crusaders, with their cross-legged effigies. From the intelligent verger I learned a lesson in knight-errantry. If the effigy on a knight's tomb has its legs crossed near the ankle it signifies that the deceased was engaged in but one campaign in the Holy Land ; crossed below the knee it signifies two expeditions, and at the thigh, three. If the hand grasping the sword appears palm up, the knight returned from the wars alive ; if knuckles up, he was brought home dead.

Every year a grand musical festival, lasting a week, is held in turn at Worcester, Hereford and

24

Gloucester cathedrals.   Several oratorios are produced each year, and the event is a notable one
in musical circles.

Worcester is also famous for a royal porcelain
factory, established one hundred and thirty years
ago, where the most artistic wares produced in
England are turned out.

It is the practice in Worcester, and in many
other parts of England, to suspend all business
and close the shops at three o'clock every Thursday afternoon, when the streets are as quiet and
deserted as on Sunday.

We leave Worcester for Stratford - on - Avon
(pronounced thereabouts Avon, with a long a),
the birth and burial place of the immortal Shakspeare, twenty-five miles distant.   We traverse a
beautiful agricultural country.   Stratford is situ-
ted on a branch line in the county of Warwickshire.   It is a large market town, with broad and
well laid out, but irregular, streets, and many
old-fashioned houses.   It is a neat, clean place,
and is evidently an object of much pride to its
inhabitants.   We follow a long, curving street
leading away from the station, turn to the left
into Windsor street, and then by an acute angle
to the right into Henley street.   A few doors
from the corner on the left hand side stands
Shakspeare's house.   It is a long two-story-and-
attic building, with dormer windows in the roof

and four low, broad windows filled with small diamond-shaped glass set in lead, in each of the other floors. The house is built of a framework of oak, filled in between with plaster, such as was so common about three hundred years ago. There are two doors opening from the street. We step up to the first and ring the bell. An old lady opens, and proceeds to show us through the house, the fee for which is a shilling each. Scores of people visit the house daily. The room we enter from the street is the former kitchen, with an immense stone fireplace on one side, stone floor, and low ceiling. When the house passed out of the Shakspeare family this room was long used as a butcher's shop. Behind it is a similar room, probably the family sitting room. Over the kitchen, and of course fronting the street, is the room in which the great dramatist first saw light, April 23d, 1564. It is a large room, with ceiling that cannot be more than seven and a half feet high, and the walls and ceiling, and even the glass of the windows, are literally covered with the names of visitors, though the practice is now no longer permitted. Except a few articles of old-fashioned furniture of about the Shakspearean period, the room is bare. In the room over the sitting room above mentioned, the ceiling was so low that it has been taken out for the comfort of visitors, exposing to view the rafters of the attic story above. With this exception the house has been put back as nearly as possible into the condition in which Shakspeare saw it, and the greatest care is exercised for its future preservation. Some adjacent houses have been pulled down to lessen the fire risk, and what heat is needed is supplied by hot water pipes, the hot water for which is brought under ground from premises some yards distant. Not so much as the striking of a match is permitted in the house. The other half of the house is used as a Shakspearean museum, in which are collected a great many relics of the family, a number of pictures, many autographs, and an extensive Shakspearean library.

At the end of Henley street we turn to our right into High street, two blocks down which, on the left hand side, formerly stood the elegant mansion which Shakspeare, when he became well off, purchased, and in which he spent the last nineteen years of his life, and ultimately died. Some remains of the foundation are still to be seen, and are carefully preserved by the citizens of Stratford. The indignation of the people against its last owner, who some years ago pulled it down, is hardly yet abated. The site has since become public property, and is protected by an elegant iron fence. Turning to the left at this point, a walk of a block brings us to the river, on the bank of which stands the Memorial Theatre, erected a few years ago to commemorate the three hundredth anniversary of the poet's birth. Connected with the theatre are picture galleries, library, and reading room, the whole being designed ultimately as a dramatic college, though this portion of the scheme has not yet been put into effect.

Following the bank of the river for a few hundred yards, we come to the interesting parish church of Stratford, in which Shakspeare lies buried. It is an interesting old building, situated in the midst of a large churchyard which extends on one side quite to the margin of the Avon. The central tower must have been built for an earlier church than the one existing, and must be fully eight hundred years old. The transepts are the next oldest portion, being of Early English Gothic of about the year 1200. The nave, or portion of the church west of the central tower, is in the Perpendicular Gothic style, and is said to have been built about the year 1400. The date of the chancel is put at 1480. In this chancel, just in front of the communion railing, lie in a row the tombs of the Shakspeare family, a plain, flat stone marking each. That to the left, as we face the altar, is the tomb of Shakspeare's wife, better known by her maiden name, Anne Hathaway.

Next comes that of the poet himself, with this inscription :

GOOD FRIEND, FOR IESVS SAKE FORBEARE
TO DIGG THE DVST ENCLOASED HEARE ;
BLESTE BE YE MAN YT SPARES THES STONES,
AND CVRST BE HE YT MOVES MY BONES.

On the wall of the church just over Mrs. Shakspeare's grave is the monument to her husband. His half-length figure in stone, painted, is represented in the act of writing. Above is his coat of arms, the whole being surmounted by a skull. The inscription shows that he died on the 23d of April, 1616, aged 53.

As the reader is aware, there has always been a good deal of controversy as to the proper spelling of Shakspeare's name. The difficulty has arisen from the very illegible way in which the poet wrote it himself, and the probability that he did not himself always observe the same spelling.

CHAPTER XXXVII.

A FEW miles from Stratford is Warwick
(pronounced Warrick), famous for its castle, the best preserved old baronial castle
in England. It is situated on an abrupt hill overlooking the Avon, and is surrounded by a beautiful park of about one thousand acres. It is
owned by the Earl of Warwick, who resides there
a portion of the time. When away from the
castle the building and grounds are open free to
the public, though a small fee is expected by the
attendants who show you around. It will be
remembered that a portion of the castle was accidentally burned about ten years ago, but this has
since been fully restored. We first pass the porter's lodge by a gate which opens to our knock.
A long, winding, shady walk, cut for some distance through solid rock, leads up to the draw-
bridge and gate tower of the castle. The gate
tower is fitted with two heavy portcullises, or
heavy iron gratings, which, sliding in grooves in
the stone walls, were formerly lowered when dan-

ger threatened from without. The gate tower passed, we find ourselves in a spacious courtyard with a great oval lawn in the center. To our right and left are strong towers of defense one hundred and fifty feet in hight. The left side of the courtyard is occupied by the private and state apartments of the castle, a series of elegant Elizabethan Gothic structures. Midway their length we pass through a spacious porch, up a broad flight of stone steps, through a massive oaken doorway, and we find ourselves in the great hall.

The walls are of stone, the floor of marble, and the ceiling, some thirty or forty feet high, of carved oak. The wall opposite the door of entrance must be fully eight feet thick, and the windows in it look down upon the Avon a hundred feet below. Around the hall are ancient arms and armor, and other trophies. From the great hall we pass through a series of large drawing rooms, all looking out upon the Avon, and all filled with rare inlaid cabinets and tables, pictures by such artists as Rubens, Vandyke, Rembrandt, Holbein, Murillo, Wouwerman, and others, rare porcelain, articles formerly the property of the unfortunate Marie Antoinette, and other objects rich and rare. The last room of the suite contains a bedstead, a trunk, and other articles formerly belonging to Queen Anne. Returning, we pass through a long gallery filled with arms, and a private chapel used by the members of the family and servants of the castle.

Among the objects of interest in the park is a large antique marble vase, twenty-one feet in circumference, found in the ruins of Hadrian's villa at Tivoli, in Italy, the same place where the famous Venus de Medici was discovered. In the park also are many fine cedars of Lebanon, some of which are said to have been brought from Palestine by the Crusaders hundreds of years ago.

Two or three miles from Warwick we come to Leamington, famous, like Bath, for its medicinal waters and its concentration of wealth and fashion. It is beautifully situated, has fine, broad streets, and hundreds of elegant villas in great variety of architectural design. In the upper part of the town stands a large oak tree, surrounded by an iron fence, which the natives assure us has been demonstrated to be the exact geographical center of England.

Three or four miles still farther on is Kenilworth, the seat of the castle of that name, immortalized in Walter Scott's novel, Kenilworth. It is a stately ruin. One portion called Cæsar's tower, dating from about A. D. 1100, is an immense square, bastioned stronghold, with walls sixteen feet in thickness, yet notwithstanding this prodigious strength only three sides remain stand-

ing.   At the farther end of the court-yard are the
roofless walls of the great hall, which no doubt
Queen Elizabeth graced with her presence, and
which in its perfection must have been a very
beautiful structure.   The doors and lofty windows are of the best periods of Gothic art and
some rich sculpture still remains.   Another portion of the castle, known as Leicester's tower,
evidently once contained several palatial suites of
apartments, with pleasant bay and oriel windows,
and fire-places, the carved mantels of which still
remain.   Altogether, Kenilworth castle is a very
extensive and interesting ruin and well worth a
visit, especially if one is posted in its historical
associations.   For the greater part of its existence
it has belonged to the crown, but has frequently
been given to royal favorites.   Thus Queen Elizabeth bestowed it upon Robert Dudley, Earl of
Leicester, who, readers of English history will
recollect, was vain enough to aspire to the hand
of his royal mistress, and to gain that end was
accessory to the putting out of the way of his
secretly married but lawful wife, the fair Amy
Robsart.   The whole story is entertainingly told
in Walter Scott's Kenilworth.

  Next we come to Coventry, a large and busy
manufacturing town, famous for its ribbons.   It is
also a place of rare antiquarian interest.   It possesses two very large and fine old churches, St.

Michael's being almost a cathedral in size. Both were built between the eleventh and fourteenth centuries, and from the soft character of the material of which they are constructed—the red sandstone that so abounds throughout England, are so badly weatherworn as to present the most ancient appearance of any churches I saw in my travels. Close by is St. Mary's hall, built of the same stone, with ceiling of oak, the latter being as black as ebony, from age. The hall was built in 1397—nearly a century before the discovery of America by Columbus. It contains many portraits of royal personages, some ancient tapestries made by the nuns of Coventry, and a throne of carved oak, as dark as the ceiling, used by Henry VI. and his queen upon one occasion when they held a parliament in Coventry. At the time of our visit to St. Mary's hall, one hundred and thirty old men were just being paid a weekly dole of four or six shillings each, in accordance with a provision made some centuries ago by a charitable citizen of the place who left lands for the purpose. As the value and rental of the lands increase the number of recipients is gradually enlarged. They were a very respectable looking lot of old gentlemen. By another ancient bequest a certain number of loaves of bread are distributed to as many poor people each Sunday morning in the porch of St. Michael's church.

Coventry also contains a great number of very old houses, many of them very curious and picturesque, with their carved timber framework and overhanging upper stories, such as were so fashionable in Queen Elizabeth's time.

Did the reader ever hear of Lady Godiva? Well, as the story goes, a good many centuries ago there lived in Coventry a tyrannical old earl named Leofric and his beautiful wife, Godiva. The earl greatly oppressed the people of Coventry, who were all his tenants, or perhaps, more correctly speaking, serfs. In their misery they appealed to the tender-hearted Godiva, who interceded with Leofric in their behalf. The monster at length consented to lighten the burden of the townspeople, but on the one condition that Godiva should ride in mid-day through the town in a state of entire nudity. Of course he supposed she would not comply with the terms, but the plucky woman was bent on accomplishing her mission at whatever cost, and ride she did, and thereby earned for all time the gratitude and worship of the people of Coventry. One chronicler relates that the ride was taken on a market day when the streets were crowded with people; but popular tradition has it that an order was previously given for the people to stay indoors and keep their blinds tightly closed; and it further adds that one curious individual who did venture to look out was immediately struck blind. He is known as Peeping Tom, and his effigy, leaning out of a third-story window at a prominent street corner, with eyes strained to their utmost, has long been a conspicuous landmark of Coventry. Until within the last few years there was an annual festival in Lady Godiva's honor, one of the features of which was a grand procession through the streets, led by a woman on horseback dressed in flesh colored tights. The last such show took place in 1878.

Birmingham is the fourth largest place in Great Britain, and boasts a population of about four hundred thousand. It has fine streets, elegant stone buildings, splendid shops, fine public edifices, and altogether is an attractive place to visit. It is comparatively a modern city, and has no historical associations. It is famous for its manufacture of hardware, steel pens, bronze and brass work, fire-arms, jewelry, pins, buttons, machinery, and many other products of metal, and has long enjoyed the cognomen of "the Toy Shop of Europe." One of the lions of Birmingham is its Town Hall, a fine Grecian structure, seating between two thousand and three thousand people, and furnished with an immense organ, upon which a free organ recital is given every Saturday afternoon, whereby a popular taste for music is cultivated. It was in Birmingham that Rev.

John Angell James, the great congregational
preacher and author of various religious books,
lived and labored in the early part of the century.   We attended services one Sunday evening
at Carr's Lane chapel, erected by this earnest
man in 1819.   It is a large, plain, brick building
with broad galleries extending around three sides,
and high old-fashioned pews, over the tops of
which only the worshipers' heads can be seen.
The organ is raised slightly above the floor at the
rear of the octagonal pulpit, which stands out a
little way into the body of the church and is surrounded by high seats for the choir of forty or
fifty voices.   There are numerous memorial tablets on the walls.   The church is now served by
the Rev. R. W. Dale.   The services on this occasion began with a seven verse hymn, a long chapter from the Old Testament, an anthem by the
choir, a long prayer, a hymn of six verses, a
chapter from the New Testament, another long
prayer and another hymn—the entire opening
services occupying little short of an hour.   Then
came an earnest *extempore* sermon of fifty minutes, and a closing hymn and prayer.

From Stratford-on-Avon to Birmingham we
have been altogether in the county of Warwickshire, a beautiful portion of England, and one
inhabited by as courteous and polite a people as
are anywhere to be found.

Birmingham is situated on the border line between Warwickshire and Staffordshire. Northwest of it, in Staffordshire, stretches away for twenty miles the famous "Black Country," so called because in all that region there is scarcely a field, tree, or blade of grass—nothing but coal mines, iron furnaces, rolling mills, railway tracks, canals, rows of dusty dwelling houses for the laborers, with great heaps of ashes and cinders for scenery. The contrast between the approach to Birmingham on the one side and the departure from it on the other is very striking.

I enjoyed a short chat with a very agreeable and intelligent Birmingham manufacturer. He, in common with his class, bewails the hard lot of England in working out the free trade problem single-handed and alone, and admitting freely the products of other countries, while her own products are excluded from their markets. Still he concedes that the free trade theory is the correct one, and confesses that notwithstanding the disadvantages under which England labors in this respect, she was never more prosperous than at present. Money is abundant and cheap, profits are not to be complained of, and wages in most branches of manufacture are satisfactory. The gentleman alluded to had visited America recently. "Yours is the dearest country in the world," he remarked. "A dollar scarcely goes

farther with you than a shilling with us. Your
protective system is putting some money into the
pockets of your manufacturers, but at a tremendous cost to the public at large, who pay double
prices for everything they consume." No doubt
he was right, and America would be richer and
our people individually better off were we to follow England's example, and emancipate trade
from the barbarous mediæval restrictions which,
in contempt of the teachings of science and the
spirit of the age, we continue to hamper it with.

Some fifteen miles north of Birmingham is the
city of Lichfield, a quiet little country place of
about seven thousand inhabitants. Only cathedral towns are called cities in England, and thus
the rustic little Lichfield is a city while Birmingham, with its four hundred thousand inhabitants,
is only a town. Lichfield cathedral is only of
medium size, thirteen of the twenty-four English
cathedrals being larger, and ten smaller, but it is
one of the most perfect. It is purely Gothic, and
its erection covered the period between 1150 and
1350. Its chief peculiarity is its three beautiful
stone spires. The church suffered severely at the
hands of Cromwell's army, and its central spire
was entirely destroyed by their batteries, but at
the restoration it too was thoroughly restored,
and is now undergoing a still further restoration.
Lichfield is another instance of the nave and choir

not being in a right line with each other; and here
another explanation is given of the eccentricity,
differing from the one given at Bristol. A gentleman connected with the cathedral is strongly of
the opinion that taste in architecture was more
highly developed at the period when these bent
churches were erected than at any time since, and
that the deflection was made purely with æsthetic
purpose. The effect in looking down the nave of
one of these churches is certainly greatly height-
ened by the deflection, for on one side at least the
entire range of columns and arches is brought
into the perspective, while in a perfectly straight
edifice the more distant arches are lost in a con-
fused jumble. I was inclined to favor this latter
theory, but there is still another peculiarity in
these old churches not so easily accounted for.
In many of them, including Lichfield, but principally in the churches of Norman style, the columns and arches of the nave incline outward as if
spread by being imperfectly anchored together at
the top. But, with the immense thickness of the
walls of most of the Norman churches, and the
absence of cracks that would indicate a giving
way, it is difficult to believe that they were not
originally built as we see them. In the case of
St. James's church at Bristol, the columns not
only incline outward, but to an even greater
degree backward from the chancel, so as to have,

25

in nautical parlance, quite a rakish appearance.
The west or front wall also overhangs several
feet, but nowhere is there any indication of its
having shifted into that position. The intelligent
sexton of St. James's was of the opinion that the
Normans were unacquainted with the use of the
plumb rule, but my Lichfield friend would have
it that this too was a matter of taste, and not of
accident. In the fine old churches of Stratford-
on-Avon, and St. Michael's, Coventry, the de-
flected choir or chancel is very strongly marked.

Lichfield Cathedral has a number of very
beautiful modern tombs and monuments, which
enjoy a freedom from dust and dirt that would
astonish a Londoner, but none of any personages
in whom my readers would be likely to feel an
interest, unless it be two marble busts of Johnson
and Garrick, erected to their memory in one of
the transepts. The Dean of Lichfield is Rev.
Edward H. Bickersteth, the well known poet,
the author of "Yesterday, To-day, and Forever," and other works.

Lichfield was the birthplace of Dr. Samuel
Johnson, the lexicographer and literary autocrat
of the last century, and the house in which he
was born in 1709 is still standing on a corner
facing the market place. In front of it has been
erected a colossal marble statue of the great man.
It was while living in this house that Johnson's

father, who was a peripatetic bookseller, once desired his son to attend his book stall on the market of Uttoxeter, a town a few miles distant, when himself confined at home by sickness, a duty which the young man as a matter of pride declined to perform. In after life, oppressed with remorse at his undutiful conduct on this occasion, he imposed as a penance on himself the standing bareheaded for a whole day in Uttoxeter market place exposed to the inclemency of the weather and the gibes of the rabble. The incident is commemorated by an indifferent bas-relief on the base of the monument.

Leaving Lichfield, we journey northward to Lincoln, passing through Burton-on-Trent, the greatest ale-brewing place in the world, Nottingham, the famous lace manufacturing town, and Derby.

CHAPTER XXXVIII.

LINCOLN, the capital of the large eastern county of Lincolnshire, is a rural place of twenty or twenty-five thousand inhabitants. It is situated on high ground, but is surrounded by a flat, level country. On the summit of the hill stands the cathedral, one of the largest in England, being five hundred and seventeen feet long. It was built in the twelfth century, and is a good example of the Early English Gothic style. About 1280 the choir was extended eastward in the decorated style, of which it is also a very beautiful example. In the western front may be seen some remains of the original Norman church, built eight hundred years ago. No additions or changes have been made in the building since 1482. Lincoln cathedral is easily remembered by its three lofty square towers, the one at the intersection of the nave and transept being two hundred and seventy feet high. It is a noble church, but has no particular associations interesting to an American. The only tomb I noticed worth mentioning was that of Elizabeth Penrose, author of the Markham's History of England, commonly used in our schools, the name Markham being a *nom de plume*.

From Lincoln we hasten on to Hull, the third seaport in England in respect of importance. It is a place of about one hundred and sixty thousand inhabitants, on the river Humber, near its mouth, and it has extensive docks and a large foreign trade, but chiefly with the Dutch and Danish ports just across the North sea. Its full name is Kingston-on-Hull, the Hull being the name of a smaller river that joins the Humber at this point. Besides its shipping interest, it is largely engaged in the manufacture of linseed and cotton seed oils. It is interesting as being the birthplace of William Wilberforce, through whose efforts slavery was abolished in the British colonies on the first of August, 1834. A tall column, surmounted by a statue of the philanthropist, has been erected to his memory. The house in which he was born is still in existence, but is now used for offices.

The Pole family, of which Cardinal Reginald Pole, Archbishop of Canterbury during Queen Mary's reign, was a member, were also residents of Hull.

Twelve miles north of Hull is the town of Beverley, famous for a parish church known as Beverley Minster, in size and stateliness quite the peer of many of the cathedrals. The church was originally founded about the year 700, and the existing church, which is kept in excellent repair, is about seven hundred years old. Beverley Minster is celebrated for the quaint wood carvings with which its interior fittings are ornamented.

From Beverley we proceed to York, the seat of one of the two archbishoprics of England. There is nothing remarkable about the place except its old wall, which is kept in good repair, and the summit of which forms a pleasant promenade, its ruined abbey, and its cathedral, the latter reputed the largest in England. I must own, however, to being rather disappointed in it, it nowhere approaching in beauty and interest either Lincoln, Lichfield or Worcester cathedrals. Its wooden vaulting, so constructed because its walls were not strong enough to bear the weight of stone, is a great defect, and in 1829 came near causing the entire destruction of the church. In that year an insane man named Martin secreted himself in the church, and in the dead of night kindled a huge bonfire of the books and benches just in the vicinity of the organ and choir stalls. The flames spread to the roof of the choir, which was entirely destroyed. Luckily the rest of the church was saved. In the crypt under the nave may be seen some remains of an old Saxon church built twelve hundred and fifty years ago, and also the bases of the finely sculptured columns of a later Norman church, which next occupied the site. The present edifice was erected between 1220 and 1470—too late for the best period of Gothic art. It is rather famous for its windows, some of which are of immense size and mostly filled with antique glass. The great east window is thirty-two by seventy-seven feet in size, and its glass dates from 1408. I observed no very remarkable tombs in the cathedral, unless it were that of the wife of a professor of theology who, as the Latin inscription states, died in her thirty-eighth year and after her twenty-fourth confinement.

The city wall extends almost entirely around the city. It is six or eight feet thick and from ten to twenty-five feet high, according as the ground is elevated or depressed. Its summit is finished with large flag stones and it has a parapet about four feet high with embrasures at intervals along the outer edge. The inner side of the promenade that runs along the top is unprotected. The wall does not follow straight lines or uniform curves, but jogs in and out in a very irregular manner. There are several imposing gateways with towers, barbicans, loopholes, and every other means of ancient defense. The city, which now contains about forty thousand inhabitants, has

spread to a considerable extent beyond the walls.
York has a sleepy and old-fashioned air and,
from the dirty colored brick with which it is
mainly built, wears rather a gloomy appearance.
It has an old castle to which modern additions
have been added from time to time, and which
serves for a court house and county offices. It
will be remembered as the scene of the trial in
Warren's incomparable novel "Ten Thousand a
Year."

Tradition has always asserted that the Roman
emperor Constantine the Great was born in York,
A. D. 274. In recent times it was the home of
George Hudson the linen draper who, about
thirty-five years ago, threw down his yard-stick
and made himself the railroad king of Britain.
Railroads were made or ruined according as he
accepted their presidency or refused the same.
In a short time he made an immense fortune, but
soon after, when reaction and panic seized the
railway share market, he became the scapegoat
for the unwisdom of the period, and died at last
miserably poor.

From York we journey to Ripon, twenty-five
miles west, passing *en route* Knaresborough, the
location of the famous dripping well which in a
year or two petrifies any object brought in con-
tact with its waters. Ripon is the seat of a bish-
opric, and has an interesting little cathedral,

built in large part in the latest Norman and very
earliest Gothic style. Its transition architecture
is indeed quite unique, and in its stalls it boasts
the finest wood carving in England. The subjects
of some of these carvings are very curious; as,
for instance, Punch (Pontius Pilate) trundling
Judy (Judas Iscariot) in a wheelbarrow to Hades;
a big pig playing the bagpipes and two little pigs
dancing to the music; a fox in a pulpit preaching
to two roosters, and many other like grotesque
subjects, all of which, in the minds of the monk-
ish designers, were, no doubt, thought to convey
useful lessons. About four centuries ago the
central tower fell and crushed one side of the
choir, which was thereupon rebuilt in an entirely
different style from the corresponding wall opposite, and we thus have the architectural curiosity
of a church with one side of Early English Gothic
the other of Perpendicular, a style of three
hundred years later. The chapter house is of
early Norman work, fully eight hundred years
old, and under the church is a rude Saxon chapel
affirmed to be twelve hundred and fifty years old.
The latter is a small room perhaps ten feet wide
and fifteen long, arched over at the top, and all
of stone. It was probably only designed for private devotions. Its most curious feature is a hole
about sixteen inches square penetrating a massive
wall on one side and connecting with a passage

way behind, the use of which hole, known as St.
Wilfred's Needle, is thus described : In the olden
time, when a woman went to confess, if the priest
doubted her truthfulness he required her to creep
through the hole.   If she had been chaste, she
got through easily enough ; if otherwise, she
stuck fast.   In modern times the superstition has
grown up that the woman who passes through St.
Wilfred's Needle will be married within a year,
and the verger assured us that it is no uncommon thing for twenty females a day to be dragged
through.   Certain it is that the sides of the hole
are highly polished by the centuries of attrition
with female garments.   The verger tells of one
young lady who, having passed through the Needle, received an offer of marriage three days
after, and forthwith brought her sister, that she
might share her good fortune.

Two miles from Ripon is the celebrated ruin
known as Fountains Abbey, probably one of the
most extensive monastic ruins in England.   The
abbey buildings are said to have formerly covered twelve acres.   It is one of a great number of
such ruins scattered over England.   These abbeys
were generally of great antiquity, some, as in the
case of Fountains, dating from the early part of
the twelfth century.   They generally consisted of
an extensive group of massive stone buildings, in
the erection of which much delicate art was

expended. At the Reformation the abbeys were dissolved, the monks turned adrift in the world, and the property first confiscated to the crown and then sold or granted to various royal favorites. To their new owners the buildings were often useless, unless for the material they contained, which might be re-employed in the construction of more convenient abodes. They hence for some generations became the stone quarries for the neighborhood. If a load of stone was wanted for any purpose the abbey was resorted to, and fine old clustered columns and richly mullioned windows would be ruthlessly battered down to supply it. Roofless and exposed to the weather, they soon became overgrown with ivy, the insinuating roots and tendrils of which disintegrated the stone work, and furthered the work of decay. In this deplorable condition they were found by the art-appreciating nineteenth century, and for the last two generations as much zeal has been expended in the care and preservation of these old ecclesiastical remains as formerly had been in their destruction. They usually form the center of attraction of some nobleman's park, having been carefully explored by expert archæologists, dangerous places strengthened, fragments set up in something near their old positions, and a continual guard kept over them to prevent the slightest acts of renewed vandalism.

Within and without the walls, the ground is covered with a soft, green turf, which contrasts very
prettily with the grey stone of the edifice, and
and the blue sky above, which forms the only
roof.

At Fountains, as in all these old· abbeys, the
church is the central and principal building. It
is cruciform in shape, with a lofty square tower
rising at the extremity of the northern transept
to the hight of a hundred and sixty-eight feet.
The church is in the Norman style, with massive
round columns and semi-circular arches, except
where at a later period alterations and additions
were carried out in the Early English Gothic.
The Lady chapel, or extension eastward, is peculiar, in forming as it does a second transept, or T,
to the choir.   The same existed originally in Lincoln Cathedral, and still exists in Durham, and
seems to have been a favorite style in the northern part of England at the end of the twelfth and
beginning of the thirteenth centuries.   Along
the eastern wall of this terminal transept were
arranged five, seven, or nine altars, dedicated to
as many different saints.   This portion of Fountains Abbey is in the pointed style, and must
have been exceedingly beautiful.   The other
buildings of the abbey, judging from the foundation walls which remain, were very extensive.
They comprise cloisters about three hundred feet

in length, with dormitories on the floor above, an immense refectory or dining hall, a kitchen with two fire-places each sixteen feet wide from jamb to jamb and six feet deep, a chapter house for the business meetings of the monastery, with a library and scriptorium, or writing room, on the floor above, a hospitium or guest-house, a house for the abbot, with a great hall rivaling in magnitude those of the proudest barons, a dungeon for criminals, for the abbot also exercised civil jurisdiction over the surrounding conntry; and a great many other buildings of which the uses are not clearly apparent. The abbey, originally founded in 1132 by an order of monks more ascetic than the Benedictines, seems early to have become rich, powerful and luxurious. We are told that the abbey possessed sixty thousand acres of land all in one body, besides other property. The dissolution took place in 1539, and the estates were sold by Henry VIII. for what would to-day be a merely nominal sum, to the ancestors of the present owner, the Marquis of Ripon.

From Ripon we continue our journey northward to Durham, passing on our way through Darlington, a large manufacturing town famous as one of the termini of the first railroad ever built for general traffic, viz., the Stockton and Darlington, constructed by George Stephenson, and opened in 1825.

Durham is a beautifully situated little city on the sides of the hills which rise from the river Wear, the tops of which are crowned by the castle and cathedral. The see of Durham was formerly one of the richest in England and yielded its bishop an income of about $200,000 a year, but latterly the revenues of the bishoprics have been to some extent equalized, and his lordship of Durham now has to struggle along with $40,000 a year. Durham is one of the oldest, best preserved and most interesting of the English cathedrals. It was built about the year 1090 in the most highly developed Norman style, and is much more highly ornamented than most of the Norman churches we had previously seen. The walls are of great strength, and the entire building is vaulted with stone. About the year 1250 an eastern transept, similar to that described in connection with Fountains Abbey, and known as the Nine Chapels, was added in the Early English style; and, with the exception of the central tower and here and there a window inserted at a later date in the Perpendicular style, the edifice remains as its thirteenth century builders left it. Its two western towers are very fine specimens of the Norman-Gothic transition period.

Durham Cathedral is famous as the burial place of two Saxon worthies whose works and fame have survived a thousand years. These are St.

Cuthbert, of Lindisfarne, and the Venerable Bede, the ecclesiastical historian of the Saxon period. The latter died in the eighth century and his remains were brought to Durham in the thirteenth. His tomb, a plain slab of stone, bears this inscription :

"Hac sunt in fossa Bædæ Venerabilis ossa."

Green, in his "History of the English People," gives a touching account of the death scene of this holy man. "Two weeks before the Easter of 755 the old man was seized with an extreme weakness and loss of breath. He still preserved, however, his usual pleasantness and gay good humor, and in spite of prolonged sleeplessness continued his lectures to the pupils about him. Verses of his own English tongue broke from time to time from the master's lips. The tears of Bede's scholars mingled with his song. 'We never read without weeping,' writes one of them. So the days rolled on to Ascension-tide and still master and pupils toiled at their work, for Bede longed to bring to an end his version of St. John's gospel into the English tongue, and his extracts from Bishop Isidore. 'I don't want my boys to read a lie,' he answered those who would have had him rest, 'or to work to no purpose after I am gone.' A few days before Ascension-tide his sickness grew upon him, but he spent the whole day in teaching, only saying cheerfully to his scholars, 'Learn with what speed you may. I know not how long I may last.' The dawn broke upon another sleepless night, and again the old man called his scholars around him and bade them write. 'There is still a chapter wanting,' said the scribe, as the morning drew on, 'and it is hard for thee to question thyself any longer.' 'It is easily done,' said Bede; 'take thy pen and write quickly.' Amid tears and farewells the day wore on to even-tide. 'There is still one sentence unwritten, dear master,' said the boy. 'Write it quickly,' bade the dying man. 'It is finished now,' said the little scribe at last. 'You speak truth,' said the master; 'all is finished, now.' Placed upon the pavement, his head supported in his scholar's arms, his face turned to the spot where he was wont to pray, Bede chanted the 'Glory to God.' As his voice reached the close of his song he passed quietly away."

St. Cuthbert's tomb, in the rear of the high altar, was formerly enriched with a magnificent shrine, which, however, was demolished at the Reformation.

Durham castle, formerly the residence of the bishops of Durham, is now used for the college or university which is under the control of the diocesan authorities.

From Durham we continue northward, passing Newcastle-on-Tyne, one of the greatest centers of English coal mining—whence the expression, when articles are carried to a place where they are extensively produced, "Carrying coals to Newcastle." Near the border line between England and Scotland we are in full view of the North sea, and just off the shore catch a glimpse of Holy Island and the site of the Lindisfarne of St. Cuthbert. A little farther on we cross the Tweed, the boundary line between the two countries, and are in the old town of Berwick-upon-Tweed, pronounced Berrick. The terminal "wick" is an old Saxon word meaning harbor or port.

CHAPTER XXXIX.

WE skirt the eastern coast of Scotland till the Firth of Forth is reached, then, trending westerly, follow the south bank of that noble estuary till near Edinburgh. The Scottish capital lies south of the Forth, and two or three miles distant from it, the intervening space being a level plain. On the nearest bank of the river is the port of Leith, formerly a separate town, but now quite united with Edinburgh by the building up of the intermediate space.

Edinburgh itself is built on two parallel ridges extending east and west. The northern ridge or the one nearest the Forth, rises at its eastern extremity into a lofty eminence known as Calton Hill. The southern ridge rises similarly at its western extremity, which is surmounted by Edinburgh Castle. On the crest and sides of this ridge stands the old city of Edinburgh. On the northern ridge the new or modern city has been built. The valley between, contains the railway stations, market buildings, and pleasure grounds

known as Princes Street Gardens. The two
sections of the city are connected by high bridges
spanning the valley. The southerly or castle
ridge slopes down gradually from the castle
until, opposite Calton Hill, it is altogether lost in
the lower level of the valley. At this point
stands Holyrood Palace. Still further south, but
beyond the limits of the city, is a third lofty
ridge known as Salisbury Crags, above which
towers a peak eight hundred and thirty feet high,
known as Arthur's Seat.

Calton Hill forms a public park, and commands
a magnificent view, both of the city and surrounding country with its background of distant
mountains. On the top of the hill are several
monumental structures, including a tall tower to
the memory of Lord Nelson; small Grecian temples to Burns the poet, Playfair the mathemati-
cian, and Dugald Stewart, a philosophical writer;
and an unfinished copy of the Athenian Parthenon, intended as a memorial of the battle of
Waterloo. The funds, however, ran out when
only the front colonnade had been completed, and
work stopped short at that point.

On the ridge extending westward from Calton
Hill stands what is called the New town, which
is, without exception, one of the finest cities in
Europe. The streets are broad, well paved, and
clean. Public squares and gardens are numerous

and well cared for. The houses are of squared
stone and wear a highly respectable mien. Princes street, which extends along the brow of the
ridge and overlooks the old city across the ravine,
is one of the most attractive retail business streets
anywhere to be found. The shop windows are
wonderful in the great variety and beauty of their
contents, so that indeed it takes a lady a whole
afternoon to get from one end of the street to the
other. The view from Princes street across the
valley is very picturesque. At our extreme right
stands the castle. In front, over the tops of the
tall houses, rises the crown-like summit of St.
Giles's Cathedral. At our left can be seen the
lofty summit of Arthur's Seat. All along the
foreground are tall eight and ten-story buildings
with curious gables and extinguisher-shaped turrets, forming a picturesque panorama.

On the slope of the valley, near Princes street,
stands the Scott Monument, one of the finest
monuments to a private individual that modern
times have produced. It consists of a marble
statue of Sir Walter Scott, surmounted by a magnificent Gothic canopy and spire two hundred
feet high. There are also in the new city a great
number of other monuments to public men of the
present century, some very imposing.

In this part of Edinburgh is the new English,
or Episcopal, cathedral, probably the finest

Gothic church edifice of modern times. It was built under the supervision of Sir Gilbert Scott, in the Early English style, and is a very beautiful and meritorious structure. Its cost has been about $600,000, a sum equivalent in the amount of building it will accomplish to two or three times that amount if expended in America. The larger half of the cost was defrayed by an Edinburgh lady, who thus prevented her heirs quarreling over and squandering her fortune.

While the new city is in every respect so beautiful and attractive, Old Edinburgh is quite the reverse. Take High street, for example, which extends along the crest of the castle ridge from the castle down to Holyrood palace, though for the latter portion of the distance it is known as the Canongate. It, of course, lies parallel with Princes street. It has few intersecting streets, but a great number of courts, closes or wynds— narrow passages running under the houses and communicating in the rear with narrow open courts surrounded by lofty buildings. The buildings on High street are six, seven and eight stories high, massively built of squared or rubble stone, and in quaint and very irregular style, most of them being two hundred years old and upwards. Judging from the great number of children that swarm the streets, nowhere else in the wide world can there be so large a population

crowded into so small a space.   And such a dirty
population !   Even on High street, to say nothing
of the wynds, one must be careful where he sets
his foot, and if at all of a weak stomach he will
do well to hold his nose as he passes the entrances
to the wynds or closes.

It must not be understood that all the southern
part of the city is of a like character with High
street and its purlieus.   On the contrary, one of
the prettiest parts of Edinburgh lies just beyond.
As in our western cities, the houses in this portion are built with considerable ground about
them, which is prettily laid out in lawns and
flower-beds.   The houses themselves are uniformly of stone, and are built with much architectural taste.   Taken as a whole Edinburgh is
certainly a beautiful city.

Edinburgh Castle had its origin in a very early
period.   One small chapel contained in it, dates
from the middle of the eleventh century, it having
been built for Queen Margaret, wife of Malcolm
III., who died in 1093.   Malcolm and Margaret
were the parents of David I., the model king of
ancient Scotland.   He founded the abbeys of
Holyrood and Melrose and many other ecclesiastical establishments, the centers of civilization and
learning of that early period.   Part of Edinburgh
Castle is quite modern.   It possesses little of
interest beyond the fine view it commands,

though there is shown there a suite of rooms occupied by Mary Queen of Scots, in one of which, a mere closet in size, she gave birth to James VI., afterwards James I. of England. In another room of the castle is preserved the ancient regalia or crown jewels of Scotland, which the jealousies of the Scotch people prevented being taken to London on the union of the crowns. To quiet public apprehension the old crown, sceptre, and sword of state—no very rich display compared with the English crown jewels—were boxed up and deposited in a strong room of the castle, where they remained for one hundred and ten years, until they were forgotten, or at least till their existence was considered doubtful. Then, through the instrumentality of Sir Walter Scott and other antiquaries, the old chest was broken open and the jewels were found intact. An old fifteenth century gun, made of bars of iron secured by bands, known as Mons Meg, from its having been made at Mons, in Belgium, is also one of the curiosities of the castle.

In High street, about midway between the castle and Holyrood, stands St. Giles's Cathedral, a very old church, but one so mutilated at the Reformation and by a bungling restoration fifty years ago, that it has lost all appearance of antiquity, and, excepting its crown-shaped spire, nearly all its artistic beauty. Up to the present

time it has been divided by partition walls into
two parish churches, but these walls are now
about to be removed, and a more discriminating
restoration proceeded with. A large share of the
cost of this work is being borne by William
Chambers, the famous publisher of "Chambers'
Edinburgh Journal," "Information for the People," and the well-known "Chambers' Encyclo-
pædia." Mr. Chambers' place of business, by
the way, is just across High street from the cathedral, and overlooks Princes Street Gardens and
the New town, as brass plates containing the
name W. & R. Chambers on several doors indicate. One of the most fascinating biographies
of the past decade is that of Robert Chambers,
the junior member of the firm, who died a few
years since. The two brothers began life about
half a century ago in the most humble manner,
with no resources but their native Scotch industry
and thrift. Being fond of literature they gravi-
tated into the publishing business, and founded
their weekly journal, which speedily became a
prodigious success, and ultimately acquired for
them a large fortune. The biography alluded to
is worthy the perusal of every aspiring young
man.

St. Giles's has, since the Reformation, been a
Presbyterian church. We attended services there
one Sunday. The minister wore a black gown

and bands, such as we are used to in some Episcopal churches. There was a large choir and
organ, but all the congregation joined heartily in
the singing. The people stood up to sing and sat
to pray. The prayers were *extempore*, but were
strongly interlarded with expressions from the
English liturgy, and closed with the most ritualistic *ah*men. Indeed the longer prayers were
each in fact a series of shorter ones, rather than
a continuous petition. The programme of the
services was as follows: Singing of a psalm,
prayer, Old Testament lesson, chanting of a psalm,
New Testament lesson, prayer, another psalm, sermon of twenty-five minutes, psalm, prayer, collection and benediction. It was noteworthy that
almost every member of the congregation held a
bible in his hand and followed the minister in the
reading of the lessons.

In the south transept of St. Giles's is the tomb
of Regent Murray, the half-brother of Mary
Queen of Scots, and regent of the kingdom during part of her imprisonment. Readers of Scottish history will remember that he was assassinated at Linlithgow, in 1570, by Mary's partisans.
He was a wise and moderate ruler, and his death
was a great loss to Scotland.

In the middle of the street, on the south side of
St. Giles's, is the grave of the famous Scottish
reformer, John Knox, marked only by a small

square stone, level with the pavement, with the letters I. K. 1572, in brass, let into it. It requires careful looking to find it at all.

A little farther down High street, on the left hand side, is the house formerly occupied by John Knox. It is a quaint old place, projecting far into the street, with a low ground floor, now occupied by a tobacconist's shop, stone steps to the second story, and three stories above it, each projecting farther into the street than the one below. The roof is a queer jumble of gables, dormers and chimney-pots. On the corner is a little stone image pointing up to the word God, cut in the wall in four different languages. Where the sign should be, just over the shop front, are the words:

LOFE. GOD. ABOUE. AL. AND. YOUR. NICHTBOUR. AS. YI. SELF.

The house was built in 1490 for a Scottish nobleman. When Knox was pastor of St. Giles's he secured it for a manse, and here he resided till his death. The house has in late years been restored interiorly, and it is kept for exhibition to strangers. Ascending the outside steps we enter a large room used by the great reformer as an audience chamber, and from one window of which, looking up High street, he was wont occasionally to preach to a crowd on the sidewalk below. The next story contains his bedroom, a large parlor richly wainscoted with carved oak panels, and a small closet projecting into the street, which served as his study. The chair he occupied in the latter still stands in its old corner. Other furniture of the period has been collected in the other rooms, together with a number of miscellaneous curiosities associated with the Reformation period. John Knox was born in 1505, was educated for the priesthood, and became a professor in the university of St. Andrews. In 1542 he joined the Reformers, and it was mainly by his earnest and vigorous preaching, and by the influence that he gained with the masses, that Scotland, from being a stronghold of catholicism, became of all countries the most uncompromisingly protestant. Knox was a most remarkable man for the recklessness with which he assailed the enemies of the reformed religion, no matter what their power. To the royal family he was on occasions positively insulting. It seems almost miraculous, in view of the rough times in which he lived and the slight regard in which human life was held, that he was not summarily put out of the way. But his life seems to have been a charmed one, for, although several conspiracies were formed to murder him, and once a bullet did come whizzing through his parlor window, aimed at the spot where he was wont at that hour to be sitting, he escaped all perils and died at last, in 1572, a natural death in his own house.

Leaving John Knox's house, a little further on we come to the Canongate parish church, an ugly old building, in the churchyard of which lies buried Adam Smith, author of the "Wealth of Nations," one of the ablest works on political economy ever published.

At the foot of the street, the Canongate, we come upon Holyrood Palace, famous chiefly for its associations with the beautiful, but misguided and unfortunate, Mary Queen of Scots. It was originally an abbey, founded in the twelfth century by the pious King David I. It had long been used more or less as a royal residence, when James IV., grandfather of Mary Stuart, added to it the present palace. James soon after married the Princess Margaret, daughter of Henry VII. of England, and of course the sister of Henry VIII. This was in 1503. Ten years later he fell in battle with the English at Flodden Field. He was succeeded by his young son, James V., during whose reign the Reformation in Scotland made considerable progress. James's wife was Mary of Guise, a French princess, and their only child, the future Queen Mary, was born in 1542, only seven days before her father's death. Mary's early life was spent in France, where she was married to the Dauphin, or heir apparent to that kingdom. Upon his early death she returned to Scotland, and was received with great loyalty by her subjects. This was in August, 1561. All went well till her marriage to her cousin, Lord Darnley, a young English nobleman, in July, 1565, when the Scottish court at once became a hot-bed of intrigue. Darnley embarked in pursuit. of royal powers, and the Scottish nobility plotted against both Darnley and the Queen on account of the husband's overweening pretensions.

Mary's private secretary was one Rizzio, an Italian, who was also a great favorite with her on account of his musical talents. Darnley early became jealous of this man, and in less than eight months after his marriage organized a conspiracy to assassinate him. It was on the 9th of March, 1565, that, with a large party of armed men, he burst into the Queen's private rooms where she was supping with a party of friends, Rizzio being in attendance, and in her very presence assaulted and slew him. The blood stains on the floor, in the large outer room whither they dragged him, are still plainly visible. Later Queen Mary had this portion of the room partitioned off from the rest, so as to hide the ugly spot from her vision, and thus it happens that the scene of his death is now a narrow passage way. Three months after the murder the Queen gave birth to her only child, afterwards James I. of England. Mary lived unhappily with Darnley, but there seem to be grave doubts of her being accessory to his

murder, which occurred on the 31st of January
following—but little more than ten months after
the Rizzio tragedy. Darnley, who was in ill-
health, was lodging for quiet in a secluded house
known as Kirk of Field, on what is now part of
the university grounds, when, early in the morning, a large quantity of gunpowder was exploded
in the cellar, and that was the last of either the
house or Darnley. The horrible deed was fixed
on the Earl of Bothwell, but he managed to
secure an acquittal upon his trial, and within
four months had procured a divorce from his own
wife and had married the widow of his victim.

Then Mary's more serious troubles began.
Bothwell treated her like a brute, and her nobles,
scandalized by her conduct, and dreading the
power and ambition of her new husband, rose up
in insurrection. In less than a month from the
date of her marriage she was a prisoner in Lochleven castle, and Bothwell a fugitive in the Ork-
ney Islands, where he ended his career as a pirate.
A year later she escaped from Lochleven, and
rallying her friends ventured a battle with the
insurgent lords. She was defeated and fled to
England, to meet there an imprisonment of
eighteen years, which was to terminate only with
her tragic death. While living, as a Catholic,
and the next heir to the throne of England, she
was constantly the center of intrigue for the

removal of Elizabeth and the restoration of the Catholic religion. Queen Elizabeth finally relieved herself of her constant anxiety by cutting off her troublesome captive's head.

Mary's private apartments at Holyrood palace are open to the public on payment of a small fee. They occupy the third story of the north or left hand wing of the palace, as we stand facing it, and consist of a large audience room, a good sized bedroom, a little five by nine dressing room in one of the round towers that ornament the corners of the building, and which are so conspicuous in all pictures of Holyrood, and a supper room of like diminutive size in the other tower. Darnley's apartments were the exactly corresponding ones on the floor below. The rooms are far from elegant, the ceilings being comparatively low, the wood work clumsy, and the panes of the windows small with sash bars an inch thick. The walls of some of the rooms are wainscoted with wood entirely up to the ceiling, and in others are covered with faded tapestry made to fit the various spaces. The floors are bare and the furniture old, uncomfortable and inartistic. Such were royal apartments in Scotland three centuries ago.

The palace of Holyrood consists of a single quadrangle, with a plain building of Italian architecture three stories in height extending around its four sides. An arched piazza extends all

around the quadrangle on the ground floor. The
buildings on the south side contain the state
apartments, and the rooms occupied by Queen
Victoria when she visits Edinburgh. The historic
apartments, including those above described, are
in the opposite or north side of the palace.
Among these is a long picture gallery containing
portraits of most of the kings of Scotland from
the year 330 before Christ, down to the close of
the Stuart dynasty. The authenticity of many
of the older portraits is beclouded by the fact
that they were all painted by one artist. Adjoining the northeast corner of the palace is the
ruined chapel of the former abbey of Holyrood,
and which, down to the period of the Commonwealth, was the royal chapel of the palace. It
was burned by Cromwell's soldiers in 1650. In
1758 the building was restored, but such a quantity of stone-work was put into the vaulting and
roof that the walls gave way under the weight
and the building became the utter ruin we to-day
see it.

Probably no city in the world is better supplied
with schools and colleges of a high grade than
Edinburgh. It also has an art school and very
excellent public gallery of paintings. The latter
contains a few old masters, but the works are
mostly those of Scottish painters. There is also
a gallery of casts of ancient sculpture, and a very

interesting museum of antiquities. In the university is another extensive museum of arts and sciences somewhat similar to that at South Kensington.

Riding on a street car one day, I asked a gentleman beside me what might be the population of Edinburgh, "Really, I cannot inform you," he replied, then turning to an old gentleman next to him, he put the same question to him. The old gentleman did not know either, and asked a third party, who was not sure, but thought about fifty-eight thousand. With some trouble I ascertained that it was two hundred and eighty-five thousand, including Leith, but I was impressed with the little interest Edinburghers seem to feel in the growth of their beautiful city.

CHAPTER XL.

THIRTY-FIVE miles south of Edinburgh is the little village of Melrose, the site of Melrose Abbey, famous from its association with Walter Scott's "Lay of the Last Minstrel," and his novel, "The Monastery." It is one of the abbeys founded by the good King David I., more than seven hundred and fifty years ago. In the fourteenth century it was restored by Robert Bruce, whose heart, by the way, lies buried just under the east window in the choir. In 1545 the abbey was destroyed by the English in one of their retaliatory forays across the border. Then for a long time the ruins became the stone quarry of the neighborhood. In 1618 a portion of the nave was vaulted over in a most barbarous style and converted into a Presbyterian kirk, which purpose it continued to serve down to 1810. The ruin is now carefully preserved. It consists of all the outer walls, except the west end and about half of the north wall of the nave, which are entirely gone. More than half of the columns remain standing, also a few sections of the groined vaulting, and one side of the square central tower. The tracery of the windows, and the sculptured capitals of the columns, are exquisitely beautiful, showing that the church in its perfection must have been a work of the highest artistic merit. None of the other monastic buildings are at all traceable, though the abbey before its destruction was very extensive, rich and profligate. Besides Bruce's grave, that of Michael Scott, the wizard, immortalized in the "Lay of the Last Minstrel," is pointed out in the south transept.

Two or three miles up the valley of the Tweed from Melrose is Abbotsford, the renowned home of Sir Walter Scott. When Sir Walter became wealthy, from his literary work, he purchased this estate, then a humble farm with the uneuphonious name of Cartley Hole. For eleven years, from 1811 to 1822, he gave his personal and immediate attention to the erection of the house, and the laying out and beautifying of the grounds, and succeeded in producing one of the most artistic and interesting homesteads to be found anywhere. Every portion of it is modeled after the best features of some mediæval castle, palace, or abbey, the whole forming a perfectly harmonious mosaic of antique architecture. The sculptured stone work of Melrose Abbey, Roslin

Chapel, and other beautiful ruins of the neighborhood, was drawn upon largely for models for the
interior decorations. Visitors enter by a side
door, pay a shilling apiece to the attendant, pass
through a basement ante-room hung with old
prints, up a winding stone stair, and then find
themselves in Sir Walter's study, a comparatively
small room, with book shelves all around reaching quite to the ceiling, and the chair and table
in the center which he occupied while writing all
his later novels. From the study we pass into
the library, a very large room with twenty thousand volumes filling the shelves that line the
walls. The furniture is all unique, and was for
the most part presented to Sir Walter by high
dignitaries in church and state, King George the
IV. and the Pope being among the number.
There is also a glass case containing a great number of interesting curiosities, picked up by Sir
Walter in his long career as an antiquary. Both
the library and drawing room adjoining look out
upon a beautiful lawn, extending quite down to
the little river Tweed. The latter room has its
walls decorated with hand-painted paper, hung
more than sixty years ago, and contains portraits
of many eminent historical characters. We next
pass into a long, narrow room, the walls of which
are completely covered with ancient and historic
arms. Here are the pistols of Claverhouse, the

onaluminumonaluminumonaluminumonaluminumonaluminumonaluminumonaluminumonaluminumonaluminumonaluminumonaluminumonaluminumonaluminum

persecutor of the Covenanters, the claymore and musket of Rob Roy, a pair of pistols carried by Napoleon at Waterloo, a German executioner's sword, and hundreds of other rare and curious weapons. The collection of arms and armor is continued in the main entrance hall, which we next enter, and which completes the suite of rooms open to the public. The rest of the house is occupied by a great-grand-daughter of Sir Walter, a Mrs. Maxwell. It was impossible in the brief time alloted to a visit to note even a tithe of the interesting objects with which Abbotsford is replete. It is the model home of the poet, the historian and the romancist.

About an equal distance on the other side of Melrose, and also on the banks of the Tweed, is Dryburgh (pronounced Dryboro) Abbey, another beautiful monastic establishment, founded in the twelfth century, restored by Robert Bruce, and left a ruin by the English in 1544. The church is much less perfect than Melrose, but the walls of the other monastic buildings are still in good preservation. The latter are mostly covered with ivy, and the whole ruin is exceedingly pictur- esque. In one bay of the north aisle of the church, the vaulting of which still remains per- fect, are the tombs of Sir Walter Scott, his wife, son, and son-in-law and biographer, Lockhart, each being marked by a block of solid Scotch granite, with a simple inscription on the top, and all inclosed by an iron railing. It will occur to the reader that there is a peculiar appropriateness in the great poet and novelist thus finding his last resting place amid the romantic ruins of an ancient abbey.

Between Melrose and Dryburgh are the Eildon Hills, which the reader of the "Lay of the Last Minstrel" will remember the imps of Michael Scott clave in three in a single night, when, pestering him for further employment, he ingeniously set them to work twisting ropes out of sea sand. From this place also can be seen in the distance the Cheviot hills, which form in part the boundary between England and Scotland.

About ten miles southeast of Edinburgh is the hamlet of Roslin, or Rosslyn, as it is variously spelled, with its ruined castle and famous chapel. The castle must at one time have been very extensive, and a place of great strength both from its position, almost entirely surrounded by deep valleys, and from the thickness of its walls, but nothing now remains of it but several tiers of vaulted chambers, which were probably the kitchens, storehouses and dungeons of the establishment. The chapel was built by the Lord of Roslin in 1446, and is one of the most remarkable pieces of architecture in Great Britain. It was originally intended as an abbey church, with

RUINS OF DRYBURGH ABBEY, SCOTLAND, THE BURIAL PLACE OF SIR WALTER SCOTT.

transepts and nave, but only the choir or chancel was ever finished. It is a small affair, but very massively built and excessively ornate. In the whole interior there is scarcely a square foot of surface in the stone work which is not elaborately carved, and as there is no repetition of the designs, the reader may imagine what a study the building presents. Even the vaulted ceiling is richly carved in what is known as diaper work, in a variety of patterns. Not only are the capitals of the columns diverse in every instance, but the faces of the columns themselves. One of the latter, known as the Apprentice's Pillar, is a rare piece of workmanship. It is a fluted column with a wreath of foliage spirally encircling it. The legend is that the builder of the chapel found his skill unequal to this column, and went to Rome for further instruction in his delicate art. Upon his return he found that an apprentice lad had undertaken and completed the difficult job, whereupon in a fit of envious hatred he killed the poor fellow with his mallet. The arches, too, are cuspated so elaborately as to present quite a stalactite appearance. The building is in the Gothic style of architecture, but its excessive richness of ornamentation suggests the influence of a Spanish or Moorish taste. For two hundred years the chapel was neglected, windowless, and exposed to the weather, but has lately been put in repair, and services are now held in it every Sabbath.

These were all favorite haunts of Sir Walter Scott, and frequently figure in his works. It may not be out of place here to refresh the reader's memory in regard to the history of this remarkable writer. He was the son of a lawyer, was born in 1771, and was himself educated for the bar. From early life he was fond of antiquarian studies, and was a ready versifier. In 1805 he published the "Lay of the Last Minstrel," and at intervals of two or three years, "Marmion," "The Lady of the Lake," and his other poetical works. His poems were received with great favor by the public. In 1814, when his popularity seemed to have passed its zenith, he suddenly appeared in the role of novelist, "Waverley" being his first production, whence the title, "Waverley Novels," commonly applied to the entire series of his works of fiction. The enormous expense he was at in establishing his seat at Abbotsford, and the lavish hospitality he there indulged, with perhaps some reckless speculations, brought him to financial ruin in 1826, his debts reaching $750,000. As an honest man, he refused to compound with his creditors, and devoted the remainder of his life to indefatigable literary work for their sole benefit. His writings during this period were much inferior to those of the era of his prosperity, but he accomplished his end, and the last dollar of his indebtedness was paid by his executors soon after his death, which occurred in 1832. Sir Walter Scott's works are alike famous for their purity of style, their richness in historic fact and incident, and their admirable portrayal of the manners, customs, and modes of expression of the mediæval period. No man is more worshiped in Scotland than he.

From Edinburgh we take the train for Stirling. The reader will frequently have observed after a rainstorm how, under the shelter of every pebble in the gutters, a little ridge of sand or mud forms itself, which gradually diminishes in size as it recedes from the protecting pebble. So when, at some very remote period, a great flood of waters washed out the valley of the Forth, it encountered two sturdy rocks which withstood its fury, behind each of which a sloping ridge of alluvial deposit formed itself—two instances of what geologists call "crag and tail." Upon these two rocks castles were ultimately built, and upon their sloping tails cities grew up, which in turn have been the capitals of Scotland. One is the castle and city of Edinburgh, the other the castle and city of Stirling, the latter being situated thirty-six miles farther up the river, or northwest of the former.

Next to Edinburgh, Stirling possesses more

historical interest than any other place in Scotland. It was the scene of two very early and memorable victories gained by the Scots over the English. In 1297 William Wallace here won the battle of Stirling Bridge, to commemorate which a noble monument in form of a tower with coronal spire, very like that of St. Giles's cathedral, conspicuously surmounts a neighboring hill. Seventeen years later (1314) Robert Bruce won the great battle of Bannockburn within sight of Stirling castle, and this a tall flag-staff commemorates.

The oldest existing portion of the castle dates from 1424. The Stuart family made it a royal residence, and in 1480 a fine building, still in good repair and in use as barracks for the garrison, was erected within its walls for the sittings of the Scottish parliament. Sixty years later James V., father of Mary Queen of Scots, built adjacent to it a sumptuous palace, which still stands, forming the principal building of the castle. It is rather richly ornamented on the outside with statues, and has a court in the center called the Lion's Court, because originally lions were kept at large in it for the amusement of the inmates of the palace, who could look down upon them from the windows surrounding the court. The openings through the massive walls through which the lions were fed are still to be seen. In 1594 James

VI. (James I. of England) built a royal chapel
within the castle walls, which is now used as an
armory.

The view from the ramparts of Stirling Castle,
three hundred and sixty feet above the river, is
most superb. On all sides is the level and highly
cultivated valley, through which flows the little
tortuous Forth, bounded in every direction by
beautiful hills. Such views are rarely to be seen
out of Scotland.

A little below, on the castle slope, is the old
Grey Friars' church—an old abbey—in which
both Mary and her son, James VI., were crowned
in infancy. Down in the town is a house which
belonged to Lord Darnley, and which served as
the nursery of his son, the infantile King James.

Stirling bridge has always been known as the
key to the Scottish Highlands, so from the time
we leave Stirling we may regard ourselves as
strictly in the Highlands. About twenty miles
brings us to Callander, a pleasant little town in
the valley of the river Teith, one of the larger
tributaries of the Forth, with which it unites near
Stirling. Callander lies just at the gateway to
the Scottish lakes, and is a popular summer resort.
Dozens of handsome stone villas were, at the
time of our visit, going up for the accommodation
of sojourners. The place also boasts one of the
best managed hotels in Britain. It bears the

imposing name of the Dreadnought, and is kept by an unmarried lady.

Who has not read the "Lady of the Lake," Sir Walter Scott's most popular poem? Well, this bit of country we are now in, is the scene of the thrilling events therein described. Loch Katrine is the lake in question, and an island of considerable size near its foot is known as Ellen's island. Here is the mountain of Ben Venue and here Loch Achray, through which the waters of Katrine flow on their way to join the Teith. A little below is Lanrick Mead, the rendezvous of the Clan Alpines, and still below is pointed out the traditional spot where Roderick Dhu and Fitz James held their memorable combat. The reader will recollect that the last scene of the poem is laid in Stirling Castle, which we have just left. So every inch of the way is intimately associated with the legends of the poem and is wonderfully full of interest. The good king who brings the tragic story to so sunny a close, it may be interesting to remember, was James V., father of Mary Queen of Scots.

We leave Callander about nine o'clock in the morning in an open coach drawn by four horses, for the famed Trossachs or Trosachs, as the name of the romantic glen that forms the outlet of Lake Katrine is variously spelled. The lake is ten miles distant, and the route affords us a splendid introduction to real Scottish mountain scenery.

The mountains of Scotland are unlike either those of our own country or of Switzerland in being entirely bare of trees. From base to summit they are covered with purple and brown heather. Much of the intervening land and often far up on the sides of the hills is peat bog, which, even for purposes of pasturage, has to be drained. This mountain country is very pretty though somewhat dreary-looking. It pastures large numbers of highland sheep, all, both ewes and wethers, with horns, and all with jet black noses. Highland cattle, too, we see, small and hardy, with hair several inches long. They have what they call farms up in this region, but raise nothing but hay and a few potatoes. One farmer we met who paid between three thousand and three thousand five hundred dollars a year rent for his mountain ranch, upon which he simply pastured about four thousand sheep. The land hereabouts is all owned by the Duke of Montrose, and though what an Illinois farmer would consider worthless, still brings him a good revenue, as may be judged by the rental of the farm above mentioned, and by the proceeds of the sale of the shooting rights. For the right of shooting grouse on one tract five or six miles square his grace receives four hundred pounds, or two thousand dollars per

annum, and there are plenty of sportsmen who
can afford to pay that sum for three or four
months' shooting. The grouse season lasts from
August 12th to about December 10th.

The famous Trossachs are nothing remarkable
after all to an American. They consist simply of
a wooded valley, bounded by sharp, bristling
mountain peaks, and extend for about a mile and
a quarter to the foot of Loch or Lake Katrine.
Plenty of just as good scenery of the kind can be
found in Vermont and New Hampshire, but in
Britain people travel hundreds of miles to see the
Trossachs.

So with the lakes. Neither Loch Lomond nor
Loch Katrine can compare with Lake George.
They are very pretty lakes, however, narrow, and
edged in with mountains, the principal of which
is Ben Lomond, three thousand two hundred feet
high. Along the shores are numerous pleasant
and picturesque residences and popular hotels.
A steamer carries us from the Trossachs to the
head of Loch Katrine, where we take another
coach, five and-a-half miles, to Inversnaid, at the
head of Loch Lomond. Another boat takes us
to Balloch, at the foot of the lake, and thence
we go by rail to Glasgow, passing *en route* the
ruins of Dumbarton Castle on its rocky hill.
The whole trip from Edinburgh to Glasgow, via
the Trossachs, can be accomplished in a day.

CHAPTER XLI.

GLASGOW began its career as a religious and educational settlement about thirteen hundred years ago. Its existing cathedral is over seven hundred years old, and its university over four hundred and thirty. Its earliest trade was in connection with the fisheries. Then Glasgow took a leading position in the Virginia tobacco trade, and grew wealthy. With the invention of the power loom she went largely into cotton manufacturing, and to-day works up nearly a million pounds of raw cotton per week. Later she embarked in the iron and ship building trade; and thus has grown up a great commercial and manufacturing city of between seven and eight hundred thousand inhabitants, reckoning its dependent suburbs.

Historically, Glasgow has not much to boast of, though it was the scene of the battle of Langside, waged between Mary Stuart, after her escape from Lochleven castle, and her rebellious nobles, and in which she sustained the defeat

that led her to throw herself into Queen Elizabeth's hands.   In January, 1812, it saw the test
of what the Scotch claim to have been the earliest
successful steamboat, the Comet, constructed by
Henry Bell, between whom and Robert Fulton
there must ever be a division of the honor of
being the first to use steam successfully for vessel
propulsion.

I spent a Sunday in Glasgow and attended
Established Church of Scotland services at the
cathedral, and at two o'clock (all the churches in
Glasgow have their second service at two and
Sunday school at half past five) dropped in at the
Free church of St. Columba.   The Presbyterians
of Scotland, by the way, have no prejudice
against saints in naming their churches.   St.
Columba's was the church over which Rev. Norman McLeod was pastor from 1836 to the time of
his death, in 1862.   A fine bust of him stands in
the vestibule.   Both English and Gaelic services
are held in this church.   The contrast between
the services at the Established and the Free church
was very noticeable.   The former had an organ
and well trained choir; the latter discard the
organ but have some of the best congregational
singing I have ever heard, led by a precentor who
sits at a table just below the tall pulpit.   At the
Free church the services were conducted much as
our Presbyterian services are at home.   The

prayers were purely extemporaneous, and very
warm and earnest, and the sermon plain, practical
and strongly evangelical.   At the cathedral, on
the other hand, the prayers were made up of a
number of short petitions, some of them taken
bodily from the Episcopal liturgy, and all of them
containing much of its language, while the sermon, though scholarly, lacked in depth and earnestness.   I could not but be impressed with the
idea that the religious life of the country is in the
Free rather than in the Established church, which
seems to have no such decided mission of its own
as suffices to keep it from hankering after the
æsthetic forms of the church of England; as for
instance the chanting of the psalms, the introduction of an anthem in the middle of the service,
adaptations from the liturgy, etc.

Glasgow cathedral is quite an old one (built
1175), but has recently been restored.   Only the
choir is used for worship, the nave serving as a
magnificent vestibule.   There are no walls, however, separating the two portions.   The music is
superb, the large organ and choir being well supported by the congregation, and the effect being
enhanced by the size and construction of the
church.

Just at the back of the cathedral is the principal cemetery of Glasgow, the Necropolis, as it is
called.   It occupies a hill overlooking the city,

28

and is beautiful both in its location and monuments. The most conspicuous of the latter is a short Doric column surmounted by a stone statue of John Knox, the whole being dedicated to the memory of the reformers and protestant martyrs of Scotland, including George Wishart, the teacher of Knox, who was burned at the stake at St. Andrews in 1546.

Like Edinburgh, Glasgow has its High street stretching away from the cathedral in the direction of the river, and like Edinburgh's High street it is filled with barefooted and bareheaded women gossiping on the sidewalks, and with barefooted, dirty-faced, crying children, to an extent that makes it anything but a pleasant thoroughfare to traverse. But the old part of Glasgow is very insignificant as compared with the new sections, in which the streets are broad, clean, and run parallel and at right angles, as in most of our American cities. The buildings too, are, as a rule, more elegant than in any other city of Great Britain, and stone is almost exclusively the building material. The Italian renaissance style generally prevails, and this gives Glasgow an air of modern elegance rather than one of mediæval picturesqueness. It is every way a fine commercial city, nor is it lacking in artistic aspirations. In the square, in front of our hotel, we counted no less than twelve statues of as many eminent personages.

In the center stands a tall column, surmounted by a statue of Sir Walter Scott, to the right and left of which are equestrian statues of the Queen and Prince Albert. Among the other statues are those of Dr. Livingstone, Robert Peel, James Watt, and Sir John Moore, the hero of Corunna, who was also a native of Glasgow. The churches of Glasgow are nothing extraordinary, but the new university building, in the Gothic style, situated just below the city, is a very striking edifice.

The Clyde, which, within the recollection of persons still living, could be crossed by wading, has now, by the enterprise of the Glasgow people, been so deepened and dredged out that the largest ocean steamships sail right up to the wharves of the city. Unfortunately, in accomplishing this end, the current of the river has been destroyed, and the Clyde, through the heart of Glasgow, is a mere pool of stagnant sewage. The river is crossed by several fine bridges, below which the wharves are lined with sea-going steamers bound for all parts of the world. Still farther down the river lie the shipyards, unequaled in extent by those of any other port in the world. The yards are but a short distance apart, and at each three or four iron vessels are on the stocks, and the hammering of the riveters is one continuous clatter.

Glasgow is well supplied with water by an

aqueduct from Loch Katrine, thirty-four miles
distant; notwithstanding which more drunken
people are seen on the streets than in any other
European city we have visited. The extreme
prevalence of intemperate habits in Scotland,
even among women, is illustrated by the necessity
for the last clause of the following sign, which I
noticed on a house in Dumfries:

MRS. CROSBIE,
Certified Midwife—Qualified in Accouchments.
Terms Moderate—Total Abstainer.

Leaving Glasgow, a two hours' pleasant ride
through a very hilly country—it would be
hard to find a ten-acre field of perfectly level
ground in the whole distance—brings us to
Dumfries, a town of twenty thousand inhabitants near the mouth of the river Nith, a few
miles from the Irish sea, almost at the extreme
southern edge of Scotland. Dumfries is principally famous as having been the later home
of the poet Burns, and the place of his burial.
His house still stands just as he left it eighty-
five years ago. It is an unpretending two-
story building, on a narrow street, and only a
few steps from the cemetery where he is buried.
In the cemetery stands the old parish church,
built one hundred and forty years ago in the
peculiar Scottish Presbyterian style, nearly
square, with gallery on three sides, and a tall

pulpit holding but one person on the fourth. A charge of three pence per head is made to see the Burns mausoleum. It is a plain dome supported by Ionic columns filled in between with glass. Inside is a life-sized relief in marble representing the poet holding a plow, with an angel swooping down upon him. In the front of this relief is a slab in the pavement bearing this inscription :

In memory of

ROBERT BURNS,

Who died the 21st of July, 1796, in the 37th year of his age,

And

MAXWELL BURNS,

Who died the 25th of April, 1799, aged 2 years and 9 months,

FRANCIS WALLACE BURNS,

Who died the 9th of July, 1803, aged 14 years,

His sons.

The remains of Burns removed into the vault below, the 19th of Sept., 1815,

And his two sons,

Also the remains of

JEAN ARMOUR,

Relict of the poet,

Born Feb., 1765, died 26th Mar., 1834.

And Robert, his eldest son, who died on the 14th May, 1857, aged 70 years.

A visitors' register is kept in the mausoleum, and the number signing it is very large, particularly of Americans. On the river bank, a short distance below the cemetery, is a pleasant walk shaded by large elms, which is pointed out as a favorite resort of the poet, and where no doubt many of his poems were inspired.

Looking up the river from this point, we see a very ancient stone bridge, said to have been built in the thirteenth century by the mother of John Baliol, King of Scotland.

The good people of Dumfries seem to be excessively given to hospitality, if they may be judged from the courtesy of a gentlemanly seedsman, who, simply to show politeness to strangers, left his store and walked with us to his nursery nearly half a mile away just to gratify a desire expressed in a three minutes' acquaintance to take home to America a root of Scotch heather. And not a penny would the good burgher take for all his time and trouble.

They have many curious expressions in the highlands of Scotland, as for instance, in denominating a butcher a "flesher." The sign on a vacant lot near Glasgow, "This property to be Fued," puzzled us till we found out that a Scotch fue is a perpetual lease. The practice is very common to fue or lease land for building purposes for a term of nine hundred and ninety-nine years, the rental remaining the same throughout, and the tenant's rights being as absolute as if he owned the ground in fee simple, so long as he pays his rent annually.

In half an hour's ride from Dumfries we pass

Gretna Green, the southernmost town in Scotland, and just at the English border. Gretna Green was long famous as the goal of runaway couples from England, who could there be married under Scottish law and thus exempt themselves from the restrictions and formalities that the laws of England imposed. So extensive did this surreptitious marrying business become, that the people of Gretna Green provided regular facilities for it, and it indeed became the principal industry of the place. And this has continued to within the memory of the present generation. But railways and telegraphs have destroyed the trade of Gretna Green just as they have of hosts of other ambitious towns.

This reminds me that I never attended church in England on Sunday without hearing the bans of one or more couples published. No one can be married there, unless by special license, without having the bans thus publicly read in the parish church on three successive Sundays. Hasty or secret marriages are thus impossible. So, too, no marriage can ever be performed after twelve o'clock noon, up to which time it is presumed by the law that people are sober and have their wits about them.

We cross the river Solway, and are again in England. The Solway, by the way, is memorable as being the scene of several cruel executions

of Covenanters during Charles II.'s reign. The
gay and frivolous monarch undertook to force
episcopacy upon Scotland in spite of the intense
conscientious prejudices of the Scottish people.
Many gave up their lives rather than worship
God out of a prayer book, so much did they consider it as tending to a relapse towards Roman-
ism. Among these were several young maidens,
who were led out into the sands at the mouth of
the Solway at low water, bound to stakes, and
left there to drown when the tide should come in
and cover them.

CHAPTER XLII.

SOON after passing the river Solway the train
enters the splendid station at Carlisle. The
castle at the time of our visit was closed to
the public, so we had to content ourselves with a
visit to the curious old cathedral. It is a queer
architectural jumble. Originally a Norman structure of the eleventh century, the choir was pulled
down in the fourteenth to give place to a larger
and more beautiful one in the pointed Gothic
style. In connecting it with the central tower
and transepts the old arches were walled up and
new ones cut through to suit the new structure.
The result is a curious confusion of Norman and
Gothic moldings and fragmentary arches. Later
an attempt was made to carry up the tower to a
much greater height, which caused the piers to
settle at least a foot, with the effect upon the
semi-circular arches of the adjoining bays of the
nave and transepts that may be imagined. Such
queerly distorted arches are probably nowhere
else to be found. To save further disaster thirty

feet of the tower had to be taken off. Still later,
to wit, during the rebellion, about the middle of
the seventeenth century, to provide stone for the
fortifying of the city, four-fifths of the nave was
pulled down, and thus the church was left in a
sort of stump-tail condition, with a nave of only
two or three bays. Despite its mutilated state
the church is very interesting for the history that
can be read in its stones.

It is further interesting as being the burial
place of William Paley, D. D., the author of the
well-known "Evidences of Christianity," and
other popular theological works.

We are now in Cumberland, a county of charming landscapes. Beautiful green hills, thrifty
hedgerows, spreading trees, picturesque thatched
cottages, ivy-grown old castles, romantic baronial
halls and ancient church towers peeping out
above the foliage, greet the eye every rod of the
way.

We branch off from the main line to visit the
old ruin of Furness Abbey and, close by, the
modern town of Barrow-in-Furness, which has
grown up within forty years, from the proximity
of valuable mines of iron ore. Barrow is on the
sea coast, and very extensive docks have been
constructed there. It is likewise the seat of the
most extensive Bessemer steel works in the world,
and of extensive ship-building interests.

In England iron ships have entirely superseded wooden ones, and steam has almost as entirely supplanted sail power. Only now and then is a sail vessel built on the Clyde or the Tyne, while steamships are turned out by the score, and a wooden-built vessel is a very exceptional thing indeed. If well taken care of an iron vessel will last for a century at least. Iron is cheaper than wood in Europe for all purposes to which it can be applied. One application which I noticed was for telegraph poles.

Noting the great consumption of fuel in the manufacturing districts of the north of England, I inquired of a large operator if he had no fears of the exhaustion of the British coal fields. "None at all!" he replied. "We have only to go a little deeper from time to time, and fresh veins are reached. It will be centuries at least before the coal fields of England are worked out."

He then went on to tell me of one mine the workings of which extended under the sea for a long distance. In sinking the shaft for it great trouble was experienced from the inflow of water. At one point a stratum of rock one hundred feet thick had to be penetrated with a hundred and fifty feet of water overlying it. But English engineering was equal to the task. The shaft was thirteen feet in diameter and a hole of that size was literally drilled through the entire one hun-

dred feet of rock. The method was substantially
the same as that employed in sinking oil or salt
wells, but the bit or cutting tool, instead of having an edge a few inches wide, had thirteen feet
of cutting edge and was itself an immense inverted
T of iron weighing a great many tons. This by
a powerful engine was alternately raised and
dropped, with a gradually revolving motion, until
the stratum of rock was entirely cut through.
The shaft was then tubed with iron, the water
pumped out, and further sinking proceeded without anything more than the ordinary trouble
from water, the stratum of rock that had been
pierced effectually shutting out all from above.

From Barrow we proceeded to Liverpool, passing through Wigan, a famous colliery district.
At Liverpool I had occasion to visit the post-
office. The English postoffices very little resemble
ours, but are more like banks. The delivery system is so general and complete that a very few
pigeon holes suffice for the "general delivery,"
or *poste restante*, as the Europeans call it. The
principal business, therefore, of the postoffice, or
at least of the part the public has to do with, is
the receipt of telegrams—the uniform price of
which for twenty words to any part of the country is a shilling, or twenty-four cents—the issue
and payment of money orders, the receipt of
money on deposit and repayment of the same

with interest when called for, the purchase and sale of government stocks, and the insuring of lives. The policy may be questioned of government thus engaging in the life insurance business, but there can be no doubt of the propriety of its thus offering the broadest facilities for taking the poor man's savings in sums of from one shilling up to thirty pounds and paying him interest upon them with all the guarantees of safety that attach to loans to the government.

Money orders are issued at much lower rates than with us. For sums under ten shillings ($2.40) the charge is two pence (four cents), for sums up to ten dollars it is six cents, and it only reaches ten cents where the amount exceeds fifteen dollars. Another kind of postal order is also issued by which twenty-four or thirty-six cents can be remitted at a cost of one cent; ten, twenty or thirty shillings at a cost of two cents, etc. Why cannot we have an equally liberal system in this country?

At Liverpool we bid good-bye to European soil and go aboard our homeward bound steamer. The number of passengers coming this way is very large, and it takes a long time to get all the baggage aboard. At last we weigh anchor and steam down the Mersey. In a few hours we are in the rough sea of the channel, and in something less than twenty-four hours put in at

Queenstown for the mails which have been forwarded thither by rail.

Our homeward trip was a rough one, partly because of westerly winds, but mainly because our steamer was sailing light or simply "in ballast" as to cargo. Going out the steamers are heavily loaded with grain, flour and other agricultural products, but coming this way, owing to our protective tariff, which keeps out foreign products, cargoes are hard to be obtained, and the railroad iron and a few other things that do offer, have to be carried at merely nominal rates. The result is the farmer's grain has to pay double for transportation what it would if return cargoes were obtainable, and thus in one particular, at least, does the entire cost of protection fall upon the shoulders of the tillers of the soil.

Under a different system England with her twenty-five millions of inhabitants would look to us almost for her entire bread supply, for grain is raised there under great disadvantages. The great drawback is the excessive moisture of the climate, which keeps the crops green and prevents their ripening. Thus when the wheat and oats reach a degree of maturity which in America would betoken the putting in of the reaper in a few days at farthest, in England and Scotland you see them remain for weeks without apparent progress towards ripening. This is terribly discouraging to the farmers, especially after the cool and shortening days of September arrive.

But the same damp climate that is so prejudicial to the grain crops makes the country at all times beautifully green and renders it one of the gardens of the world in its wealth of flowers. Every house down to the meanest cottage has its flower garden, or if that is impossible, its window sills are filled with pots of geraniums or other plants, and all seem to flourish so admirably and to be so prolific in bloom.

The striking contrast in the scenery between England and the continent lies very largely in the hedgerows. On the continent no ground is wasted on partition fences of any kind, and one may almost travel all day without seeing a fence, while in England the farms are not only fenced, but are cut up into very small fields, and of the most irregular shapes imaginable. Then for fences the hawthorn hedge is almost universally used, with a picturesqueness of effect not easily described.

Another striking feature of the country is the admirable roads they are able to maintain. The country roads, as well as the residence streets of the towns and cities, are all macadamized. Being graded, a layer of broken stone is spread over the surface with a little gravel. A hose is then turned on and the whole thoroughly saturated with water. Then a heavy steam roller passes over backwards and forwards till the whole is as smooth as a floor and as solid as native rock. The road will then last for years without further repair. When it does become uneven the process of restoration is very simple and cheap. A gang of men with pickaxes go over it and loosen up the old stones, some new ones are added, with a little more gravel, more water, and a day of the steam roller, and the street is as good as new. The steam roller has become as indispensable to the English road-makers as the pick and shovel, and it might well be introduced into this country more generally.

Notwithstanding that England has to import most of her grain the cost of living is much less than with us. Nowhere in this country do the bakers' shops furnish such nice bread and cakes and at such cheap rates. At Glasgow I was able to procure a substantial lunch of buns and Banbury cakes with a glass of milk for the trifling sum of six cents. House rent, I think, can scarce be more than a third what it is with us, while clothing and almost every necessary of life is very much cheaper—even commodities imported from America being often retailed at lower prices than at home. On the whole, upon a given income people live more comfortably in England than in America. Of course for people with large families and without capital, and for those engaged in the too well beaten avenues of trade, there is a serious repressing influence at work in excessive competition; but, perhaps, not much more so than in our own country. For men of brains, push, and energy, I fancy there are quite as good opportunities in England as even with us. Certainly a great number of people have been pointed out to me who beginning life in the humblest circumstances have become wealthy.

And living cheaply, the British people do not overwork themselves. Walking through Glasgow, for instance, at half past nine in the forenoon, we see scarcely half the stores open, and at the time of our visit most of them contained notices in the windows that they would be closed altogether on the following Thursday, because, forsooth, *the Queen was going to visit Edinburgh* on that day. I went into a barber's shop at Edinburgh after four o'clock one Saturday afternoon, and was coolly told I would have to come again on Monday, as they did no work after four. At Bristol a case came to my notice where a dressmaker was summoned to appear before a magistrate and fined for simply *permitting* one of her assistants, who did it of her own free will, to work after four o'clock on Saturday, the law being peremptory that work-people must not be kept later than that hour. I verily believe that, despite the low wages of the British workmen, they are fully as well paid in proportion to the work they accomplish, as our own; though, irrespective of the amount of work done, our American wages sound fabulously high to them. On the continent it is different. In Antwerp, girls are employed in the cotton factories sixteen hours a day for the pittance of two francs, or thirty-eight cents a day. On the other hand, the clamor in England now is for the reduction of the hours of the legal working day from ten to nine.

And this reminds me that, judging from external appearances, there is in Great Britain but a mere fraction of the lawlessness and criminality that we are exposed to at home. I presume the laws are there more rigidly enforced than with us, for in almost any part of London ladies can be out up to a late hour in the evening unattended; no householder ever for a moment worries himself about burglars; no one ever dares to claim another party's baggage on the railway platform, although there is no check used, and every one is allowed to take what baggage he claims without a question being asked; room doors at hotels are rarely locked during the day, and murderous assaults are scarcely, if at all, more numerous than cold-blooded, willful murders, which, of course, is a phase of crime that no laws or penalties can check. Dishonesty is severely dealt with in England, whether it be the case of the boy who pilfers an apple, or the bank teller who misuses the funds with which he is entrusted. That assaults are less numerous than with us, is, perhaps, owing in large measure to the restrictions that are placed upon the carrying of firearms of any sort. To carry a gun or pistol without a license is a serious offense. Still, there is no infraction of personal liberty in the matter, for anybody of any degree of respectability can procure a license upon simply paying a fee of thirty shillings ($7.50). Those who need weapons do not mind the tax, while those who have no lawful use for them are naturally chary about applying for licenses. The system is a good one, and something like it would be a fine thing in our own country.

Ten days at sea, and we sail up the beautiful harbor of New York. We stop an hour or two at quarantine for medical examination, then proceed to our landing pier. Here every passenger has to sign a declaration setting forth the number of pieces of baggage he has, and whether or not they contain dutiable articles, and to what amount. Then inspectors go through the baggage and verify the truth of the declaration. If deception has been attempted the goods are confiscated. Otherwise an appraiser sets a value on

the articles that should pay duty, and the same
is collected on the spot. In general, the duty
and expenses bring the cost of everything up to
about what would have to be paid at home for
the same article, so it only pays to bring back
such things as cannot be purchased at home.

New York looks very dirty in contrast with
the cities we have seen abroad, and the whole
country unpicturesque and prosaic, and one of
the first things we do on reaching home is to
resolve that, sooner or later, we will repeat the
trip.

INDEX.

THE END.